FUGITIVE FAITH

ECOLOGY AND JUSTICE SERIES

FUGITIVE FAITH

*Conversations on
Spiritual,
Environmental,
and
Community Renewal*

Benjamin Webb

ORBIS BOOKS

Maryknoll, New York 10545

Copyright © 1998 by Benjamin Webb.

Published by Orbis Books, Maryknoll, New York, U.S.A.

Library of Congress Cataloging-in-Publication Data

Fugitive faith : conversations on spiritual, environmental, and
  community renewal / Benjamin Webb, [interviewer].
        p.   cm. — (Ecology and justice series)
      ISBN 1-57075-170-6 (alk. paper)
      1. Environmental sciences—Philosophy.   2. Environmental sciences—
Religious aspects.   3. Environmental responsibility.
Environmentalists—Interviews.   5. Social scientists—Interviews.
    I. Webb, Benjamin, 1954-   II. Series: Ecology and justice.
    GE40.F84   1998
      179'.1—dc21
                                                    97-45882
                                                    CIP

To My Wife Sarah

Contents

PART 3
RESTORING AND RE-STORYING

PART 4
THE RESURGENCE OF SPIRITUAL, ENVIRONMENTAL, AND COMMUNITY RENEWAL

Foreword

BILL McKIBBEN

Every year we have a "Blessing of Animals" at church. It's a pretty low-key, rural, Methodist sort of affair: a few horses and cows, eight or nine dogs, a number of cats, a frog or a turtle, usually some stuffed bears, and always a mosquito or a blackfly caught specially for the occasion. We stand around in the rutted parking lot trying to keep the dogs from mayhem, and then the preacher says a few words, and as the Sunday School teacher I get to toss in a piety or two. We sing a hymn, and everyone takes their animals home so they can come back for the worship service later.

We don't do it because animals need our blessing; they wear so much more naturally than us the blessing of their creator. Instead, it's to remind us how richly blessed we are by the sheer sweetness of the world we inhabit—by the patient love of dogs and cats, by the spring riot of the frogs, even by the whine of the mosquito. Half the hymns in the hymnal repeat the same refrain: God's love and power made manifest in flowers, trees, winds, waves. "For the beauty of the earth," indeed.

And so it is somewhat surprising how long it has taken religious communities and movements to wake up to the environmental predicament. Perhaps it's taken us so long because it is simply too painful. For a true rationalist, if there is such an animal, the fouling of our air and water would be stupid, uneconomic, unproductive. But for someone who professes to believe in a creator, the ongoing destruction of creation is blasphemous. We wipe out a hundred species a week; we alter the very temperature of the planet with our habits and industries; we play God in a way that no person could even have conceived of just a generation ago. And we play God in a particularly mindless and destructive way.

This book, and the intellectual and emotional movement it chronicles could not be more timely. If our environmental problems are ever to be solved, we need to draw on precisely the resources of community, of tradition, of literature, and of love expressed so deeply in these interviews.

The dilemma I have studied most thoroughly—global climate change—results from too many people living at too high a level. They are overwhelming the planet's systems. That result comes from the very fact of economic expansion that our governments, our schools, and our businesses all exist to support. We are encouraged at every turn to be idolatrous, and we can now read our appetites in every cubic meter of air, in every heat wave and drought and windstorm.

Synagogues, mosques, and churches are nearly the only organized institutions that can posit some end, other than accumulation, for human life; therefore they may have a central role to play in dealing with these issues, in helping us remember that there are other, better, routes to satisfaction. Faith communities, at least potentially, represent one of the few counter-culture forces in this society. That's why the voices contained herein are so important; as they reshape the dialogue of theologians—and of environmentalists—they offer glimpses of a different path.

Somehow we need to get our civilization on to that other road. It may bear off only slightly at first from our present course, but eventually it will take us far, far from our current directions. Far away from "It's the economy, stupid!" The reflections contained in this book are every bit as relevant to that task as a new design or a new international treaty. May they spark a myriad of other conversations, and even a myriad of conversions, conversions to something older, newer, sweeter, and more sustainable than our present life.

Preface

If Wallace Stevens was essentially correct when he said that "we don't live in a place but in a description of it," then one of our primary tasks today is to enrich our description of Earth in order to inspire in us greater affection and better patterns of care and fidelity. Of course, a better understanding of ourselves and our responsibilities is integral to that task.

This book takes that insight to heart in a series of candid interviews with people who are calling us back to right relationship to the world, away from desecration and destruction, to what cultural historian Thomas Berry calls the "great work" before us, reverence and restoration.

In these pages you will find political and spiritual leaders, environmentalists and agriculturalists, naturalists and scientists, writers and poets, all of whom are enlarging our sense of the sacred to embrace nature and daily life. Each of them conveys a passionate conviction about the decisive interface between nature and human spirituality as realities embedded in one another. Out of this conviction we hear them express their views about the practical link between spiritual, environmental, and community renewal as an antidote to the disintegration so evident in our urban and rural areas.

While each interview is unique, there are recurring questions: (1) What are the central challenges facing us? (2) What resources do we have or need to have to address them? (3) What drives the passion and sustains the work of those being interviewed? (4) What do they think they are contributing toward a cultural solution? I have grouped the interviews into four sections. Each interview, however, is an organic whole that may overlap and echo the comments of others.

At its heart, this book addresses our need to make sense of the shift in human perceptions we are living through, to find meaning in it, and to be encouraged to walk that path faithfully. When institutions fail to guide us in this respect, we sometimes turn to mentors to inspire us, and that is the role I see these interviews playing for many of us.

Each of these thought-provoking conversations invites us to go deeper in ourselves, and by way of example makes it more permissible to express one's heartfelt concerns and hopes in conversation with others. As our public discourse steadily improves around these matters, we may find such conversations more significant than we can imagine. For as sociologist Robert Bellah has said, "We need conversation in cold times to prepare for the time when widespread social transformation becomes possible."

Acknowledgments

I want to thank Michael Lerner and Jenepher Stowell of Commonweal for their moral support from the beginning, and for the material support they provided through the Jenifer Altman Foundation. Such generosity of spirit gave me the freedom to pursue my convictions in this beloved project.

Warmest thanks also to The Regeneration Project (a project of the Tides Foundation) where this undertaking was conceived, and especially to my co-founder and colleague, Sally Bingham.

My thanks also to Rob Lehman at the Fetzer Institute for much needed material support at midstream, along with Buz Brenton and the Ahrens Family Foundation.

I am deeply indebted to many capable assistants along the way who helped with translations, transcriptions, typing, and editing: Gerry Duckitt who works with Pra Kru Pitak Nanthakun, Terri Phipps on the staff of Grinnell College, Sherri Lindgren, Mimi Kingsbury, Loree Rackstraw, and especially Sarah Webb for her excellent editorial support.

I also offer thanks to the staff of the Grinnell Public Library and Burling Library at Grinnell College for their assistance, along with professors David Campbell and Brad Bateman at Grinnell College, and Laurie Lane-Zucker and Emerson Blake at the Orion Society, all of whom encouraged me in this work.

I especially thank those who consented to interviews, whose company was a pleasure and whose conversation was inspiring. I stand in your debt. Any errors are mine alone, and all satisfactions are gladly shared.

To my many hosts around the country during the course of these interviews, I extend thanks for your gracious hospitality, but none more than Jerry and Carol Wehr who know the sacrifice of real hospitality. Thank you for your safe ark, and your prayers.

I especially want to extend my heartfelt thanks to John Neff and Jamie Brodie for their everlasting friendship and spiritual support along the way. I also offer my gratitude and appreciation to Bill Burrows, my editor at Orbis, who believed in this project from the start and patiently waited for its completion, and to Orbis Books where I am convinced this book belongs.

My deepest gratitude to those who first taught me about people, land, and community: Tom and Sandra Grissom, Russell and Rose Harrod, Kevin and Lois Flood, Wendell and Tanya Berry, Robert and Amy Amunrud, Mike and Alice Jessen, Maurice and Jeannine Telleen, and Bob and Ruth Dougherty.

To my wife Sarah and my children—Hannah, Phoebe, and Zoe—who have endured my absence in too many ways the past few years, I thank you for your abiding love which has sustained me. Much of the energy that has driven me to complete this book is connected to my love for you all and my deepest hopes for the future of all children. As each of you seeks to follow your calling in life, I pray that I will always be there to support you on your path, as you have supported me.

PART 1

EXAMINING THE SPOILED CONDITION OF OUR PHYSICAL AND MORAL ENVIRONMENTS

Reforming Our Institutions of Meaning

ROBERT N. BELLAH

Robert Bellah is Eliot Professor of Sociology at the University of California in Berkeley and an internationally respected public philosopher and sociologist of religion. Together with four American colleagues, he co-authored the 1985 bestseller, Habits of the Heart, *which redefined the terms of America's debate about individualism and social commitment, along with its sequel,* The Good Society, *which helps us better understand the institutions through which we live and how we might take responsibility for them and ultimately transform them. Together, these two books join the great tradition of social analysis, begun by Alexis de Tocqueville's* Democracy in America, *by showing us how to understand and talk about American society, which is the beginning of knowing how to solve our problems. Bellah is also the author of such earlier classics as* On Civil Religion *and* Beyond Belief, *with its groundbreaking essay on "Religious Evolution," a subject to which Bellah has returned in his current research and writing. "Religion is generic to the human species," he said at one point. "It's not a question of the presence or absence of religion. Religion is going to be around. Tradition is going to be around. It's a question of what kind of religion. What kind of tradition. So that is our task."*

BW: You have said that most of the threats to the planetary ecosystem are the results of habitual ways of relating to the natural world, ways dictated by institutional arrangements that obviously need to change. But aren't many of these bad habits of fairly recent origin? Wasn't it partly the worldview and values associated with Modernity that shaped our most destructive personal and institutional behaviors? Is this where we went astray?

RB: While I certainly think that Modernity has produced a quantum leap in our destructive impingement on the environment, I think it needs to be stressed that the human species has been a problem for a very long time. For one thing, human beings have occupied almost every ecological niche on the planet since before history began. When the European explorers set out, they found human beings everywhere, even in the middle of the Pacific. So ecological damage does not begin with Modernity. The Pacific Islands are an example of serious consequences, with destruction of bird species everywhere and the cutting down of coconut palms on Easter Island, all of which drastically reduced the population to a small percentage of what it once was. Agriculture has also been very destructive in many places for ages. We have evidence from Central America, going back a thousand years, of the destruction of whole valleys by overt cultivation. And China, too.

BW: Yes. Dale and Carter, in their book *Topsoil and Civilization*, confirmed that soil erosion has been a problem around the world since ancient times.

RB: With the invention of petroleum-powered machinery, particularly the automobile, we're clearly in a whole new situation. But I think it's worth remembering that these problems have a continuity that pre-dates Modernity, and that so-called tribal peoples have not necessarily been so sweet to the world in which they lived. This is also true today of cultures that have a profound sensitivity to nature. I know of no culture as sensitive to nature as Japanese culture, whose people are tuned to the seasons, appreciate the cherry blossoms and the leaves turning, and go to nature all the time as a source of refreshment. But the Japanese are ruthless polluters. It's as though their sensitivity to nature and their economic life are totally disconnected. So you don't need to persuade them that nature is important. You need to persuade them that nature needs to be protected. Those are two different things.

BW: So we are reminded that these problems, though greatly magnified today, didn't originate with Modernity. But aren't there some particularly flawed ideas and assumptions about society and nature that undergird the modern program of human betterment?

RB: Yes. I think it's what Albert Borgmann, in his classic book *Technology and Everyday Life*, calls the "control paradigm." That there is nothing we can't control is the presupposition behind a great deal of technology. It's a kind of hubris, a kind of triumphalism. It is what Albert calls "regardless power," a power without concern for the consequences. When you get powerful enough technologically and you have this ideology, the consequences are terrible, not only ecologically but sociologically. You don't care what happens to people any more than you care about what happens to nature.

BW: So the great modern problem is that our means of controlling the earth have outstripped our moral capacity to recognize the consequences.

RB: The means determine the ends, which is just the opposite of what ought to be the case in normal human activity.

BW: In his book *Cosmopolis: The Hidden Agenda of Modernity*, Steven Toulmin made the case that Modernity was largely born over the short span of 50 frantic years in 17th-century Europe, an age marked by widespread social, economic, intellectual, and religious crises. I wonder what can be learned from that earlier moment of cultural crisis that would help us avoid repeating earlier mistakes? What lessons can we draw from the history of Modernity's origins that would help us in this transitional period?

RB: Well, Steven accurately describes that situation of extraordinary upheaval. It was the most violent century in European history—with the exception of our own century—and very heavily involving religious conflict. Coming out of the Reformation, these struggles were tearing Europe apart. And so there was an effort, through the use of reason, to construct ways of thinking— philosophical, scientific, and so forth—that would transcend the religious conflict and therefore bring order. It was a rather harsh kind of order from Steven's point of view. Very formalistic, abstract, quasi-mathematical, and with consequences for all subsequent history.

BW: An attempt, as Toulmin puts it, to "wipe the slate clean" and start anew.

RB: Exactly, because the traditions were killing people. They were all fighting with each other. And we certainly do see the resurgence of religious primordialism in a variety of forms of conflict today, although I don't really think the 20th century is a terribly good analogy. I suppose the extreme technical messianism of the late 20th century is somewhat parallel to what Toulmin describes in the 17th century. That somehow through the computer and the World Wide Web and so on we're going to solve all our problems. That we don't need tradition. We hardly even need human beings. Just the lone individual and the computer will be the answer to all our problems.

BW: So the lesson is that we won't get out of our present dilemma by merely technical means. There are always unavoidable moral issues to be faced.

RB: Indeed.

BW: Do you remember Toulmin describing how Renaissance humanism gave way to scientific rationalism in the 17th century? Is there anything that can be said with confidence about the respective roles of philosophy, science, and religion as Modernity was being forged in the 17th century that is worth remembering in today's quest for a "good society"? By "good," I mean a society and economy that doesn't imagine it can improve itself at the expense of the basic earth system on which it depends, or by enlarging the gap between rich and poor.

RB: I think one precedent we *ought* to have learned is that wiping the slate clean is not going to do it. The effort to construct society entirely on the basis of critical reason has turned into a nightmare and contributed in the 20th century to some of the greatest forces of unreason in human history. Human beings are rooted in community and tradition, and if that isn't respected the consequences are going to be movements like Nazism and extreme religious nationalism and other such things. Even in the university today, which is probably one of the most secular segments of the whole society, there's an increasing willingness to entertain the notion that religion is generic to the human species, that it's something we better take seriously with some degree of respect, rather than imagine it's on its last legs and we can just forget it. So I think we have learned some lessons. It's not a question of the presence or absence of religion. Religion is going to be around. Tradition is going to be around. It's a question of what kind of religion. What kind of tradition. So that's our task.

BW: Are you saying that the notable feature about our modern hubris has been this effort to run away from the religious nature of our being?

RB: Entirely. And of course much of our education is based on a stark and stunning separation of the sacred and the secular, to the great impoverishment of our intellectual as well as our moral life.

BW: Yet you see that wall of separation breaking down within the greatest of our secular institutions?

RB: I would say it's being questioned. I don't think structurally it has been broken down by a long shot. Of course part of the irony of our situation, given that most of higher education through most of history was designed to train people for the clergy, is that religion is now pushed to the margins. Departments of religious studies have the lowest prestige and are apt to have the highest ratio of students to faculty. Because they have low prestige, the professors in those departments are often more positivistic than people in other fields and least apt to go to church in order to prove that they are true blue intellectuals and real academics. So departments of religious studies can turn up to be part of the problem rather than part of the answer. And, of course, we have banished theological education to the margins of university life for a very long time. So bringing religion into some real dynamic interchange with the whole secular culture of the university is very much a project of the future. If I see anything hopeful it is just a few budding signs, a willingness to open one's mind, rather than any real structural shift as yet.

BW: This is a long-term project.

RB: Very long-term. We may not live long enough to succeed in it if current trends of human destructiveness continue.

BW: I've heard you speak passionately in the past about what you have called our massively false belief in unlimited material progress and endlessly rising material affluence. Yet while this cultural belief in progress is enshrined in our political economy and cherished by both left and right, it has absolutely no warrant in the biblical tradition. So there is this huge clash of values between scripture and our dominant institutions of power and control. Yet in practice even organized religion has pretty much made peace with our economy, which may account for why many people feel religion offers no real alternative in practice. How do we make sense of this? Why such a gap between the story we affirm and actual religious practice?

RB: Well, of course, the religious tradition has given us a powerful orientation to the future, and millennialism at this moment is obviously lurking barely off-stage all over the place. Christianity, in a perverted form, has contributed to this notion by taking the Kingdom of God idea and secularizing it, falsely promising that we're going to create endless material progress and a society where everybody is going to be happy. It's a perverted secular version, to be sure. But I do think that some of the dynamism behind material progress comes precisely from the biblical tradition which has a powerful lineal conception of history. We move forward in time. It's not a cyclical view. So that can be secularized into a notion about material progress that knows no limits. I heard someone at a conference in Mexico argue convincingly to me that the advanced world—Europe, U.S., Japan—just to hold our own ecologically, ought to turn to living standards of circa 1950, perhaps allowing the rest of the world to catch up a bit. Because the notion of us improving our living standards along with the rest of the world is a clear shortcut to total disaster. Yet politically that argument is almost an impossible suggestion. What politician in any advanced industrial country, by suggesting we should return to living standards of the 1950s, can expect to get a hearing or be considered for re-election?

BW: Which surely underscores why we cannot count on the Left or Right to address these substantive issues. It will have to come from other places of leadership and deeper places within ourselves.

RB: Exactly. On the other hand, I think that if the standard-of-living issues were presented in a way that linked them to quality of life issues, there would be more public willingness to consider the alternatives than is currently imaginable. There have been polls which asked people, "Would you be willing to have a smaller income if you could live in a place where you weren't afraid to go out at night and felt you could trust most people?" And people, by and large, will say, "Yes." In other words, a relentless concern for maximizing one's known material position without regard to the kind of society in which you live makes sense only in a situation where you have absolutely no confidence in the rest of society. And therefore you need security guards, you need to live in gated communities, etc. But not because you really like that. You might really like something else and would be willing to accept a lower standard of living if you could live in a place where people were fulfilled together. And that would mean relying on public provision a lot more than we now do.

A few years ago, I met the executive of a very large Swedish insurance corporation, probably among the more highly paid executives in Sweden, who told me he does not own a car. Stockholm is designed so that everyone lives within walking distance of green space. Everyone lives within walking distance of easy public transportation. When they go to the country for the weekend or take a couple of weeks off in the summer, they rent a car. But they don't need to own a car. Imagine what that would mean in a society where wealthy people can afford two or three cars, yet they don't have any because everyone can count on public provision. Imagine living in a place that is so beautiful that you don't always have to go to some other place to find beauty, where in your own city there is safe, quick, public transportation that is actually much more convenient than owning an automobile.

BW: Sweden sounds like everybody's paradise, but I know there's some truth in your description.

RB: They do have a lot of problems of their own, but you see what I mean. If you organize life in such a way that you can feel fulfilled and happy and prosperous without this immense array of energy-consuming equipment in every household—above all the automobile, which is the single most destructive things we possess—I think it could be sold. But in this society there is almost no leverage for that.

BW: You're suggesting that polls and studies indicate a willingness among Americans to make some sacrifices and changes, provided we could address some of the social and environmental issues that would make us feel like we're getting more out of our common life together.

RB: Yes, that's right. But there is bad news too, as we describe in our new introduction to *Habits of the Heart*. Our civic resources are way down, even since that book was published a decade ago. Public trust is way down. Membership in civic organizations is way down. So we live in a society where people are increasingly motivated by fear and defending their most immediate interests precisely because they don't trust our institutions—certainly not government, not business—and less so one another. The two institutions in which people have not lost confidence, despite everything else, are the Church and the army.

BW: The Church and the military? What a curious pair of institutions in which to place our trust. One, I suppose, expressing our deepest hopes, and the other perhaps an expression of our deepest fears.

RB: Yes. The sheer order and coherence of military life appeals to people when they're living in chaos. Another deep irony at this moment in history is the use of our troops in Haiti and in Bosnia as peacekeepers. Using the army in this way is one of the best things we are doing in the world.

BW: Yet there is also among Americans this residue of trust in our religious institutions. If we want our political and institutional leaders to help us address the question of what we now mean by a good society, a good community, a good life, what role do our local churches and faith communities play in the politics of meaning? For instance, you've said that we need conversation in cold times to prepare for a time of social transformation. What role might local churches and faith communities play in helping us talk about the things that really matter, in helping us give sustained attention to these issues and possibilities?

RB: I think they are our last best hope. Religious people are often amazed at the amount of confidence I have in the Church, for instance. It's not that I have so much confidence in the Church; it's that I have even less confidence in anything else. The local parish or congregation is for many people in this society the only voluntary group that connects them to the larger society aside from their job. The declining membership in all kinds of organizations that is now apparent is even showing up in a modest decline in religious membership. But it is much more modest in religious bodies than in any other kind of voluntary group. So people are still involved and engaged there, which is why it is incorrect to think of ourselves as a secular society. We know from comparative work in Europe that not only is religious membership much higher in the U.S., but more importantly there is a much higher percentage of American laity actively engaged in their local parish—about 25 percent in America compared to 5 percent or less in European countries. So if Americans belong to a faith community, they are far more likely than Europeans to be engaged in committees and take on actual projects that contribute to society's betterment.

There is also a recent study by Sydney Verba and others, which we refer to in our new introduction to *Habits of the Heart*, which shows that civic skills—the capacity to have influence in U.S. society—correlate highly with income, above all, with education, and occupation. People who feel confident speaking in public, who feel confident in writing their congressperson, picking up the phone and calling a government official to make their views known, tend to come from the high end across the board. This is probably one of the reasons why conservatives are powerful now, not because they are numerous but because rich people happen to be conservative. The only exception to this high correlation is active engagement in religious associations. It turns out, for instance, that African Americans active in their churches have civic skills comparable to whites with much higher income levels, because their churches are teaching them how to speak, how to run a meeting, how to raise money, etc. And so they make themselves felt in community and society. This is the only thing that crosses class lines. Otherwise correlation with class and civic participation is extraordinarily high.

We don't have something like the British Labour Party. We've never had a humanistic socialist tradition in this society. Labor unions have been pushed to the wall and are ever smaller. So aside from the Church, what is there that speaks for most people? With 98 percent of the money given for political campaigns coming from 2 percent of the population, almost all our civic or political life is controlled by monied interests. This means that our whole political system is just totally skewed to the most affluent Americans. The one thing that makes a difference is our local churches and religious membership.

BW: In the past we had many small communities in this country that nurtured the kind of leadership skills and civic volunteerism you say is now reserved to local faith communities.

RB: It's still important, and relative to other societies strong in this country. But all the indications and trends are downward. So aside from religion and religiously associated groups, there isn't a lot to be optimistic about.

BW: So while political leadership obviously needs to be involved in the change process at some stage, we're talking about deep cultural changes that must come from the base, from such people and institutions as we would find in any community, from religious lay persons.

RB: I don't totally agree with that. The local congregation can only do so much. An enormous amount depends on the minister, the rabbi, the pastor, the priest. And given the ethos of American religion for quite some time, the dominant note has been therapeutic. Those who never let us forget the poor outside our door and beyond our borders are unique. Most churches have a limited grasp that they are part of a larger world. If the Body of Christ is only a nice liturgical symbol but has no concrete sociological or political meaning, then where is that leadership going to come from? Even if people are engaged. Even if people are learning civic skills. What are they going to use them for, except the defense of their own immediate interests? So leadership from the clergy is absolutely critical. Without it there is no particular reason to be optimistic at all.

There is another layer, too. I think there is a tremendous responsibility for religious intellectuals to take leadership in linking religious traditions to the problems of the world in which we live. We need people who can speak to the religious community and to the general community at large. Everybody points out that we don't have any Reinhold or Richard Niebuhr or Paul Tillich anymore. Well, why don't we? Why is it that we need to call forth people who can take that role, who can articulate something that the local pastor can pick up and do something with? So it's the whole structure. It's not just the local congregation. The local congregation is a great resource, but it can be totally pacified if the leadership takes this therapeutic line, that "it's my spiritual journey" and that's the end of it.

BW: Do you see any signs of a promising shift?

RB: Yes. I see signs all over the place. There is a lot of sensitivity and awareness. *Christian Century* devoted its Spring '96 issue, including its cover, to "Radical Individualism: Habits of the Heart Revisited." They have a big chunk of our new introduction in there. And if you read *Christian Century*, or *Commonweal*, or *Tikkun*, you'll see three American journals that are more on top of most of these issues than any other secular or religious journal you're going to find. So it's there, and though they don't have the clout they had a generation or two ago, it's not gone. To the extent that ideas are fed into local parishes through such journals, it's not missing. There are effective people among religious intellectuals, maybe not as famous as they might once have been, but there are voices and a presence. But we're also constantly fighting this privatization which affects religion as much as everything else. This withdrawal, of trying to go on one's own private pilgrimage and forgetting about the rest of the world. So it's not all good by far, but it's not all bad either.

BW: Lacking that prophetic voice—and I would add Abraham Joshua Heschel to your distinguished list—are people seeking that challenging moral perspective from sources other than our traditional theological leaders?

RB: Who are you thinking of? Because I don't think the secular intellectuals who can speak to a large public are very conspicuous either. You have a voice like Wendell Berry, but he is not primarily a university intellectual or a major influence in American life. And it's hard to think of any on the side of religious intellectuals. The public intellectual of any stripe is not easy to discern today. University intellectuals are primarily oriented to their own special fields and what other professors think of them, not whether they are having an impact on the larger society. Again there are exceptions, but it's not a high-water moment for serious intellectual engagement with the world.

BW: So what do you urge people to pay attention to in this spoiled social environment where there are not obvious public leaders in our midst?

RB: I think we have to seriously consider religious community since it is the best organized community at the local level, provided we can encourage each other through that community to think about the problems that are facing us in the larger society, not at the expense of spirituality, but out of an understanding of who we are as the people of God. For instance what might the eucharist really mean? What might the post-eucharistic prayer mean when it says, "Let us go forth into the world to do the work that is given us to do"? To really do what the liturgy is calling us to do means we have to think about the environment, about civic life, about redressing social wrongs.

BW: In other words, spirituality with a practice and a practicality.

RB: Exactly. But that practical concern brings us back to the source of our being. It's a constant process of renewal and engagement. And I'm not saying that never happens. It does to some degree in many, many places. Did I tell you about this community organization, this group of about twenty-five parishes, about half Catholic and half Protestant, in economically poor and marginal parts of Oakland, California? These people are definitely linking their religious commitment to the life of Oakland and the larger society on issues like education, basic safety, etc. They are mainly helping people in these parishes feel that they have a voice, that they can be listened to, that they can make a difference in their community. They've had their setbacks, but by and large it's a remarkably positive story. And the only basis for successful community organizing is the parish! Many secular groups that are suspicious of religion have tried to organize these minority and poverty areas, but they get nowhere, literally nowhere! The only ones that succeed are parish-based, because that is where the people are and who the people trust. Again, the key dimension is the pastor. If the pastor supports this, it is going to go. If the pastor is against it, it won't go. Maybe it ought not to be that way. But let's face it, the clergy are absolutely critical.

BW: So there you have yet another good example of ways in which local congregations, in this case by banding together, can be simultaneously effective at both spiritual and civic renewal.

RB: Yes. They never have a demonstration without prayer. And it is sincere prayer. They really do combine their spiritual and their political concerns. Have you read Jonathan Kozol's book, *Amazing Grace*? Kozol describes an Episcopal parish in South Bronx that is astounding. It is the last place I would have expected to find an Episcopal parish, but it is the only ray of hope in that place. Coming from our upper-class white denomination, to find that we have a presence in a place like that is very moving.

BW: I look forward to reading it.

RB: In terms of religion and contemporary society, I have picked up from Jürgen Habermas a way of phrasing a problem that is helpful. He makes the distinction between what he calls the "lifeworld," which in his peculiar way he says is steered by language. And in contrast to the lifeworld, there is what he calls the "systems," which are the administrative state and the market economy, one steered by power and the other by money. Non-linguistic media are doing the steering. The way Habermas describes our current situation is that the systems are invading and colonizing the lifeworld.

This is happening in every institution. I had a student whose father resigned from directing the Denver Jewish Community Center because the president and board of that center were more oriented toward the bottom line than to what he viewed as Jewish ethics. Just to give you one example, they wanted to cut the budget for child care and increase the budget for the health club. The child care program was for very needy people. The health club was for upscale people to work out, you know. Why? Because the one was making money and the other wasn't. My student was just astounded at that. And it's happening to hospitals. At lunch, Ann Swidler was telling me that Sloan-Kettering may close—probably the single most important research hospital in the United States—because it's losing too much money. The notion is that we cannot provide money for medical research because now medicine is expected to turn a profit.

Look at higher education. In many, many places tenure-track positions are being reduced as they hire these short-term people for a few years and throw them out. It's exploitation. It's an academic underclass, as well as exploiting graduate students to teach when the chances of their landing a job after getting their Ph.D.'s are increasingly bad. So in every part of our society is this invasion and colonization of the lifeworld, as Habermas calls it, in our case more by the market economy than by the state. In the Soviet system it was the state that was doing the colonizing, and in our society it is increasingly the market that is so invasive.

BW: And increasingly in all societies it is the market economy that is colonizing, especially with the spread of a global economy.

RB: Yes it is, Ben, but it is so much worse here in America than anywhere else. It is just a quantum difference. These are global trends to be sure, even north of the border, where Canada is going through the same thing. But it is much more severe and omnipresent here in America. I have a daughter living in Germany and I can tell you there is pressure on the social support system there, but it is so much more adequate than ours is, or ever was! Yes it's a global trend! But there is just no serious resistance here anymore. In almost every other advanced country there is serious resistance. We argue in the new introduction to *Habits* that our lack of resistance has to do with this extraordinary ideology of individualism.

BW: Which started with us, the first truly modern nation. We are the proving ground and impetus for this experiment the world over.

RB: But any society that doesn't have a viable lifeworld isn't even going to be able to reproduce itself. Without systems that work, based on some degree of trust, people won't ultimately honor their contracts, social or economic. If you're producing a situation where nobody trusts anybody, then you approach system collapse. So I guess what I'm trying to say in using this lifeworld/system analogy, which I think is a powerful way of putting it, is that right at the core of the lifeworld is the Church. And this puts a heavy responsibility on the Church whose life is organized linguistically—where language and story are its only resources—to take the initiative in response to these pressures and try to fight back. We have all this talk about the family. But the family, as we know, is an extremely fragile institution, an extremely vulnerable institution. The economic pressures on the family today are destroying it, just cutting it to shreds. Families can't operate without some larger context, and the most immediate context for the family is the local parish. So that's another way in which the Church contributes to the viability of the lifeworld in the face of these pressures, in our case, from the market economy.

BW: Our residual trust in these religious institutions makes me think that we instinctively and correctly sense they are our last chance by which to express a meaningful life together. Because they represent the rallying place for the struggle of the lifeworld to resist the systems, in essence the struggle to assert a sacred view of life versus one that is simply reduced to a society full of consumers.

RB: Profane in the deepest sense. Yes, I think that's where we are. And maybe in this millennial mood, at least some people in the Church will begin to see it that way.

Prospects for Enduring
Economies and Cultures

WILLIAM K. REILLY

William K. Reilly was Administrator of the Environmental Protection Agency under President George Bush. Reilly has written and lectured extensively on environmental issues and is highly respected on both sides of the political aisle. His personal integrity and outspoken views in public occasionally put him at odds with the president he served in those years. Reilly elevated the international priority at EPA, headed the U.S. delegation to revise the treaty that protects the ozone layer, and led the U.S. delegation to the Earth Summit conference in Rio de Janeiro. An early advocate of market-based incentives in environmental regulation, he used this principle to integrate the national enviromental and economic agendas in the Clean Air Act of 1990 and in several incentive-based regulatory programs for toxics, pesticides, and energy conservation. Before his tenure at EPA, he was president of the World Wildlife Fund and the Conservation Foundation where he pioneered debt-for-nature swaps with Costa Rica and Ecuador. Reilly is an alumnus of Yale, holds a law degree from Harvard and a master's degree in urban planning from Columbia, and he is a Catholic. He said at one point, "Environmentalists are fundamentally groping in the same direction as Catholic social teaching, because they are both looking for a system that values community more, one that involves an ethical extension of community that includes economy and nature as part of the same moral enterprise."

BW: I understand you began your conservation career with the President's Council on Environmental Quality just before Earth Day 1970.

WR: I have always been interested in development, in the edges more than the wilderness. I tend to think that the excitement, the frontier, the creativity is in the edges. A lot of biodiversity is in the edges, too. That happens to be a fairly productive area of the environment.

BW: When you say the edges, what do you mean?

WR: Well, where nature has some boundaries. Where the deep forest yields to meadows and more open lands, and where the countryside begins to open to the city. I've often thought the most creative problems in the environment are to figure out how to fit people and development into nature, to accommodate to nature, rather than simply to protect unspoiled or pristine nature, as important as that is. The task of conservation, it's always seemed to me, is really a task of creation. And especially in the developing world, where the development imperative is fundamental, the challenge is to make sure that development is infused with respectful values regarding nature, not to oppose it altogether.

BW: I am struck by the excitement you find along the edges of things. I want to talk about another edge and its significance, where religion and the environment merge. But first I'd like to discuss the global environmental crisis as you see it, and the American role in it. In an interview with Steven Lerner prior to the Earth Summit, James MacNeill said that despite our best efforts, there has been a steady increase in the frequency, scale, and impact of environmental disasters worldwide since the late 1960s. With population now expected to double in 40 years and economic activity expected to increase five-to-tenfold in that time frame, he said the chance of a progressive ecological collapse is very real unless people and institutions begin to change fairly radically. This sounds like a profound challenge for human civilization. What is your perspective? Are we facing something unprecedented in scope and urgency?

WR: There is a reading you can make of current trends which is very negative and hopeless, and it goes pretty much like this. There are 5.5 billion people in the world today. Conservatively we can assume that number will become 8 billion or so in 40 or 50 years, perhaps leveling off around 12 billion. In many parts of Africa and Asia we already see extreme stresses, depleted environments, rates of erosion that are serious, a fall-off of agricultural productivity despite the use of fertilizers. Fish stocks are also under stress. We're approaching the limits of what we can take from the sea. All of that I think is true.

Nevertheless, there are some very promising signs and I don't think that we should ignore them. The world is vastly freer than it was just a few years ago; there is reasonable ground for optimism and confidence in that. And if you take different parts of the world one by one and look at the prospects for successful adaptation of enduring economies and cultures, the prospects are better in Eastern Europe—with the single exception, and a large one, of Russia, where the jury is still out. In Latin America things are more promising than they have been in many years with more free countries, more market-oriented countries, with NAFTA and the prospects of a unified trade area possibly reaching out to Chile and Argentina and eventually other countries. The populations of some of these countries—Mexico is a good example—are not likely to be as high as had been projected as recently as the late 1970s. Birth rates have even come down in the Philippines and in Korea and in other places where they used to be very, very high. The economic prospects for China look very good at the moment, as they do for Vietnam, which has been an economic backwater, a place of virtually no freedom.

Africa is the place for which we have no answer, where, except in South Africa, the facts seem to offer little hope for near-term economic improvement or long-term adequacy of resources and biodiversity. I think there could be ecological collapse in some places, West Africa in particular, in part because of chaotic and unstable social and political systems.

Now that may sound like a rosy scenario overall, but I think it's one that is reasonably fair to the facts in those places that I mentioned. The world has known famine and plague and distress for a long time, and I think it is in our future. But I don't despair of our capacity to get it right in some substantial parts of the world either.

BW: But can the planet sustain a material consumption rate on the part of billions more that conforms to present U.S. patterns?

WR: I have a problem with the American or affluent northerner, saying, "We have five and a half billion people and it's going to double, so there's no way we can stand to have other countries aspire to the level of material comfort we have." From a policy point of view that is not helpful, and it's a didactic that seems to me utterly unjust and ineffective. I'm extremely uncomfortable with what I call the " 'let them eat bread' philosophy of romantic underdevelopment," and it also infuriates people in the developing world. That's just what they suspect we think, that we want to hold them down so that we can continue to heat up the atmosphere. It is especially infuriating when it is said by people who show no signs themselves of moving their per capita emissions of greenhouse gases anywhere close to what they are in the developing world, where they are often one-tenth as much as they are in the United States. So I honestly take a lot more positive encouragement from the development dynamic than I think most environmentalists do. I think it will be good for people and good for the world that many of these societies develop. I think we'll see some of the problems that we fear become less serious as affluence becomes more widespread. We will see parts of the world that now look very stressed and overtaxed begin to look more like what we would consider appropriate and productive. Now the other slant you can take on the issue is to say that even if the prospects for market economies, for material abundance, for higher standards of living, better health care, and longer lifespans are real for many of these countries, the stresses that would be placed on the global ecosystem call all that into question.

BW: That's my question, too.

WR: While the consumption patterns that we have are arguably not sustainable for much of the rest of the world, I'm not sure the answer is sackcloth and ashes. We could choose a more austere life and abjure the automobile and a lot of other comforts we have—the large amount of space, the second homes, the airplane travel—but I don't see a lot of us doing that, even environmentalists. I'm reminded that Dennis Meadows and Herman Kahn once had totally opposite philosophies with regard to the limits of growth. Dennis Meadows thought that early in the next century we were going to crash against a ceiling that would limit our consumption of resources. Herman Kahn thought that we were going to see a sort of "S" curve of basic satiety or social sufficiency, of a sense that we had done it with material affluence and that we would then begin to lower very considerably the portion of the resources that we consumed relative to our per capita numbers or our expenditure of money. In fact there is some evidence that this is true; it does seem to be happening. The material component of a dollar increment of product is less than it was twenty years ago. The energy necessary to produce it is down to about 40 percent. It's possible that we could become more efficient with less material, depend more on technologies to get at certain kinds of problems, become more information-oriented and create value in that way in the future. I think that is perfectly reasonable. It may be that we will ourselves provide some instructive experience and lessons for the rest of the world as well.

So I think our hope for the long-term future—if the hypothesis of climate change proves out as I suspect it will—has to be to achieve lower population ceilings, especially in the developing world. To say we have to have fewer babies to prevent stressing the earth's systems is not a friendly message in many parts of the world, particularly coming from affluent northerners. But I think it is a reasonable hope given the direction of material improvement, since the two typically correlate. As people get better off they have fewer children. We also need to develop Chinese cars that are not as stressful to the environment as our cars are, that do not consume the kind of fossil fuels that ours do. Just as we were able to convince the Chinese to use substitute technologies in 300 million new refrigerators, rather than using ozone-depleting chlorofluorocarbon compounds as a refrigerant.

BW: So you're more optimistic than MacNeill?

WR: There's no question in my mind that for much of the developed world, management of the environment is something we have achieved. We may not have solved all the problems, but if you look at the large indices of environmental health in the U.S., the levels of sulfur dioxides and carbon monoxides in cities are down a third from where they were twenty years ago. Particulates are down two-thirds. Lead, one of the worst pollutants, is down 97 percent, largely as a consequence of our having phased it out of gasoline, and that's happening in Europe as well. The Great Lakes are vastly healthier than they were twenty years ago. The fecal coliform counts, nutrient counts, and algae blooms are all way down. Many of our rivers support fish life that they haven't supported in a hundred years. Some of them have concentrations of PCBs or dioxin that are worse, it is true, but they are alive and back, and PCB and dioxin concentrations are coming down too. We have about a hundred million more cars than we had twenty years ago, but the cars are about 98 percent cleaner. So in the developed world, in the United States, I think environmentalists make a big mistake crying doom and acting as though the glass is always half empty when in fact we have filled it quite a lot more than half way.

The problems we are talking about are developing world problems or global ecosystem and climate disturbance problems. The Montreal Protocol was tremendously encouraging because it suggests that when the world does in fact encounter a major disturbance and sees that the science is compelling, it responds. We're straightening out the problem of upper atmospheric ozone. In terms of carbon dioxide, the fundamental byproduct of combustion which drives our economies and transportation and everything else, I learned that Kyoto Electric was experimenting with ways to strip the molecule and to separate the carbon and sequester it from the oxygen, which is then allowed to go out the stack. It's not yet economical, but it's not beyond the capacity of humankind to figure out ways to do that. I don't think environmentalists should dismiss technology just because it creates so many of these problems when it has the capacity to solve them as well. I guess I am more hopeful than MacNeill.

BW: Without dismissing the legitimate claim that developing or undeveloped countries have to achieve a better life, isn't it a little difficult to imagine replicating a world of nation-states as materialistic and wasteful as ours? For instance, Fred Krupp of the Environmental Defense Fund [EDF] has said that the U.S., with only 7 percent of the world's population, is probably causing around 60 percent of the damage to the global web of life, and that one American has the equivalent environmental impact of nearly thirty people in the undeveloped world. Even you have pointed out, when comparing the U.S. to Germany, Japan, Switzerland, and Italy, that we waste two to three times more per person and use two to three times more energy per person than do people in these developed countries. Is this a reasonably accurate picture of the U.S. role in waste and consumption?

WR: I think it's a one-sided picture. The amount of municipal waste we have is under 200 million tons. I tend to think that it says something about our attitudes and our philosophy regarding nature that we allow ourselves to be so profligate in its use, but this is more a criticism of us personally than it is something that the earth cannot withstand. I don't think the amount of wood products or plastics that we are using are themselves taxing the earth severely. I really don't. The argument that Americans are responsible for so much of the stress and pressure on the world I think neglects a lot of things. American forests, in fact, are more plentiful, cover more land area, contain more biomass today than was true a hundred years ago. Our farms are very productive and fertile. People argue that they're too chemical intensive and a lot of other things, but by worldwide standards we are not doing too badly in that area. We are not, as they are in Chiapas and Oaxaca and a lot of other places I've been in the developing world in recent years, burning our hillsides just to expand grazing land or establish land tenure and ownership.

To a very large degree we are living within our means. I think it is true that we are profligate with energy use. But we have been sufficiently productive to be able to compensate the rest of the world for supplying what we need. As a former official of the U.S. government, I can't count the number of times I have heard Third World officials rail against American consumption practices in public, and then take me or colleagues aside and plead with us to increase consumption of their tin or coffee or their oil or their products of one sort or another, in what would seem a totally hypocritical way, but was really just a way they had not reconciled. It's popular to say that we Americans place most of the stress on the planet, and yet where is this stress? I think that population and poverty pressures in fact are very stressful and do result in erosion and played-out land and lost fertility. But we're not doing much of that, and we're not honestly responsible for a lot of the countries that do it. There is a sense of victimization that you sometimes hear in the Third World, that somehow it's the developed countries that are driving this whole process. But it's not the developed countries that have caused them to have so many children. I mean, let's be honest about some of those choices that they are making. It's not the developed world that has foisted corrupt governments on so many of these places. It's not the developed world that has prevented them from having free trade or free markets which would have liberated a lot of creative energies and entrepreneurship in their cultures and I think brought them to a higher standard of living and lower population numbers and all the rest. I think that more than a few problems have been created by the people there themselves. Look at some of the countries like Argentina that used to be a huge exporter of grain, or Chile, now that they've moved to these extremely unproductive latifundia and suffered the social consequences and inequities there.

I am someone who believes that the moral contribution of the United States has been positive on balance: that we have advanced freedom; that we have created conditions for growth and economic development for ourselves and others, even affluence in many parts of the world; and that, by and large, our political influence has been benign. So I am less prepared to say that the United States is somehow implicated in 60 percent of the world's environmental problems simply because it consumes so much more in the way of resources. We ought not to lose sight of the fact that consumption of resources is powering economies and improving the lives of people in many parts of the world in a global economy. Environmentalists have to get that straightened out in their heads. Were we not to be consuming at the level we are, there would be a very severe worldwide recession, or possibly depression. Now some will come back and say, "Yes, that's the problem with the economic signals and incentives that are built into the system that we have."

BW: That's right. In fact, MacNeill, economist Herman Daly, Bruce Rich at EDF and others contend that the only way to avoid ecological disaster and achieve sustainability is to make the transition from growth-based economies to a steady-state economy at every level—regional, national, and international. The vision they are working toward is for the world's economy and the Earth's ecology to become intermeshed at all levels.

WR: I think it's worthwhile to try to influence those economic signals and incentives to become more sustainable. But it's not a trivial problem. It's a difficult thing to rejigger the worldwide economy, and you don't do it responsibly without stimulating a lot more efficiency. I think there are vast possibilities for greater efficiencies, certainly on the part of Americans in the use of all sorts of resources, particularly energy. I don't think we've even begun to plumb the depths there. Amory Lovins at the Rocky Mountain Institute is very practical and specific about different kinds of glass we can use, different materials for automobiles, different ways to build houses that require virtually nothing more than solar heat. He grows bananas at 7,500 feet in the Colorado Rockies and has had his second crop this year with no use of fossil fuels, all with a little greenhouse construction. Those things we have not had to do and so we haven't done them. But as a matter of national self-interest and responsibility for consumption of these resources, which are going to become scarcer over time, I think we have to do it and we can do it.

It struck me as astonishing that even after the Kuwait war we didn't institute any of the measures designed to reduce our dependency on foreign oil. That is a blind spot with Americans. Yet this is possible for us. The prospect is also very real for then making these efficiencies available to the economies that are being built almost from the ground up, to some of the developing countries which are going to have countless more factories and automobiles and refrigerators and appliances and all that. But we have to do this somewhat gradually. I guess I've never been a fan of most revolutions. As I said before, I think ecological collapse in some places is likely, especially in parts of West Africa. But I don't despair of our capacity to get our political and social systems right with the environment in some substantial parts of the world either.

BW: In terms of improving our political, economic, and social systems, let me ask you about religion and the environment as sources of instruction. When I look at the social disintegration, environmental destruction, and moral confusion that surrounds us, and ask myself where we might turn for reliable instruction, it's clear to me that one source is nature, what we might call ecological wisdom. I seem to recall that, as EPA administrator, you made a point of constructing agency priorities based on principles of ecology by elevating the status of your scientific advisory board.

WR: Yes. I started something called "ecological mapping" which is designed to get a fix on ecological conditions and trends. For instance, to what degree is the country healthy and fertile according to the kinds of organisms we can find in the soils, according to the birdlife and wildlife of one sort or another? I think that's very important for us as a mature country that wants to have a long-term relationship with its land. In many places it looks like we're short-termers, even in the very places where the opportunity would seem to be the largest, where the real money is. You look at the mess that has been made in much of Florida, which is an ecologically delicate place, a sensitive place, a beautiful place, and can support a lot of life. But Florida is a place where the groundwater has been contaminated, the architecture has been monotonized, and it ends up being a not particularly attractive living environment. That has social manifestations, too. The movement toward walled cities and enclaves, toward guarded and gated cities, is extremely unattractive in our culture. We know what it responds to, but the idea that you can somehow turn in and avoid contact with the larger society is not very healthy. These things are related.

BW: So sensitivity to nature is not just a matter of aesthetics but of real practicality in developing enduring civilizations. Yet a transformation through ecological literacy may not be enough given the human challenge before us. You've referred publicly to another stream of meaning that is flowing in to join and reinforce ecological wisdom, the spiritual wisdom and moral values of the world's great religious traditions. As these two cultural resources and their principles converge, is it your hope that we will draw on them to help shape a more just and enduring economy?

WR: I think that the crisis of our time is much more a spiritual one than an ecological one, quite frankly. The absence of meaning that prompts us to fill our lives with material goods should be more distressing to Americans than ecological degradation.

BW: Are they unrelated, these crises of community, of overconsumption, of environmental destruction, of spiritual malaise?

WR: They very well may be related. This may be what a lot of moralists in the environmental movement are getting at when they say that excess material consumption is a response to a spiritual vacuum. This not only afflicts Americans. It's due to a loss of meaning and faith worldwide. Yet it's clear to me that if you want to reach people, Americans or anyone else, you don't do so just through their minds. You impel their hearts. And I think the hunger for spiritual values and significance of a religious sort is a very fundamental one, and environmentalists would do well to recognize it and to appeal to it. But it has always struck me as interesting that environmentalists in the U.S., who are hugely tolerant of Third World indigenous people and their religious beliefs, are extremely intolerant of traditional religious systems such as Christianity, particularly fundamentalist Christianity. I said this at Yale to the Campus Earth Summit in response to all the talk about Rush Limbaugh and why he has so many followers.

I said that what might just be differences of opinion to others seem to that group to be matters of fundamental moral value. Religious fundamentalists believe that a lot of environmentalists' values are deeply flawed. Why is that so? One reason for it, I said, is that they are religious and they believe that you and a lot of other American environmentalists have contempt for their religious values, their outlook, their belief system—and you do. In other words, there is an insufficient tolerance for our own traditional belief systems which, in the case of Christianity, represent one of the very few sources of authority for questioning material consumer society. So in that sense it's not logical for environmentalists to have this kind of outlook. They ought to be building bridges to those groups. In all the great religions, there is a basis in religious authority for doing what they want to do, for respecting the created order. And these Christians ought to be receptive to environmental arguments that are based on scripture, for which they have tremendous reverence. Yet that is not obvious to a lot of environmentalists.

BW: But isn't there evidence of a growing spiritual hunger that expresses itself in the convergence of religion and ecology?

WR: Most religions have environmental projects of one sort or another going on. I think the churches have become increasingly sensitive to environmental stewardship, and have tried to draw upon those elements of their authoritative tradition that reinforce responsibility for nature. I've read some very good theological treatises on the book of Genesis and other books of the Bible, and on the lives of the saints and prophets, where theologians are drawing out of them principles for reconciliation between humans and nature. So Christianity is looking for parts of its tradition that appeal to the awareness, which is new in this century, of our capacity to alter the global ecosystem. It's not that Christianity is so guilty of these problems. You'll find the same problems—significantly worse than in the U.S.—in China, in India, and some of the Buddhist countries, which ostensibly have in their religious tradition and culture a great reverence for nature. I don't say that to castigate them, for they are also at another stage of development. But I don't think those cultures have done much better at pioneering better environmental records than those influenced by Christianity. However, I do think there are plenty of correctives to draw upon within all of the religious traditions. I take a lot of encouragement from the Franciscan and Benedictine traditions in Christianity, both Umbrian saints separated by several centuries who had very different contributions to offer. I also happen to think the traditions that come down from both of them are very uniquely present in the United States, particularly the Franciscan influence.

BW: Haven't you said that the modern American environmental movement can trace its roots to a conservation ethic which goes off along those two branches?

WR: Yes. Before Francis, I'm not aware of anything quite like the intrinsic respect for nature that he advocates, that nature had rights in and of itself, even birds and animals which had no apparent utilitarian value. Lord knows where he got it, but I think it began with him. This Franciscan notion of intrinsic value is very much in evidence in American conservation efforts. The Benedictine outlook, which has been equally productive, was more utilitarian in terms of its concerns with sustainable use of resources. But both of those are very rich traditions that are insufficiently appreciated by today's environmental movement or the Church.

BW: And both of them are rooted in expressions of religious community.

WR: Which is instructive itself. Because while we hunger for a spiritual support system, we also sense we have constructed in our country communities that don't work satisfactorily. We are disturbed by the excessive levels of violence, of family fragmentation, of personal loneliness and alienation in America. I think we live more atomized lives than many more traditional cultures, even those of some wealthy countries, like Italy. There is now an unavoidable social pathology that has been driven home to us, and we are paying the consequences.

BW: So there are consequences to our radical individualism.

WR: Yes. Excessive individualism makes managing the environment more difficult. Everything is harder, from confronting peoples' attitudes toward their right to alter wetlands, for example, to the regulation of gun ownership. But I think there is also in this country a very large sympathy for religion in the main, a feeling that we would be a healthier country with healthier communities if we were a more religious country, and a sense that our traditional religions offer us more guidance in steering our way through these difficult times than perhaps we've appreciated.

BW: You've been a public official and leader for many years and must have a feel for how social movements and their moral claims get heard in high places.

WR: Well, the source of most moral authority in this country is from religious traditions and institutions, and the capacity to draw on a religious tradition and appeal to religious values is very important to the success of a lot of policies. But I often had the sense that our religious communities were failing to give to their adherents an understanding of the fundamental moral issues affecting their use of land, for example. If we had more help from the ministers and priests, you would get more reverence for certain circumstances of land which would suggest certain uses and preclude others. That would balance individualism's claim to do whatever I want with my own land or be compensated accordingly. Individualism is really not fully attuned to the needs that the land demonstrates on its face.

BW: I want to pick up on what you were saying about the still real moral force that exists in our religious institutions, in their people and leaders. You once drew an analogy between this movement—of religion and the environment—and the Civil Rights Movement. When men and women of faith marched against racism, you said they helped create a new reality by adding a strong current of moral indignation to the milder current of legal reform. Is that analogy instructive to this new movement?

WR: If you look at church attendance in this country, especially the strength of some of the more fundamentalist, evangelical, or charismatic groups, you have to respect this dynamic. You have to see that the moral force is still there. Sometimes the Church loses a certain appeal because it's perceived as not sufficiently concerned with environmental problems, for example. But there's no question that a lot of the moral energy that young people might once have invested in church activities of one sort or another they now invest in environmental action. I would argue there is today a larger convergence of those two attitudes; they respond to the same kinds of ethical convictions and needs and perceptions.

BW: Perhaps young people today recognize the divine presence in the ordinary things of nature. Their moral energy is directed to the resanctification of nature, which ultimately has a lot of practical consequences. This reminds me of your public lecture at Stanford. You said the ecological problem in America is not so much a few primary polluting sources, but a large number of small pollution sources—scattered, diffuse, and individual. Together, these individual sources now exceed all industry sources. The problem this presents, you indicated, is that these individual behaviors don't respond well to compulsion or regulation, to appeals to law, or economic incentives. If not these avenues, then what kind of appeals will engage us and enable us to change the way we lead our lives?

WR: There is an ethic in this society, one that strongly supports the environment. All the polls indicate a very substantial foundation for environmental support on the part of the public, in the range of 85 percent. Yet I think we appeal too little to that ethic. The companies which deal directly with the consumer, the public, are very aware of this. The CEO of Proctor and Gamble said to me once, "We're not doing these things because the law makes us do them. We're not designing compostable diapers and recyclable plastics because the law makes us do them. Our consumers demand that we do them!" If that's the case, the power of information is much greater than we had thought. Simply informing the public about the consequences of their behavior can be very efficacious. That was the point behind a number of voluntary programs at EPA, such as annually publishing measures of emissions or toxic substances, even those that do not exceed maximums. This published information helps provide a moral incentive to neighbors, stockholders, plant employees, newspapers, congressional representatives, and ultimately companies to get these toxic levels down. This is how you build an ethic in the culture. We've yet to figure out how to do that for non-point source pollution which is now the source of more than 50 percent of the water quality problem in this country.

BW: Is most of that from agricultural sources?

WR: A fair amount of it is from agriculture, the consequence of either cultivation practices or excessive deposits of fertilizers and nutrients of various sorts that end up in the bays, the rivers, the groundwater, and ultimately the fish and food we eat. But it's also coming off construction sites, peoples' roofs and parking lots, and a lot of other things that involve individual behavior. And though people aren't evil, we sometimes resist regulation because the costs of controlling erosion can add up. But there are other sources of pollution, like the oil we throw away each year which amounts to sixteen times more than was spilled by the Exxon *Valdez*. And the smog checks we resist which may render 600 to 800 dollars' worth of air pollution control equipment on our newer cars useless. It's one thing to get automakers to install this equipment; it's another to get the drivers of these cars—some of whom may be environmentalists—to take responsibility for maintaining them. The challenge of positively affecting personal choice is harder to get at in terms of public regulation than the regulation of PG&E's power plants. And yet only individual behavioral changes will really make a difference here. But if people understand why we're doing it, if they have information and incentives, I think environmental regulation in general becomes less onerous.

BW: So there is a large reservoir of environmental goodwill on the one hand, and on the other hand some pretty obvious resistance to change beyond a certain point. How do we impel hearts and overcome our resistance to greater personal responsibility?

WR: I think we're very strong environmentalists when it comes to Exxon's behavior in Prince William Sound, but a lot less so when it comes to changing our own motor oil. That's natural, it's human, but I think we need to confront our own behavior much more directly than we have. Ultimately, I would also argue that we need to acknowledge the importance of rearranging the tax burden in the country so that we reinforce economically some of these ethical attitudes toward, for example, wasting energy. If the climate-warming theorists are correct, the oil problem is destructive and certainly exposes us to greater dependency on other countries, all of those being reasons to shape up. If prices were more encouraging of better behavior, then I think the country would be better off. But you don't want to bet the Taj Mahal on peoples' environmentalism when you start talking about energy taxes, or controlling oil prices, or smog checks, or landowners' behaviors toward their wetlands and their rights to develop it. Those programs at EPA where I came into direct confrontation with the consumer or the owner of wetlands or the driver needing a smog check were the most difficult programs that we ran. Those were the places where we had to acknowledge that the general public is more difficult to regulate than General Motors.

BW: If individual choice and responsibility is the new frontier, the new challenge in environmental management, can the religious traditions help us develop new habits of heart?

WR: Well, I think the religious tradition offers an ethical system that is coherent and a source of authority which to many people is very compelling, probably much more so than government. Government of course is backed by the compulsion of law, the courts and the prisons, but the religious systems reach the heart. And we haven't yet reached the heart on this, at least we haven't made the connection with personal behavior to the degree that we need to in this country. The next challenge in America is to line up our ethical beliefs with our individual practices, and I think religion is the glue, the cementing force that can do that. So I don't think Christians should be apologetic about their tradition. I think they should draw on its strengths and recognize that the basis for stewardship is there. The foundation is there in the scriptural tradition and the lives of the saints and what they stood for, and in the monastic tradition, and in some of our greater prophets and poets, for making a very compelling case to individuals.

BW: So if the world still looks to America for moral leadership, and if the new frontier or challenge has to do with how we reshape personal and collective behaviors, then how can religious communities—drawing on their own traditions—best contribute to that task?

WR: Well, there is the radical critique which comes from the Judeo-Christian tradition which is a critique of material abundance and riches, which really advocates a vow of solidarity with the poor. That is not likely to be a very popular message, but I don't want to suggest, in what I said earlier, that I rule it out. It's an exemplary tradition, in the sense that not everybody is called to it. But it causes reflection and makes us do interesting things when we confront people who have chosen a course of radical self-deprivation and service to others. The more mainline message, I think, is one of a certain respect for the created order that leads us, out of a sense of propriety and good conduct, not to do certain things which have lasting, irremediable consequences for a natural system on which both human beings and the whole system itself depends. If that sense of humility before the creation and responsibility for it were itself inculcated by our priests and ministers, then a lot of the practical choices that flow from these basically religious principles could be exercised daily in society.

BW: Our perceptions about the world really do shape our behavior, and the environmental evidence suggests that both need improvement.

WR: Yes, they certainly do. And religion—even religious pluralism—can help bridge some of these gaps, can help unify us. I have a sense that this estrangement from nature and natural systems that you see in so many people in the developed world is itself part of the larger problem. It's part of the growing impersonality in our culture, an overdoing of this individualized, anonymous, privacy-is-everything ethos. We have not fostered a sufficient sense of community and interpersonal caring and responsibility, and that translates into family breakdown. We lose ourselves in material possessions and measure ourselves by material acquisitions. I think those are related, and it seems to me that religion really works against that. Genuine religious values don't tend to be very consistent with exploitation of relationships, of either people or nature. So that's a powerful thing that religion could put to good service on behalf of environmental concerns. Some environmentalists can't see it because they consider traditionalists to be in the other camp, one of the forces of the establishment that they are trying to overthrow because they think they've created all the problems. The truth is we've all created them. I was trying to say to those Yale students that if we're not going to be hypocritical, we've got to come to terms with the consequences of our own, as well as our culture's, material consumption and high standard of living and try to turn it to good advantage, for ourselves and for others and for the future. I don't think people talk that way in public very much, but maybe we need to.

BW: So religious leadership can help the environmental community by addressing the whole pattern of problems of which environmental destruction is just one, in part by focusing on human behavior and social order, which is, after all, where most of these problems arise in the first place.

WR: Yes. Religion deals more or less successfully with these. For a long time, the encyclicals of the popes were groping for a way to intervene in a very harsh economic system. And they did that very bravely in 1890 with *Rerum Novarum*, and the social teachings of the church became very influential and a moral force in the face of a pretty ruthless capitalism. But it's my view that since the 1960s, if not before, there has been a socialist orientation to some of the encyclicals, a difficulty in understanding the degree to which capitalism has in fact fostered a more generous moral order. There is a certain amount of self-interest that is productive and natural and human and not un-Christian. But obviously it can become excessive. Environmentalists, interestingly, have the same problem. This suggests that environmentalists are fundamentally groping in the same direction as Catholic social teaching, because they are both looking for a system that values community more, one that involves an ethical extension of community that includes economy and nature as part of the same moral enterprise.

BW: If young people are turning their moral energies from church activities to environmental issues, and if both environmentalists and people of faith are groping for the spiritual support of community and ethical values that integrate nature and economy, then what does the environmental community have to offer the religious community that it needs to hear?

WR: Well, the environmental community can pose certain moral questions like, "How do we feel about the consumption of tropical timber in developed countries when this timber is being developed at the expense of biological diversity and natural systems in those countries?" And that's an important debate. But the church doesn't have any expertise to lead that debate, whereas the environmental community does. I think the whole issue of climate change, to the extent that science continues to move in the direction of validating it, is going to introduce a moral dimension into environmental choices, into our behavior, that hasn't been there before. Those are things that the church needs to learn from environmentalists, these practical behavioral decisions about whether we throw away oil or resist smog checks or develop wetlands—all of those things. The Wise Use Movement, which has very strong support among religious adherents in many parts of the country, is premised on a constitutional right to develop one's own land or property as one wishes. Environmentalists can help them understand that this is not fundamentally a very Christian outlook if its consequence is the destruction of vast amounts of wildlife, to say nothing of the lives of fishermen and others who depend upon the kinds of things that are nurtured in coastal wetlands. Those are messages that I think would be useful to address to religious thinkers, so you get a more practical intersection between religious values and daily ethics.

BW: What's been your experience and your role in this movement that is drawing religion and the environment together?

WR: I was one of the only heads of a national organization, of which there were then twenty-four in the World Wildlife Fund family, that supported holding a conference in Assisi in 1986, on the occasion of the 25th anniversary of the World Wildlife Fund. Most of the leaders in the national organizations were very opposed to it, and I thought it was interesting as to why. They were anti-religious, many of them, and they certainly didn't want to make any connections to the established religions. They thought the kind of people that would be involved were not particularly supportive of nature and environmental protection, either in Europe or most of the developing world, and they didn't trust them. I think some of them had a particularly strong feeling about Assisi and the significance of going to a Catholic country, to a very Catholic saint's home. Yet that proved to be a tremendously successful conference, and a very moving one. We had the world's major faiths each conducting a ritual, their liturgy, in the church of Saint Francis, in front of those Giottos, with beautiful light and music. We had Buddhist monks chanting; we had dance; we had a Jewish rabbi blowing the ram's horn at the entrance to the church; we had the Sistine Chapel Choir. It was one of the most beautiful things I've ever seen. And everybody in native dress, including indigenous peoples. Maori chiefs in native dress performing on certain instruments, and Native Americans. That could so easily degenerate into a feel good, everything's equal, kind of outlook. But Assisi really made the point that nature is sacred and many different traditions have their ways of acknowledging that. The scriptural foundations for the protection of nature in each of those cultures were read out to the assembly. It was a tremendously moving moment. From a practical point of view it also proved successful for World Wildlife in that its message, which has essentially been a very rationalist, very Western, very modern, post-industrial message of live and let live and biological diversity, was reinforced by appeals to the heart, by appeals to the value systems of people in the cultures where they are really making the choices that will determine whether the forests survive or the wildlife continue.

BW: So what you see in events like these are signs that we're beginning to recover an authentic voice within our religious traditions, one that has been neglected by environmentalists and perhaps insufficiently voiced by religious leaders on behalf of the environment, a story that reminds us we are immersed in nature, in creation, in the holy.

WR: Yes. I think we are finding a certain unity of belief around the shared religious significance we see in nature into which many people from different belief systems can enter. One that offers a common outlook and a principle of respect for nature as we change it, manage it, alter it, and take responsibility for it. I also find it marvelous that the patron saint of the environment is also the patron saint of the poor, and the most popular saint in Latin America.

BW: It sounds like there is the potential for common ground now between environmentalists and the religious community in the West, and solid ground for a new ecumenism and interfaith commitment centered on common ethical responsibilities for the Earth.

WR: I think it's an entirely common reference point to which we all must appeal. I have never believed in a kind of Pollyanna ecumenism, that somehow we're all going to get together one day. I don't think that's in the cards for a lot of good reasons. But there is a level at which there can be much greater mutual respect and cooperation than we have seen, and much less distrust among the various religious groups and belief systems. In nature and the environment, what better common point of reference do we have than the planet that we all share.

Earth Systems ... Human Systems

THOMAS BERRY

Thomas Berry is a historian of cultures and self-described "geologian" who taught history of religions for many years at Fordham University. Among his many published works are The Dream of the Earth *(1988),* Befriending the Earth *(1991), and* The Universe Story *(1992), which he co-authored with physicist Brian Swimme. He is currently at work on* The Meadow Across the Creek. *Berry's work and passions are well informed by his ability to draw on science, the history of cultures, and comparative religion. By making the case for the Earth as the primary revelation of the divine, he has invested the new scientific story of the universe with sacred significance. As he once said, "For religion to be so irresponsible to the destruction of the natural world reveals that religion doesn't begin to know what it is itself all about! Because this is the devastation of religion itself!" Like some of our best poets, Tom Berry makes us aware of God's presence, God's immanence in the world. This suggests, among other things, that our love and care for the Earth can be one of our finest forms of religious devotion and piety. The interview took place the day after a powerful address by Berry about the need for healing the relationship of humans and the Earth.*

BW: Your address to us yesterday was beautiful. We all had a strong sense that you were speaking straight from your heart, and so you had our full attention.

TB: Well, it is something that I have wanted to say for a long time, but never quite had the occasion. I think that any time you talk about land, about natural phenomena, about the regions of this North American continent, you get people's attention. That is what I proposed when I was invited down to the White House office for environmental programs, that if I had been writing the president's inaugural address, I would have started off with some descriptions of the North American continent. I would have talked about the Appalachian Mountains, the Great Central Valley, the Great Lakes, the Gulf of Mexico, the great deserts of the Southwest, the grasslands, the rain forests of the Northwest. I would have talked about the stars, the mountains, and the sea. The natural world here is just fantastic! The names of these things, or the identification of natural phenomenon—it is pure poetry. So why more people don't do it, I don't know. But if the president would have just started out this way, and then said, "Good people, this is where we live, and we have to have an economy that is based here, that we can long live out of, because this is all we have to work with." So, we need an economy suited to this. We also need a medical program, because we cannot have well people in a sick continent or a sick climate. Therefore our medical programs and medical education have to come out of this base, too. We also have to educate people as to the meaning of this continent, so that even our religion should become integral with this continent, a manifestation of the ultimate mysteries of existence, and so forth. The continent should provide a unifying background for all our programs and a way to unify education from the two-year-old to the doctoral level and professional programs.

BW: So you want to ground the national agenda in these realities, and make sure that the medical program is not unrelated to the economic program and the agricultural program.

TB: It's all related. Under the agricultural program is the food program, and related to food is shelter. We have to shelter ourselves in accordance with these requirements, as Amory Lovins of the Rocky Mountain Institute is suggesting. We need to live suitably in the place that we are.

BW: I heard somebody come away from a talk today disappointed to find there was nothing spiritual about it, yet I thought it was at once both spiritual and practical.

TB: Some people have a strange idea of what spirituality is these days. This rootedness in cosmology is so important. In fact, that is what is wrong with modern western civilization all the way through: its lack of a unifying cosmology. It did exist to some extent, but wasn't taken that seriously. Even with the Greeks, civilization became human-centered rather than universe-centered. With our religious tradition, the distinctive feature of the Bible is the perception of the divine in historical events. So that the divine is not perceived primarily in cosmological manifestations, as is the case for most other peoples. So, for instance, the Exodus was a springtime festival that was historicized, made into a historical event that henceforth became the reference point for the whole of the biblical world. In other words, the historical overwhelmed the cosmological. But there was a certain balance that was kept up through the early Christian ages because the natural world was considered a scripture. They talked about the two books, the book of the Bible and the book of the natural world.

BW: Up until about what time?

TB: Up until the end of the Middle Ages, up into the 16th century.

BW: So people were in essence reading both scripture and nature?

TB: Yes. In the cathedrals of the Middle Ages there is this image of the "green man," where you see the vines grow into the human form and other manifestations of nature growing out of the human form. You see these images in the face. It was a male mode of being in the natural world, rather than a feminine mode of being. And you see the human countenance formed of leaves, oak leaves. It's amazing! So western culture kept a certain rapport with nature at this time, particularly in the arts. But the break came to some extent through the Black Death in 1347 to 1349, when a third of Europe died, perhaps the most traumatic experience of western civilization. Since they had no germ theory, they could only have a moral cause of disease and death, so they figured that the earth had got wicked and God was punishing the world. The best idea was to get saved out of the world. So that's when they developed some of the morality plays, based on the idea that the only thing worthwhile is what you can take with you when you die, which are virtues. So, what's the use of trying to value anything in the world of time. The idea was to disengage from the world, in order to get into heaven. But then that led to an opposite move in the 16th century and particularly the early 17th century with Francis Bacon saying that the way to deal with the difficulties of the world is not to get out of it, but to learn to control it. To torture nature to give up its secrets so it can be controlled for human purposes. And so you get this split, between the secular effort to answer the problem by controlling the natural world, and the religious effort to be saved out of the world. So that gave us our secular/religious relationship. Now, to some extent there was a tension, but to some extent both were happy. Because those committed to the natural world didn't have to worry about the spiritual world because that became irrelevant. And the spiritual people didn't have to worry about the secular world. And so they reached a compromise.

BW: It was as though we were dividing up realms and determining who would have authority over each.

TB: That's right.

BW: And all this arose at a time of enormous human crisis, is that right?

TB: Yes. But there is another element involved in this, too. And that is the promise of the millennium at the end of St. John's Book of Revelation. It goes back to the apocalyptic tradition of Daniel and runs all the way through. The story depicts the strife between good and evil, destruction and salvation. The idea was that there would come a time when humans would transcend the human condition, a time when there would be peace, justice, and abundance. It was referred to in terms of the thousand years when the dragon would be chained. That's when you would have this wonderful period of the reign of the saints.

Then the dragon would be unchained for a brief while when history would come to an end and the celestial Jerusalem would be moved from its historical setting to its eternal setting. So what happened, to my mind, is that this put into western civilization a deep hidden rage against the human condition because a divine promise had never been delivered—this period in history when our lives would have a serenity, a peace, an abundance that was due us somehow. Since this did not happen by divine processes, we determined to raise it up ourselves, to take the planet to pieces with our technologies. To take control of it and learn how to run the planet. And so we get into this madness, this deep cultural pathology that we are into, an insane cultural situation where we destroy our air, our water, our soil. We do all of these crazy things, which then become the basis of our education and economy. We try to stave off the destructive effects on us physically by our medical technologies and all of this. But the basis of our economy is absolute madness. It is driven and controlled by the modern corporation, and there is no way of controlling the modern, transnational corporation because it gives us our jobs, pays us our salaries, it gives us all of these wonderful gadgets that we have. But the modern corporation increasingly owns the planet now, particularly after the GATT treaties go into effect.

BW: You seem to be suggesting that a twisted millennial vision has helped produce our massively false belief in unlimited material progress and endlessly rising material affluence.

TB: That's right. Except that there are only some who belong to the successful section of humanity and more and more who drop out, as well as a depletion of the middle group between the very well-off and the underclass. So this distorts the whole situation of recovery. We have this difficulty that the corporate endeavor has taken over the media, taken over the universities, taken over the government, taken over the ownership of the planet. And with the GATT treaties, this will no longer be under some manner of national controls because the nations will be forbidden to block this trading relationship, so that both productivity and trade can be expected to increase to the benefit of the power people or the money people. But this will be accompanied by a loss and an uprooting of the people that are not in the money class, so that the lower groups are just going to suffer more than ever.

BW: You paint a pretty sobering picture.

TB: Oh, a terribly realistic picture. Now, Amory Lovins has put out a program that could work. But the corporations cannot accept it because they are making their money on this other pattern and they are not going to give that up in favor of his more sane approach.

BW: Why not? I thought more corporations were embracing what he's proposing?

TB: Well, there are people who are embracing it, but the response is still pretty minimal. He can give you an instance of what's been done in Sweden and how others could do the same, but others are not about to do the same on this large scale.

BW: Are you more pessimistic now than when you wrote *The Dream of the Earth* and subsequent books that convey a sense of hope?

TB: I want people to appreciate the stark reality of what is facing us. Because people sometimes think we can get out of this easily, that if we can adopt some of these programs that seem to make a lot of sense then we'll be able to continue managing more or less the way we have. Now the question with Amory Lovins' proposals is to what extent we can expect them to be adopted? I think they need to be adopted, but I don't think they are going to be widely adopted until people are really up against some very stark alternatives. And I want these stark alternatives to be realized in their most devastating form.

BW: What do you say to someone like William K. Reilly, who was George Bush's EPA administrator? He says that we are focusing on a glass that is half empty as opposed to half full.

TB: It's not a matter of half and half. It's a case where we are about to destroy or devastate the total functioning of this planet. We have already, in this country, wiped out 95 percent of the basic forests. Now after destroying 95 percent of the primordial forest in this country, ecologists say we must save the last 5 percent, and the country says "No, we must have jobs." Well, if we have to have jobs by cutting the last 5 percent, that is pathological, that is madness. That is not half full or half empty, that is just pure and simple devastation. That is denying even a remnant of the ancient forest from the experience of coming generations. When we are poisoning our water, when the salmon are dying, that's not half and half; we are extinguishing our food supply. When we have to close down fishing off Georgia's Bank because enormous quantities of fish are being hunted to extinction, that's not half and half; it's 1 percent and 99 percent.

We need to see this reality, see it in its historical perspective. And part of the problem is the way people cite and teach history as a series of transitions from this to that, say from the Roman period, to the Medieval, to the Renaissance, to the Enlightenment, to modern technological society. And so this is just another crisis and we'll go on. That is utterly absurd. It does not even give you a shadow of an idea of what is happening now. Because what is happening now is the termination of 65 million years in the geo-biological history of the planet. And it took this last 65 million years to produce the world we know, even longer to produce the chemical balance of the atmosphere. But in a more proximate way, we are terminating 65 million years in the geo-biological history of the planet. And this is something infinitely greater than just moving from the Roman period to the Medieval period, or from that to any other historical period. To do away with 20 percent of all living species, to be doing away with 1000 species in so short a time, when it used to be that one species died in a hundred years. Species have always come into existence and passed out of existence, but at a very slow rate. This acceleration is precipitating a disastrous situation.

Now I say that we have to first understand the order of magnitude of what's happening, the starkness of this situation, that we are not going to get out of this simply by certain adaptations such as we are undertaking now. We have got to develop a whole new civilizational approach. Take our universities. Our universities are themselves a disaster. They are owned by the corporations in a sense because their money comes from endowments that come from the people that get their money from the corporate endeavor. So that they function within this context, and they train people for this context. Look at their schools of economics. They are teaching an absurd economy. Their schools of medicine are not teaching the integrity of the health of the planet, that we must establish a healthy continent and a healthy planet before we can have healthy humans. All the medical technologies and all of the genetic engineering in the world are not going to help in the least in this basic issue. Take the schools of education. They are not teaching any program that gives a child an integral education. In back of it all is the lack of a cosmology. And law, jurisprudence, really is the key to a lot of it, because we cannot do anything about it largely because of our constitution. Our constitution is based on an inadequate jurisprudence. It grants humans certain rights at the expense of the natural world. There are three basic aspects of English jurisprudence that we inherit: the participatory government, the individual freedoms, and the right to private property. And private property is the centerpiece of our jurisprudence.

BW: This is what comes from being the first truly modern nation.

TB: That's right. We have enshrined these values in the constitution and out of them this country has developed for better and worse. But these rights have been granted at the expense of the natural world. What we now need to do is accept the fact that there is a governance of the North American continent that is derived from the governance of the planet, and then learn to understand that human governance must be an extension of the larger governance of the natural world. That is why I say that we need to formally recognize this governance and formally indicate the derivative character of human governance through this constitution for the North American continent, not a constitution for the humans on the North American continent. This adaptation is required to enable humans to fit effectively into this larger set-up. It calls for a jurisprudence that is based in an acceptable cosmology. And it calls for a religion that is fundamentally based in a cosmology rather than in a Bible. Because the cosmology is the primary scripture, and, in any case, you cannot have any written scripture until you have the cosmological scriptures, because you cannot even have humans, you cannot even have language for a language revelation until you already have a cosmology with a cosmological revelation. And no amount of verbal revelation can supplant cosmological revelation. And so we have a difficulty making this transition. That's why I say we need to put the Bible on the shelf for twenty years, until we recognize the manifestation of the ultimate mystery of existence out of the sun, the moon, and the stars, and re-establish a rapport with the natural world again.

BW: Then at what point do scriptures become valid and helpful to bring about the kinds of changes you are talking about?

TB: Well, the scriptures are not that helpful right now. We cannot do without our traditional culture. We cannot do without our traditional religious developments. But we have a new revelatory experience of the natural world because we now know the universe as a sequence of emergent processes that go through a sequence of irreversible transformation episodes. The Bible, just like all traditional religions, is based on a spatial mode of consciousness where time moves in ever-renewing seasonal cycles. Yet in the Bible you have a human developmental time and a non-developmental universe. But beginning with the 16th century comes this transformation in our experience of how the universe comes into existence, and this itself represents perhaps the greatest transition in the human mind since the human mind came into being. Whereas traditional societies always have their creation stories in mythological time, not in numbered historical time, the Bible has the creation of the world numbered in historical time. So it's a case where the Bible and modern science agree. They both agree that the universe came into being at a certain moment of historical time. Where they differ is the fact that the Bible, once the world comes into being, moves into ever-renewing seasonal time like all other cosmologies, but it also records human developmental time, such as our coming into being at a certain identifiable moment. There is, then, this sense of things moving in a sequence of irreversible transformation.

It needs to be said that ever-renewing seasonal time and developmental historical time are both valid ways, and they cannot be collapsed into any single explanation. This is a situation somewhat like the theory of light, which has two explanations—either as emanations of discrete particles, or as energy waves. Now you deal with some problems in life as though light were discrete particles or segments of energy. And the other problems you have to deal with as though light were waves. You cannot collapse these into a single explanation of time. And I use this as a metaphor for the way in which the cyclical processes and the developmental processes work. There are cyclical processes in the time sequence. But I would say that the dominant understanding of time now lies with an emergent process going through irreversible moments of transformation. Yet you can understand the validity of our day/night cycle and our yearly/seasonal cycle and our larger cycles; there is no way in which we can totally discount these rhythms. There is an awful lot of wisdom that lies within that orbit, and that is the way our civilization has existed up until recent times. In fact, we have only known the story of the universe in any complete way since the 1960s.

BW: So we are dealing with scriptures that, however inspired, are nonetheless the work of human minds and are by now antiquated and flawed to some extent. Yet they are also surprisingly resilient and resonate with our experience of time and other rhythms in our lives.

TB: Yes.

BW: I want to come back to this idea of shelving scriptures for 20 years. To do the kind of task you are describing involves fundamental cultural change, both personal and institutional. Is a new cosmology enough to do that?

TB: Well, it is the basis. A cosmology is the basis of education and all of our professions and so forth. We can't begin without first understanding something about the universe and how it functions. Now the difficulty is simply that we do not take this new story of the universe seriously. And we don't take it seriously because the Genesis story is the basic story for religious people in the West, and it has become the sacred story. Now we have been presented by the scientists with this other story as mechanistic, as random, as meaningless. So that is the obstacle. What we have to understand is that the scientists are correct in their data, but wrong in their interpretation. The universe is a psychic-spiritual reality from the beginning, as well as a physical-material reality. And the universe now reveals itself as such from the beginning and in the total process of its emergence. As soon as we can understand this as a revelatory process, as carrying the deep mysteries of existence, then we can begin to educate and understand that the laws of the universe are the laws of the Earth, are the laws of life, are the laws of humans. Right now we begin with human reason and ask how human reason dictates good and evil and all of that. We don't see any continuity between the function of the universe and the function of the human. But there is a single continuity in this process. It has gone through these discontinuity episodes of transformation, but the continuity passes through the whole process, and humans belong to the universe, we belong to the Earth. We belong to history as well as the larger dynamics of the universe. When I say, "Put the Bible on the shelf for 20 years," I mean we need to put it aside until we understand this.

BW: The human species has reached a crossroads where it has never been before.

TB: Oh, absolutely.

BW: I have an image of a cultural "rite of passage" that lies before us. I don't presume to know what this involves, but I want to put the question to you this way. What do you think it means for us to come home again, as the prophets always used to say, to "return and live"? How can humanity make this enormous passage?

TB: Well, it is not going to be easy. My proposal is that we have to think in terms of a terminal Cenozoic Period and an emerging Ecozoic Period (a word I coined, so far as I know). With the Ecozoic we are recognizing that we have to make this fantastic transition, that we have to reconstitute our understanding of the planet and undergo a profound transformation in the way we deal with the planet. We must do what indigenous peoples do the world over. The first thing I notice about indigenous peoples when I talk to them or become acquainted with the studies about them is that they live in a universe. We don't live in a universe. We live in cities, in cultures, in traditions, in nation-states. We live in a human world. We don't live in the stars. We know the stars are out there, but so what. We don't get anything when we look at the stars. A star is a star, so what. But the wind and the directions and the natural phenomena—these mean things to indigenous people. The dawn and the sunset are mystical moments. You know where you are in the context of north, south, east, west, and in relationship to the sky above and the earth below. You have to know where you are. You have to know the seasons of the year. You have to read the trees. You have to read the natural phenomena. Because if you don't interact creatively with natural phenomena, you are dead.

BW: So we have to re-establish an intimate and practical relationship with nature in local places that also connects us to the universe.

TB: Yes, everybody. That is what Amory Lovins is really saying. If we get back to integrating ourselves with natural systems, we can function without the devastation that is now taking place. But the other thing is that we need to recognize the transformation of mind that we need to undergo. This involves rethinking our perceptions about the universe along the following lines. The first thing that needs to be done is to recognize that the universe is a communion of subjects, not a collection of objects. In other words, every being has its interior, whether it is some atom or whatever. It's a principle of spontaneity, a principle of manifestation, an energy principle. It has the capacity of relatedness. Every atom is intimately related to and influencing every other atom of the universe, no matter how distant. Not by passing through that distance, but by an inherent immediacy that exists from one atom to another no matter where it is in the universe. Now, this is happening at an atomic level or a subatomic level. And anything that is intelligible is already spirit, because to be known is to have a form, to have a structure that shapes its manifestation. We couldn't know an atom unless an atom told us it was an atom. We wouldn't know an oak tree unless it told us it was an oak tree. And the oak tells us by its form, by its shape, in all of these different ways. So, we have to restore this ancient idea of knowledge as being intercommunion. The second thing we have to understand is that the human is a subsystem of the earth system.

BW: This is the biocentric view?

TB: Yes, the biocentric view. Being a subsystem means that you cannot improve the subsystem at the expense of the basic system. You cannot advance the human economy if you are going to deteriorate the basic economy. In economic terms, it means we can't deplete or spend our capital. Most economists will tell you that over and over again—and then teach you how to destroy the planet. They act as though the planet were an infinite collection of resources. The absurdity of that is really something. But this applies in every field, because the human is a subsystem of the earth system whether it is health, or economics, or even education. We are educated by the universe, and that's why children are educated not by words, but by their experiences. They need to learn the language of the trees, the language of the natural world. And we do a disservice to children when we sit them down in a classroom and insist that they learn to read all these scribbles that we call an alphabet, and to read human language when they don't yet have the least idea about the language of the trees, of the soil, of the sky, or any of that. That would come naturally to them if we would just give them the opportunity. This is why indigenous people educate in this interaction, in this capacity for being present with and accepting the rapport with the animals, with the vegetation, and to learn to read the science of things by first learning to read the stars. Our city children never even see stars. They live in a world of concrete, of steel, of bars. A world of wheels, and machines, and noise, and pollution, and water that comes out of a tap, and milk that comes out of a bottle. Everything comes out of cans. Plastic is the world they live in. This is doing an injustice to children. It is distorting their whole psychic life. And I think that is why there is so much violence, so much turning to drugs and all of that. They have none of these experiences. The only natural experience is the sex experience. To some extent we alleviate their deprivation by giving young people access to space and to experiences that are both exciting and threatening. But now they get Disney World as their natural world at best, and Disney World is totally deceptive.

BW: So as we rethink our perceptions about the universe, it is first of all urgent that we see this overarching reality of intercommunion in all things. And secondly that we understand that the human is a subsystem of the earth system. Is there a third point?

TB: The third point is to understand that the universe is never again going to function in the future the way it has functioned in the past. In the past, nature developed magnificently, back in the Cenozoic Period of the last 65 million years when the mammals and flowers developed. Everything that we see about us, the seas and what have you, all of this was just a magnificent development. But humans had nothing to do with it because we did not exist. The difference is that from here on, almost nothing is going to happen that humans will not be involved in.

BW: In the Ecozoic Period.

TB: Yes. Because whereas we cannot make a blade of grass, there is not liable to be a blade of grass unless we accept it, protect it, foster it, and on occasion heal the conditions that prevent it from developing. So humans have new responsibilities. There is a certain cruelty in what we are bringing about for our children. I did not have to worry about the ozone layer when I was a child. These children have to worry about it. In Australia already the children, when they go out or go to school, have to wear these broad-brimmed hats, because in Australia the amounts of skin cancer are just unbelievable.

BW: Tom, I hear you saying that we have ahead of us a long, collective act of restoration, not only of restoring ecosystems in the places where we live, but also of reconstituting social and cultural systems that are more in harmony with the natural world. Is there also a spiritual dimension or capacity that has to be worked with in this regenerative process?

TB: Well, the whole thing is a spiritual dimension! The whole thing has to do with the survival of humans as humans! What I suggest is that we have to enter into what I call a metareligious phase. We cannot constitute a new religion such as might have been invented if this had happened earlier in history when we were creating the world's great religions. We can never again create a religion like the Hindu, or the Buddhist, or Moslem, or Jewish, or Christian, or whatever. We will never again have a basic religion with this type of structure and culture. That age is over. But this new religious sensitivity that we need, this new religious orientation, I expect to be associated with this new sense of the universe as a divine manifestation of the ultimate mysteries of existence. I don't use the word "God." God is a word that has been trivialized. It has been used in so many different ways that who knows what a person means by the use of the word "God." It has become pietistic and all of that, fundamentalist, and doesn't even begin to awaken in the mind what a person would want to awaken by a concept of an ultimate mystery of existence.

BW: What are we trying to awaken when we use the word "divine"? Not just a biocentric, but a sacrocentric worldview?

TB: Well, we are trying to awaken a sense of what I call the deep mystery of existence. A response to what we see when we see the stars and wonder about where the stars come from and all of that. We have all of our scientific explanations, but back of all of the scientific explanations is the mystery.

BW: The mystery out there along the curvature of space?

TB: Yes, but also in the blade of grass. It's as mysterious as anything. St. Augustine said that he considered the existence of a grain of sand a greater mystery than any other miracle he had ever seen. And so it is the mystery of existence that strikes us in ten thousand different ways wherever we look. So that we live in this sea of mystery. And that differentiates somebody that gets excited with life, that feels a meaning and expansiveness to life, compared to those that think a tree is a tree and that is all there is to it. Take an acre of land. No matter how far we go with our science in identifying and analyzing the genetic components, we will never be able to experience or write a formula for the principle that unites the different components of the genetic code, that causes them to act as a unity in sending down roots, raising the trunk, fashioning the leaves, drawing all the water and sap that is needed to nourish all the leaves, each one of them unique yet all in the general pattern. This is something that we know by intelligence, but is not subject to rational understanding. It's that mystery. Take a symphony of Beethoven. It's like trying to understand a symphony of Beethoven by analyzing the vibration of the instruments.

BW: And we can only do this through a deep encounter with our senses.

TB: Yes. You can't understand Beethoven unless you hear the vibrations. But you can hear the vibrations and understand the symphony. And that requires something else, because you hear the symphony played in time, but it's understood outside of time. Because to understand a melody, the first notes have died out when the final notes are played. But the melody is a single thing that is understood outside of time. It is heard in time, but understood outside of time. So the universe unfolds in time but it is understood outside of time. There is a trans-temporal dimension to the time process. A trans-time dimension of time. These are the things that give life its excitement. That is why poetry is so marvelous, because the poet evokes this sense of meaning in the words by the images that the poet presents. We need creative personalities that can function in the different areas of life. We need a competency such as Amory Lovins has. And he is not self-interested in that sense. He is a dedicated person. You see how he has acquired that total placidity, but he also has that playfulness where he presents the most startling things with kind of a lightness that is playful. We need more people who can do this type of thing.

And what is so interesting is how much fun you realize these people are having who are doing significant things. They like what they are doing and see the comedy of the situation. To some extent, even when I talk about all these terrifying things, I have in a sense absorbed them and their terror. I've worked out a way of identifying the disastrous dimension, doing what I can within the range in which I am able to function, yet feeling that amid all the misery it is very difficult not to be overwhelmed by the tragedy of things like Bosnia and Rwanda. We are caught in enormous tragedy. And we have to identify with the tragedy. We have to experience the tragedy, but not be destroyed by it. Because if it destroys us we cannot help. What we have to do is work for a new period. In a certain sense, the tragedy is beyond our help for the most part. We can do what we can, and we can try to help future generations by putting into motion forces that can improve the situation.

One of the things that I generally say is that my generation is responsible for this. My generation has done what no former generation could have done because they did not have the power, and what no future generation will be able to do because the world will not be so beautiful. My generation is the destroyer generation *par excellence*. And I ask myself, "How did it come about?" And my answer is that my generation has been autistic. My generation has been psychically locked into itself so that it could not get out to the natural world and the natural world could not get in. There was no feeling of rapport. There was no capacity to be present to the outer world of nature. And it has just been terrifying to see what my generation has done. I use that matter of autism because I have seen and dealt with autistic children to a certain extent, and it is something to see an autistic child. A very competent, intelligent child that cannot talk. Something traumatic has happened and he cannot give or receive affection. It's awesome. But my generation has been of that nature. How can people do all of the devastating things that they are doing and be totally insensitive to it. How can people fish out the Pacific Ocean with those drift nets 30 miles long and 30-40 feet deep that kill everything that touches them. There are something like 700 of these constantly in the Pacific Ocean draining all of the life from the sea. It is just monumental! The governments that are allowing it just feel nothing. The companies that are doing it say, "If we don't get it, somebody else will." So that is just one of the terrifying things that has happened. The president talks the same way about NAFTA. "If we don't do this, Japan will. If we don't get the jobs, somebody else will." It's ridiculous! "If we don't do it, if we don't exclude them, they will exclude us." It's a terrible argument! It portrays a humanity that deserves extinction. If humanity goes down this way, it will be something that we deserve. But the tragedy and the pathos of it is that the generation that caused the difficulty is not the generation that will suffer the consequences. My generation is not suffering the consequences of its actions. But some generation will. All future generations will.

BW: As a prophetic voice in your generation, I can't help but feel you are bequeathing to those of us who follow an important cultural analysis, even a real sense of hope from deep down inside yourself.

TB: A margin of hope. I think in attempting to understand any situation, there is implied a margin of hope. The answer to all problems has to be found in the way in which the problem is stated, by the analysis and the components of the problem. The more we get to the stark depths of what is happening, the closer we are to solving it.

Designing Systems
That Forgive Human Folly

WES JACKSON

Wes Jackson is the co-founder and director of the Land Institute in Salina, Kansas, established in 1976 to focus on ecosystem level agriculture using the prairie as a standard for developing a perennial polyculture. The Institute also freely explores the social, political, economic and religious implications for the way humans live on and work the land that sustains us. A national membership organization with 2,200 "friends of the land," the Institute issues an excellent quarterly publication called "The Land Report." Jackson is the author of New Roots for Agriculture *(1980),* Altars of Unhewn Stone *(1987), and a contributor with Wendell Berry and Bruce Coleman to* Meeting the Expectations of the Land *(1984). His latest book,* Becoming Native to This Place, *was published in 1994. "Modern till agriculture is like a highwire act. You can't expect everyone to get to the other side in safety. Natural systems agriculture is not just an alternative; it's a new paradigm in which nature's wisdom is primary and human cleverness is secondary . . . so it's more resilient to human folly. Because it's built so close to the ground, when you fall off the track, all you'll do is break your ankle. It's forgiving."*

BW: Driving through the midwest in early spring before the crops are up, it is easy to see that a lot of land is exposed and vulnerable to soil erosion. It also looks like midwest farmers are pretty dependent on just a few crops, large machinery and fossil fuels, and a lot of commercial fertilizer and chemicals. How big a role does this kind of agriculture play in our nation's environmental problem?

WJ: Well I think it is the major aspect of our environmental problem. We have about 400 million till agriculture acres of which 350 million are in the erodable category, and only 15 million are non-erodable. So just start with soil erosion, with big equipment, with corn and soybeans. Soybean ground loses a lot more soil than corn ground. Big equipment, which can't make sharp turns, forces patterns that don't lend themselves to good contour farming on erodable land. And then of course we had the horrendous flooding on the Mississippi and its tributaries in the spring of '93, the high pesticide levels measured in St. Louis, and what not. A friend of mine in California said we ought to tell midwestern farmers, "God has sent you a great cleansing; now, no more chemicals." It's a serious problem. A former student of mine and friend at the National Cancer Institute is part of a group conducting a longitudinal study on 70,000 farmers and pesticide applicators plus 40,000 spouses and children associated with the same home. It's a $15 million study over ten years that should produce some significant results. Instead of starting with the death certificate and working backwards, they are starting with people living now, interviewing them, and then watching as they drop off and tracking what they came down with. So all the way from soil erosion to cancers, I think agriculture is our number one environmental problem. It's been exacerbated in this era of the industrialization of agriculture.

BW: I want to come back to that in a moment. But first let me raise a point made by Lester Brown and the people at Worldwatch Institute. They report that we are beginning to see agricultural productivity falling off around the world, even though many of these regions have been receiving chemical fertilizers only a very short time. Are we beginning to see the same trend in the soils of North America?

WJ: Yes. The fertilizer response curve has been flattening. You don't get a linear relationship in terms of yield. That flattening of yield has been going on for some time now.

BW: While you are an advocate and defender of agriculture as the basis of culture and civilization, you've also been a critic of agricultural norms, at least of till agriculture and industrial agriculture, which are relatively recent developments in agricultural history. Why isn't this working? We've had the Soil Conservation Service for years and many inspired leaders in agricultural conservation. We've certainly had many exemplary farms and farmers. At root, what is the problem here?

WJ: Part of the problem is that psychologically we are still gatherers and hunters. But there are many factors. One is that we really weren't meant to do till agriculture on a big scale. If we were, we would have had longer arms. The second thing, as J. Russell Smith talked about, is that agriculture developed over a long sweep of time in the great river valley civilizations. The problems with nature there were worked out in relatively non-eroding land where you could do just about anything. Much later, when we carried agriculture to the hillsides, it was disastrous. That is one factor. Another is the difference in rainfall. The northwestern Europeans who immigrated to America came from areas where the norm was gentle, slow rains like the rain that fell today. But they came to the land of the thunderstorm, and cultural information is slow to accumulate. So, we are mere mortals, struggling with an ape body and trying to figure out how to be a species out of context. And modern till agriculture is like a tightwire act, loaded with the potential for human folly. Despite the fact there are a lot of good farmers, you can't expect everybody in the world to walk a tightwire 200 feet in the air and get from one side to the other in safety. We weren't meant to be doing things like that.

BW: Which explains why so many people are devoting themselves to sustainable alternatives. But you go further than others. You've been experimenting for nearly twenty years with something you call "perennial polyculture," or "natural systems agriculture," agriculture that mimics nature. What principles guide your work, and what are you discovering?

WJ: We have reason to believe that if we imitate the structure of nature, we can be granted the function. Let me explain. Jack Ewel has been working in Costa Rica where they use succession agriculture. In land that had been cleared, they were trying to apply the structural analog of what was going on in natural succession. In other words, the mimic was that you could not put anything there unless it could have got there on its own. And in one area, Jack actually mimicked the succession going on in another area by substituting vine for vine, tree for tree, shrub for shrub. They found that almost always, if they imitated the structure, they were granted the function.

I love that word, "granted." What we are talking about, I think, is getting a lot of this order—this system's potential—for free. There are so many possibilities sitting there. Take Maximilian Sunflower, which is allelopathic. Its roots exude a chemical that acts as an herbicide to kill off weeds at the seedling stage, which is to say you are using sunlight for weed control. So one of the most important insights that I will call a hypothesis at this time, not a law, is that the internal control of the system is more energy and materials efficient than an external control of the system. I can give you two examples. I already mentioned Maximilian Sunflower, which is allelopathic. Now let's imagine that we were to select for a high seed yield and the plant were to lose some of its capacity because of allocating resources to the seed that would ordinarily be allocated to weed control through its production of the herbicide. Now, instead of counting on inside physiology of the plant, we go outside it and use a mule to cultivate for weed control. That would be an external remedy, and that mule has got to graze on a different plant base. Let's say that we go even more outside the system and pick up fossil fuel that comes from a time and space external to both the contemporary and the local. Pretty soon you have something that looks like modern till agriculture and the antithesis of natural systems agriculture. To me it's as important as $E=MC^2$. The Illinois Bundleflower or the Eastern Gammagrass leaks sugar into the rhizosphere of the root, the gelatinous area around the root. That sugar is used by bacteria to fix small quantities of nitrogen. Now, warm season grasses of the wild variety all leaked sugar and all fixed small quantities of nitrogen. But our domesticated plants do not, and I think what has happened in our selection of high seed yield is that we have unwittingly selected for those plants that had tightened up and slowed sugar leakage. It might make more sense, if we are going to have a sun-powered system, to go ahead and allow the plant to leak sugar and fix the nitrogen locally, or go outside to the alfalfa field and have it provide the nitrogen, instead of using natural gas as a feed stock for nitrogen fertilizer. We're talking about natural systems agriculture, a sun-powered system, but I think we ought to explore whether these same principles can be applied as organizing principles in human community. If that were the case, think of what that would mean in terms of settlement patterns. I mean we ought to be promoting this within the National Academy of Sciences as a thing to look at.

BW: You're talking about a shift in agricultural thinking and practice that has huge implications. I presume this is a long-term project.

WJ: Just like the movement from the church to the nation-state.

BW: You're suggesting we might benefit from the inherent complexity of nature in natural systems agriculture. Can we master that complexity any more safely?

WJ: Yes, I think so, and that is the whole point. We need to build an agriculture that is more resilient to human folly. Instead of relying on human knowledge as adequate, on human cleverness, we are moving more toward nature's wisdom by taking advantage of the natural integrities. You can walk a rail and if you fall off the track, it's forgiving because of your proximity to the ground. But move that rail up into the air 90 feet . . .

BW: A tightwire with no net?

WJ: With no net. You see, we are talking about forgiveness. The worst you can do falling off the rail is turn your ankle.

BW: You are trying to model a forgiving system as a protection for human folly. This is fascinating. So wilderness—in this case the natural system of the prairie in your region—is indispensable because it informs both human culture and agriculture in practical ways.

WJ: I think we are always going to need a standard against which we judge our agricultural practices. I am not asking that everything be returned to wilderness or prairie. I am just saying that the wilderness we have ought to be protected because it has answers to questions that we have not yet learned to ask. That's the point. There are going to be a lot of questions that we will be asking of natural systems in the future. And that is why I see wilderness as the analog, that which is not made of human hands.

BW: Like the title for your book, *Altars of Unhewn Stone.*

WJ: Yes, it's the same notion. We learn faster than nature, but nature has been at it longer, and so I see wilderness as the standard. But then to manage woodlots is a second step down. We should try to manage them based on what we learn from the wilderness. But we also need to understand "woodlothood" on its own terms, as an agricultural entity, something which we must use. Looking to wilderness will inform us how to do that well. For instance, snaking logs out with a team of horses or a single horse is an alternative to clear-cutting. This is an intermediate step that is closer to wilderness, both for forestry and for till agriculture. This is not about nostalgia. I'm talking about a practical necessity.

BW: I see that. Wilderness and mountains are often characterized in scripture as holy, as a place for refreshment and discernment, as a place to which one retreats for spiritual direction, as a place from which the hard truth divined must be carried back to a disordered social world. In other words, wilderness is portrayed in such a way that suggests a strong link between spiritual and cultural renewal. And now we see more clearly, from what you and others are doing, that wilderness also instructs us about ecological renewal and restoration as well. In thinking about wilderness in the largest sense and in all its dimensions, is there a vital connection to be made, as you see it, between spiritual and cultural and ecological renewal. Is wilderness somehow at the heart of the regenerative task we face?

WJ: Yes. I see it as all one thing. Yet I am reticent to allow this partitioning.

BW: Say more about that.

WJ: I think that we shouldn't have too much God talk, and we shouldn't have too much spiritual talk, and we shouldn't have too much economic talk.

BW: You want less talk and more action?

WJ: What we need is the joy that comes from the interaction with the earth and the awe that is inspired by it. But in this partitioning era we say spirit, we say economics, we say exercise, etc. Let's just take work on the farm or work in the woods for a moment. Yes, you are getting exercise. But, as Gene Logsdon pointed out in a piece he wrote about an Amish man hauling manure, he is not only getting exercise, he is also cleaning the barn, training a young colt to be a member of a draft horse team, bringing fertility to his field, and experiencing pleasure. He is not just doing one thing. What I find irritating is the breathlessness of those who want to get pumped up by just the spiritual part of things, as well as the greed of those who will rub their hands together as they imagine the profits they'll make from pumping them up. I think that's the big mistake of our time, this tendency to partition. Of course you have all of those things on your mind. But as soon as you start talking about one and holding a conference about it, and developing a bumper sticker about it, that's when it becomes perverted. The last thing we want is bumper sticker spirituality. The last thing we want is what you might call K-mart spiritualism. Yet if we keep talking about this spirit stuff and this God stuff, it is going to be the K-mart approach. And what's the K-mart approach? Instant gratification. Shallow. Short-lived.

BW: Let me ask the question this way. What's the work that is before us?

WJ: I think the work in front of us is the first work task given our forbearers, which is to care for the garden. Now because it's the first thing commanded, maybe it's the first thing forgotten. But it is the first admonition and it is absolutely unequivocal. It is part of right livelihood. This is the thing about the people that go off into the wilderness. I like wilderness both for its own sake and as an idea. But what I want mostly is to be able to work on a place. I want to look out a window one Saturday morning while I am having my coffee and if I see a limb that needs to come off, I want to be able to jump up and go out and cut off that limb. Or I may want to put in a garden. Or I may want to do something to the house, or to the barn, and all of that is tied into economics. It is work, but it is also art. And some of it is bad, some of it is good, and some of it is in between.

BW: And what does that have to do with nature and spirit?

WJ: What I am getting at is this. You can see where the ecosystems not made by human hands have a beauty that can lift you and inform you. But what you really want to do most of the time is to be active on your own place.

BW: You want to take that inspiration, that understanding, and put it to use.

WJ: Let me see if I can put it this way. Let's say that I visit the Sistine Chapel, and I look up there and I see what Michelangelo did. And I think, well by golly, I believe I will get me a scaffold and get up there and do me some painting too. Well that would be unthinkable, wouldn't it? Nobody is going to let me do that. So I don't think we ought to be allowed to mess around with the wilderness either. But, that does not mean that I can't go home and do something on my own ceiling, and maybe do it in a similar manner. I may get some ideas out of wilderness, too. For instance, at the Land Institute there are parts that we don't even touch. Trees fall down, and they just lay there. But there is a sharp line, and just to the left of that is also an area that we mow. I like the side-by-side comparison. I want both. It's hard to say what I get out of that which is getting minimum human impact. There is more than the idea of it. It has standing. The force that's at work in there is beyond us.

BW: What do you like most about it?

WJ: Well, the wild places are kind of like Sunday. If you don't work on Sunday, the world keeps on going. That insight is the value of Sunday.

BW: The value of the Sabbath and wilderness is that we aren't working, and thus we aren't destroying things for a change. So in that way the Sabbath is equal to the wilderness in a sense?

WJ: Yes, the Sabbath is kind of like wilderness. God is at work, the same now as before the week was invented.

BW: That reminds me of organizing principles for human community again. You recently said that there may be a way in which a moral philosophy can be derived from the prairie. What do you mean?

WJ: Let's say that we are successful in developing herbaceous perennial seed-producing polycultures.

BW: Which is one of the efforts under your sustainability umbrella at the Land Institute, along with the Sunshine Farm and the community of Matfield Green.

WJ: That's right. Let's say that in mimicking the prairie we substitute a warm season grass that we have bred for warm season grassness in the prairie; a cool season grass that we have bred for cool season grassness; a legume for legumeness; and the sunflower family for sunflower familyness. Let's say that we plant those out so we get a vegetative structure that is more or less an equal representation of some average ratio we see on the prairie. And so now we have in our system a plant that fixes nitrogen, therefore no natural gas for feedstock for nitrogen fertilizer. Maybe one that is allelopathic, which again kills off plants and weeds at the seedling stage. And let's say that we have a system that we don't have to disturb much after we plant it, where at least several years go by before we have to plant again. Plowing is reduced. And because of species diversity, we have chemical diversity. So, it will take a tremendous enzyme system on the part of an insect or a pathogen to mow it down. And we also have a reduction in fossil fuel use. Who will get hurt because of this system? The seed houses which are almost all owned by pharmaceutical companies now. Companies that produce herbicides and insecticides. The farm machinery companies. In other words, the suppliers of inputs. Who is going to gain? Farmers and the landscape. In other words, inherent within the ecological model is what I think we could call the beginning of a kind of moral philosophy derived from the ecosystem. Of course, that is not to say that those supplier guys won't try to patent the ecosystem.

BW: Is this some kind of new prairie populism? A prairie-derived philosophy for a moral economy?

WJ: Well, it's tempting to start thinking that way. You see, this is not simply an alternative. This is a different paradigm. This is the equivalent of the Copernican Revolution for agriculture. Because for 10,000 years, the earth has not been very forgiving of human folly and now, by talking about imitating nature's systems and the development of a new resilience, we are acknowledging in a way that we have been kind of stupid and clumsy in the past. And that is a kind of humility.

BW: And an acknowledgment that in ecological systems there is an inherent genius at work?

WJ: Yes. As Alexander Pope put it, "to consult the genius of the place in all." From my point of view this is more important than the space program. This is the kind of research that the United States Department of Agriculture ought to carve out for plant breeders, plant pathologists, plant ecologists, entomologists, soils people, and even some computer modelers. And then once this ecological paradigm was overarching, I would even be willing to let in the gene splicers to serve in a subordinate role, to assist in the development of high seed yield. But I would not allow them to run without a governor. Instead, they would be operating under a paradigm in which nature's wisdom is primary and human cleverness is secondary. You see, in this system a bacterium would not be considered a cause of a disease but rather an agent. In other words, context would be responsible for health. In Dick Lewinton's last book, he talks about how in England the tuberculosis bacillus was first looked at as a cause. But if you look to see where it was in the last century, it was among poor people in the cities. People in the country and the rich did not get it. So the bacillus was not a cause but an agent. Now this is the kind of thing that begins to suggest itself for consideration in the new paradigm. Let's say that you have leaf spot on Illinois Bundleflower. Is it more important to know the organism that is involved in the making of leaf spot? Or to know the context responsible for leaf spot? The Monsantos will want you to identify an organism because then they can manufacture something that will kill it. But if leaf spot in Illinois Bundleflower is the consequence of not having some optimum sort of mix in the environment, then you have to talk about the cause not being the organism, but the organism acting as an agent of some disequilibrium. This is a very different way of thinking about it.

BW: From an ecological model or paradigm, you seem to be suggesting a moral philosophy can be developed that would represent a true evolutionary advance. Is that right?

WJ: Well, yes. I mean all of this stuff is, of course, subject to perversion. All good ideas have the seeds of their own destruction. I can imagine a kind of eco-fascism growing up around it. But that simply means that things have to be watched.

BW: But there is something about the ecological paradigm that is holding to a new truth, as you see it, or maybe a remembered truth.

WJ: Yes. Something that has made it through the Pleistocene is more to be trusted, more reliable than some Johnny-come-lately idea that some industrial hero comes up with. It's an extension of the old.

BW: So if we are really interested in sustainability, cultural sustainability, then it almost has to be patterned on the ancient, time-tested pattern of nature's teachings, nature's revelation.

WJ: Right. I think this effect goes all the way from agriculture to the human community. You and I are products of the Enlightenment, and there are some things that we think are just natural. The Enlightenment is so deep within us that it now comes with the milk. George Bernard Shaw said that perfect memory is perfect forgetfulness. You know some things so well that you don't know how you know them. It's like being raised to farming. You don't know how you know something. How you come to know a different worldview that now seems natural only comes with time. Aldo Leopold said in the *Sand County Almanac* that nothing so important as an ethic is ever written. Rather it evolves in the mind of a thinking community. That's why the long journey in all of this is so important. Under the entire canopy of sustainable agriculture, only one or two percent of the research is under a new paradigm. The rest are researching in the arena of smart resource management approaches.

BW: Which includes most of those working in organic agriculture?

WJ: Yes. That work ought to be done because it is good work, but it is in a way not very radical. Most sustainable agriculture research is based on trying to understand agriculture on its own terms and relies on empirical data, but the natural systems agricultural researcher would say, "What was here, and what was the arrangement of what was here?" To me, that is not arrogant. Again, to quote Pope, "Consult the genius of the place in all." By the way, I think the word "consult" is an inspired term. He didn't say "Do exactly as," he just said to consult the genius of the place in all.

BW: You once said that a sun-powered civilization, which requires the sun-powered agriculture that you are working toward, will arrive as a result of nothing less than a religious reformation. Do you still agree with that?

WJ: Yes. I would word it differently, but I don't mind standing behind that.

BW: And yet you said earlier this evening in your public address that the church has been in constant retreat. Now I don't want to equate religion with church, but what are you suggesting in all of this? Are you saying that not only does agriculture need to consult the genius of the place in all, but that every human institution needs to do so, including our religious institutions? Is that it?

WJ: Yes.

BW: So we all need to go back to the root of things.

WJ: I think we've got to look at the process of creation in which we evolved. Yes, acknowledging that there have been a lot of accoutrements added that we would not want to do away with. But, I think it gets back again to acknowledging our fundamental ignorance. Let's work with our long suit, which would be an ignorance-based worldview.

BW: In other words, let's go ahead and design human culture and agriculture around an ecological paradigm that takes account of our ignorance?

WJ: We are going to continue to be ignorant and foolish. The evidence just keeps coming in day after day. Whether it's the drive-by shootings or the population problem. Why are we unable to contain the drive-by shootings? Why are we unable to do anything about the population problem?

BW: What is your answer?

WJ: I think that we ought to have a discussion. Here is what I would put on the table. We have thrown at the population problem the products of the industrial revolution: condoms, diaphragms, and chemicals. In other words, we have thrown a technological *tour de force* at what is basically a cultural problem. I think the argument can be made that it is the breakdown of culture that has led to the population explosion. How is it that certain indigenous peoples, particularly island races, have already had effective population control programs? Or look at the Ladaki people where Helena Norbert-Hodge works, where they have practiced polyandry. Several brothers would be married to the same woman. And, I hear there are examples from the plains Indians about males going for years without sex and getting a high out of it. So, these are instances of cultural accommodation. I am not suggesting that any of those things be done elsewhere, but what I am saying is that we have not assessed or valued cultural answers. To use Steven J. Gould's phrase about Disney's Epcot Center, "It is a technological *tour de force* and a conceptual desert." And that's what we have featured in this culture, a technological tour de force that has created countless conceptual deserts.

BW: So cultural knowledge, and knowledge about nature's genius, involves a community's long and hard-won experience with a place and its circumstances. Does our difficulty in validating cultural answers have something to do with the explosion of technical information, as well as the difficulty of getting back to living the cultural answers again?

WJ: Right.

BW: You've been talking about "homecoming." Is the essence of homecoming to return to these old neglected relationships from which the cultural answers will be revealed?

WJ: Homecoming means to go to some place and dig in. What we are talking about is acknowledging that the fundamental locus is not the nation-state, or the church, or the economy, whatever that is. One can design a computer to do A, B, C, D, and E, and as a derivative it could do I, J, K, L, and M sorts of things. Call that a first order derivative. On that savanna east of the Great Rift we developed an upright stance and the ability to run. We can ride a bike as a first order derivative. But the farther one gets from a first order derivative—to the second, third, and nth order derivatives—the more one has to rely on knowledge. We did not evolve in the nation-state. If we had, there would be no such thing as a bureaucracy.

BW: We evolved in the first order and the first order is a tribal community?

WJ: Right. A tribal community close to the land.

BW: So we've been pushing the envelope for a long time.

WJ: Right. We are out there now, often in fifth or sixth order derivatives. What is it to be raising a kid in Silicon Valley, around shopping malls and little league? What kind of a life is that? They learn little, and if they do get a job they go to a store where a machine teaches them to make change or they flip hamburgers at McDonalds. That is not real work. The purpose of work, the Buddhists say, is to "come together with others in a common task in order to overcome our egocentrism." "Life is real, life is earnest . . ."

BW: ". . . and the grave is not its goal."

WJ: Yes. The purpose of work according to the Buddhists is to help us toward a becoming existence. E.F. Shumacher has that beautiful chapter in *Small is Beautiful* on Buddhist economics. He talks about the difference between the tool and the machine. A tool is that which helps you toward that more becoming existence, and a machine robs you of it. The machine is also getting between us. He made a distinction between a power loom and a hand loom. When is something a tool and not a machine? Well, the Buddhist knows.

BW: So the tool permits relationship, and the relationship permits the possibility of affection.

WJ: Yes, even affection for the tool. Think of that, the tool that you used, that you developed the affection for. Shumacher said something that stuck with me when he visited our place in March of 1977, just before he died that August. I had a bunch of patio doors—225 of them—that I had bought from a company going out of business. I used them for everything, backstops even. I was complaining that maybe I shouldn't be using the spillover of the technological revolution. He said, "Oh never mind that. Materials want to be used, and they will show you how." So you see, here is this kind of connection. Now, I am always kind of intrigued about the possibility materials present to me. It does seem as though they want to be used. One time I ran out of gas on a truck that had just one full gas tank on one side while the other side was empty. I had to siphon the gas out. I saw a piece of electric wire in there, the kind you use for house wiring, and I just pulled the other wires out and made a hose. I sucked the gas out of one tank into a quart jar I happened to have and I was able to go on. Well, here was something that had been sitting in that truck for years, just wanting to be used.

BW: It gave itself to you.

WJ: Well, yes, maybe. I mean, it was not going to be used for wiring. Now as soon as you start this kind of conversation, you are going to be accused of being some kind of mystic with all of the pejorative stuff that is associated with that. I would rather say that here was something that helped make my day. And I look upon that piece of material even yet with a certain amount of affection. Even though I will never again use it as a siphon hose and it has been ruined as a piece of house wire.

BW: And now it's become a part of your story.

WJ: Well, yes. It is a part of my story. So it has a kind of immortality. And I think that is worth honoring.

BW: I do, too.

WJ: That is where your joy comes. You know the story told over and over is the story reexamined. Time and again it gets reexamined. It's like reading Huck Finn when you're 10, 20, 30, 40, 50, and 80.

BW: New meanings are given.

WJ: New meanings. And who wants to let technology get between us and that opportunity for new meanings? We want to solve problems, not create them.

Spiritual Formation and Social Change

PARKER J. PALMER

Parker J. Palmer is a writer, teacher, and activist who works independently on issues in education, community, leadership, spirituality, and social change. Parker has been a consultant to universities, public schools, community organizations, religious institutions, corporations, and foundations. He serves as Senior Associate of the American Association of Higher Education, and as Senior Advisor to the Fetzer Institute for whom he also directs its "Teacher Formation Program." Parker has often been cited as a master teacher, and in 1993 he won the national award of the Council of Independent Colleges for "Outstanding Contributions to Higher Education." He is a Quaker and has authored many fine essays and five widely used books: The Promise of Paradox, *a collection of essays on community, education and the inner journey;* The Company of Strangers, *which deals with the renewal of America's public life and the role of religion in that task;* To Know As We Are Known, *which draws on spiritual tradition to explore the depths of knowing, teaching, and learning;* The Active Life, *an inquiry into the spiritual problems and potentials of work, creativity, and caring; and most recently,* The Courage to Teach: Exploring the Inner Landscape of a Teacher's Life. *Parker has said that western culture has for a long time been "thinking the world apart." Our task now is to "think back together the world we have thought apart."*

BW: Thomas Berry says the times cry out for reverence and restoration efforts from everybody. Yet the evidence suggests we may be stuck in an adolescent culture and having some difficulty assuming our social and environmental responsibilities. What is spiritual formation in this context, and how does it help us grow up?

PJP: It does seem that our times require a new sense of responsibility. I'm very fond of H. Richard Niebuhr's definition of responsibility as the "ability to respond." When I first heard it years ago, it was just so clarifying for me. Responsibility is not this heavy thing that comes down from on high. Not this living up to a bunch of ethical norms. It's the ability to respond—which presupposes that I first feel connected, or responding would be out of the question. We live in times that require a new depth in our ability to respond. At the same time we see all around us this fragmentation that Thomas Berry implies in that quote, which keeps us apart and keeps us out of community. So it's a Catch-22, isn't it? Spiritual formation, to put it very simply, is the process by which we reconnect with our own souls in a way that allows us to reconnect with that which is outside of us, which is other than us. When you have lost the capacity, as many in this world have, to connect with the deepest parts of yourself, then you're simply living life on the level of role, function, image, status. Whether that's living life on the level of the inflated ego or the deflated ego doesn't make much difference. It's still not the real you. But when you've lost touch with that which is deepest within you and are living from some other place, there's no way to connect with that which is authentic in other people, the natural world, the world of spirit. And therefore there is no way to be responsible, no way to respond. But the important thing to note is that this inner journey, which spiritual formation is all about in all the great traditions, if it's taken authentically, doesn't end inside yourself. You end up moving through that inner place to a place of outward reconnection. That certainly is what I've learned from Quaker tradition. And that's what attracted me powerfully to Quaker tradition. Here was a group that worships in silence, of all things, that disappears into silence. And yet, when that silence is fruitful, they reemerge into the world, as Quaker history will demonstrate, making all kinds of impact in the most difficult of situations . . . race relations, war and peace, the relations of men and women, etc.

BW: The Quaker tradition gives us quite a powerful testimony to the effects that silence and spirituality could have today. And the Quakers have no ordained leadership.

PJP: No ordained leadership.

BW: Or is it that everyone is ordained?

PJP: Right. Quakers are fond of saying that we've been accused of abolishing the clergy, but we didn't. We abolished the laity. I like that a lot. It's also, interestingly enough, a very tiny group. There are only 100,000 Quakers in the United States, and only another 100,000 around the world. What does it say that such a small group, that worships in silence, that is almost invisible on the screen of the great world religions, has such a prominent presence in the great social issues of our times? It demonstrates that an inward journey authentically taken returns you to the larger world in transformative ways. There's a great story about a stranger coming into a Quaker meeting and sitting in the silence. The stranger has no preparation for this experience, and the silence goes on and on. Finally, frustrated, he leans over to the Friend next to him and says in a loud stage whisper, "When does the service begin?" And the Quaker sitting next to him says, "As soon as the worship ends."

BW: Wonderful!

PJP: I think that about sums it up!

BW: What does this say about the relationship between contemplation and action when it's practiced?

PJP: What drew me to Quakerism was a sense that these people who sit in the silence and finally emerge with something to say really mean what they say. There's something about that inward journey that takes you to your own truth. And once you've touched your own truth, there are really only two choices. One is, act upon it. And the other is, become unwell by not acting upon it. The challenge of that choice is why we don't like the journey toward our own truth. This is a culture that does not like to sit in silence. Psychologists say that the average group in our institutions can stand about fifteen seconds of silence before somebody has to get things moving by making noise. If you try it in a classroom or congregation or a business meeting, you'll find out that's about right. I think we're afraid of something that is scary, which is that in the silence you come closer to that which is your authentic calling, your authentic gift, your authentic issues and questions, your authentic shadow, the things you're struggling with. And once you've touched those things, life will never again be the same. You either act on them or you strangle them, in which case you're not living whole. I suppose it's just easier to stay on the surface of things and not face that challenge.

BW: Maybe that explains what's going on in our culture, which some have suggested is stuck midway in its moral development. For how can we grow without first taking responsibility for our own spiritual journey, our own spiritual formation?

PJP: It seems to me there are two conditions for growth. One is that you have to experience the pain that cries out for growth. I have never grown much until I have gotten into the kind of pain that says "grow or die." Because growth is difficult, and pain is the wake-up call. And this culture of ours is certainly in pain. But the second condition, in the case of an individual, is that this pain gets mediated and interpreted by a therapist or a spiritual director or a spiritual friend who can help you frame that pain in fruitful ways. In the case of a society, I think we need institutions and institutional leaders who can mediate and interpret that pain and offer people, first of all, a good diagnosis of where the pain is coming from. Lots of people are in pain, but they don't have the foggiest idea that it's perhaps related to their avoidance of the inner journey. So we need institutions and leaders who can offer a good diagnosis, and then can frame for people ways of acting on that diagnosis. Ways of taking that spiritual journey.

Ways of understanding your life experience so that it becomes spiritual journey. We ought to be doing more of this kind of thing in our churches and schools. We ought to be doing it in our workplaces, and some of them are making moves in this direction. There are all kinds of ways of helping people understand where this pain they're in is coming from, by taking a journey toward a deeper source, a healing source. I've been doing this kind of work the last couple of years with K through 12 public school teachers. Sponsored by the Fetzer Institute, it's called "Teacher Formation." This work has been so useful to people, and so positively evaluated, that we are now replicating our little pilot project for public school teachers in five locations around the nation. We hope to replicate more sites each year over the next several years.

BW: You've been working with religious and educational institutions of all kinds for years, encouraging people to find a way to live and lead from within. Can you say more about the Teacher Formation project?

PJP: It's a way to practice spiritual formation in the context of a particular profession. We try to take seriously the notion that people have real vocations, and some have a vocation as teacher. Every one of the twenty-five folks we've been working with in the Michigan pilot project over the last two years feels deeply called to teaching. Not all of them are overtly religious people, or, at least, they didn't use that language. But each of them feels that he or she really belongs in teaching, is really committed to working with children or young people. But for many public school teachers the conditions of life are so discouraging and so annihilating to one's sense of self and self-worth. All kinds of little things, like twenty-eight-minute lunch hours and scheduled times to go to the bathroom. At the same time you're working with kids, everybody in the society is hammering you to solve problems with children that no other institution knows how to solve. Education's answer to all this is teacher training programs. Every six months they're coming up with the hot new technique that's going to fix everything, because we live in a culture that is obsessed with technique, that defines everything as an external problem with an external fix. Well, most teachers are very cynical about the in-service training they get because it has that false promise to it, that false hope. They know at some point that the problems really aren't external. The problems are much more deeply internal and even spiritual.

The Teacher Formation Program is a program that meets quarterly for two years, with eight retreats altogether, each of them four days long. There are connective exercises between the retreats that keep people connected with each other and on their own inner journey. We're trying to look at some of the inner issues that affect teaching and learning, that affect the relationship of teachers to their students, to their colleagues, and to their administrators. One of the axioms of the Teacher Formation Program is that we teach who we are, regardless of how we teach and what we teach. The moral is that if we want to help teachers grow, we have to do more than just give them the technique of the day.

We have to create situations where teachers can explore the inner issues of identity and integrity around which we all need to grow. It's not like you just settle on your identity and integrity and it's fixed for the rest of your life. Identity and integrity are evolving, and they have very much to do with the ability to respond. The ability to respond to criticism. The ability to respond to changing conditions. The ability to respond to the gifts of the other and the needs of the other. So we need to be offering workshops and retreats and simple ways of being together as teachers that will help us evoke what is inside each other, both the shadow and the gift.

BW: Shadows. For example, fear?

PJP: Yes. We've done a lot of work with the inner issue called "fear." I'm convinced that our educational system has for a long time been driven by fear and is just permeated with fear. For a long time we've believed that children don't know how to learn, despite all evidence to the contrary. I have this five-year-old granddaughter who wants to learn everything in sight. But she'll go to school next fall and suddenly the presumption will be that she doesn't want to learn unless you motivate her with fear. Learn or you'll flunk. Learn or you won't go on to the next grade. Learn or you'll have to sit in a corner with a dunce cap on your head.

BW: Yes, it's a pervasive message.

PJP: A pervasive message to students. And administrators try to frighten teachers into doing their work, so there's fear everywhere. Yet when we stop to think about it, we realize very quickly that people don't learn when they're afraid. Learning requires openness, vulnerability, the capacity to take a risk, to expose your own ignorance. And those are things that no one will do under conditions of fear, under the paralysis of fear. So we've been working with these teachers, in part taking an inner journey toward the sources of fear in our own lives. Where does this stuff come from? And how do you find ground to stand on that takes away fear? I stand in a religious tradition. I happen to be a Christian. But the bottom line of every major religious tradition is, "Be not afraid." That's not a bad summary of the Christian tradition or most others. Somehow all of the great spiritual traditions are about examining human life in order to find ground on which to stand which takes away the reason for fear.

I'm a classroom teacher from time to time, most recently having spent a year at Berea College in Kentucky as visiting professor. It's a fearsome thing to teach. There are days when things aren't going so well, when your students really don't like you very much because you're stretching them and challenging them or asking them to do things they can't see or connect with their real lives. If you don't have solid ground on which to stand, something stronger than how popular you are with your students at the moment, you're not going to be a good teacher. You get sucked into either a popularity contest or, more likely, a kind of adversarial relation with these quote "stupid young people" who don't understand how important you and your thoughts are. Since you have the power to get them into line, you end up in an adversarial and essentially violent relation with your students, which is where I think a lot of teachers end up. This is what happens if you haven't dealt creatively with that issue of fear in the life of the teacher. So we work with fear in the Teacher Formation Program.

BW: Are you suggesting this is primarily a spiritual task?

PJP: Yes. One way to put a big frame around this is to say that there is absolutely no way to deal with the realities of the external world until we've dealt with the realities of the internal world. Because the internal world and external world co-create each other.

BW: Terrified by the prospect of changing our lives—which is increasingly being demanded of us, whether by the world's resource limits, or the growing gap between rich and poor, or any number of ecological or social truths that are knocking ever more loudly on our doors—how can we imagine better prospects for outward change without facing a new inner reality?

PJP: Yes. To take that journey into and through our fears, and find something solid on the other side. You mention scarcity in natural resources, of limits to the Earth's economy and the world's resources. An important issue that we deal with is this whole dynamic of scarcity and abundance that goes on inside us as well as outside us.

BW: I'm glad you're bringing this up because of the growing recognition, initiated by ecologists and environmentalists, about very real limits to growth and the Earth's carrying capacity. Is there an inner parallel?

PJP: It very much has its parallel in the inner life. Again, I see the inner and outer life as co-creative of each other. For example, I can walk around with a fearful attitude that says, "Everything I really need is scarce, so I better get my hands on as much as I possibly can before somebody else gets their hands on it, or there won't be any left for me." This way of being defines a greedy lifestyle and consumptive economy; the consequence is that external scarcity becomes more and more real. It becomes a self-fulfilling prophecy. The flip side is that I am failing to enter into those forms of community that might allow us to share resources and live more lightly on the face of the Earth. The consequences of that are absolutely devastating. This manifests itself in our institutions also. One way to name the pathology of institutions is to say that every institution would like to convince us that the good it controls is in scarce supply, and it alone controls the supply, because the more we believe that, the more power that institution has over our lives. If Church X is the only place you can go to get salvation, because they have convinced you that salvation is scarce and only available their way, then they have enormous power over people. If the school system convinces you that you become an intelligent person only by running the gauntlet on their terms and coming out the other end successful because they control the meaning and supply of intelligence, then they have an enormous amount of power. And that's exactly what's happened with the schools. We have a huge, elaborate school system in this society. We also have a gazillion people wandering around feeling stupid, because that institution has controlled the allegedly scarce supply of human intelligence and rewarded only a few people for possessing it. But we know, from many sound studies by psychologists, that human intelligence is not at all scarce. It just takes many forms that schools don't honor. People have intelligences that go well beyond verbal or numerical ability. They have problem-solving intelligence, visual intelligence, relational intelligence, manual intelligence. But the schools make intelligence scarce by defining it narrowly, and by handing out the rewards competitively. So we're in an absurd situation where we experience as scarce those things which are actually abundant in nature because of an inner logic driven by fear that elaborates itself in our institutions and makes people feel like there's not enough to go around.

BW: It sounds like global carrying capacity is both the external product of our internal fears, and helps reinforce those fears. Does it take a spiritual recognition to see that the actual limits need not be so severe *if* we would only change our perceptions and behaviors?

PJP: Exactly. Surely there are, with some natural resources, objective, external limits on the supply. But you have to work the inner side of that street as well. Because it's on the inner side that we decide whether we are going to compete for what we can get from what we perceive is scarce—where I get more and you get less—or whether we are going to enter into forms of community that allow us to share that scarcity, and in the sharing create a new kind of abundance. It seems to me that's the key to it. I've lived for a long time among this very rarified stratum of the world's society where people have bank accounts full of money and houses full of consumer items and larders full of food, and as far as I can tell, those people—my people—don't have a sense of abundance at all. They're running scared. They think that when the bank account dries up and the food supply is gone, there won't be anybody there for them. Whether that's old-age retirement, old-age illness, or whatever. And they're right, because the self-fulfilling prophecy of their lives is that they have not been weaving the fabric of community, of mutual aid and of interdependency that in itself provides the experience of abundance. Abundance doesn't come from having a lot of stuff. A sense of abundance comes from being part of a community that will sustain you.

BW: In my past I have been part of rural cultures that are embedded in community, where the sharing and generosity that goes on within them is remarkable. We also have the testimony of the non-profit sector, the data that giving is much higher per dollar of income among the "low-income" as opposed to the wealthy. Doesn't this confirm your point?

PJP: Yes, absolutely. The only thing I would add is that I think there is, tragically, also a level of poverty below which those sharing behaviors no longer happen, and people are forced to become cutthroat and survivalist for obvious reasons. Sadly, I think we are creating more and more such situations in this world where people get pushed below that minimum threshold. But it certainly is true that once basic needs are met, if there is a rich fabric of community culture and an ethical sensibility, there's more generosity of spirit among people who learned those forms of interdependence than among those radical individualists among us who *think* we don't need it in order to get along.

BW: It's so much easier to bear everything in community. Even loss and tragedy, and the consolation and support it requires, can only come from the deepest kind of communities.

PJP: And that's abundance, isn't it? If you ask people, "Do you feel abundance in your life?," usually what they're going to report is that sense of connectedness, consolation, mutuality, forgiveness, the ability to share joys—not having lots of stuff. Just having lots of stuff is kind of scary, because stuff gets used, broken, and stolen.

BW: Your comment about forgiveness reminds me of Gary Snyder who said that in community we are bound to find at some point that we have offended someone or caused some grievous wrong, and so have to face this whole question of forgiveness.

PJP: My favorite definition of community is the one that came to me after my first year of living in the intentional community of Quakers at Pendle Hill. I concluded that community is that place where the person you least want to live with always lives. And that's the conflict Gary Snyder is talking about, that sooner or later in community, you're not only going to overstep bounds with somebody, you're going to find your nemesis there. Because we have this need to take whatever we don't want to look at within ourselves and find it in somebody else whom we then proceed to hate. So community is that place where the person you least want to live with always lives. In my second year at Pendle Hill I came up with the corollary to that axiom, which is that when that person moves away, someone else arises immediately to take his or her place! So I think part of being in community is always having to face ourselves in the mirror of another, frequently our nemesis.

BW: It's not easy looking at those shadows in the mirror, either for persons or presumably institutions.

PJP: As long as people are having those inner monologues that say, "I'm better than somebody, or I'm worse than somebody," which are spiritual issues, then the structural stuff gets undermined. The external and the internal are constantly co-creating each other. As I said earlier, we know a lot about manipulating the external world, but it's all for naught if we don't learn to work the other side of the street.

BW: So we can't address environmental problems through educational reform or transformative education without integrating spiritual formation into an ecological worldview.

PJP: That's right. Years ago I stopped being excited about what was at that time called interdisciplinary studies, because it became clear to me that if you take one objectified discipline and connect it with three other objectified disciplines, all you've got is four objectified disciplines that have made some kind of deal with each other. This doesn't constitute the kind of breakthrough that I think we're all reaching for—and the field of ecology is no exception. There is a growing sense among ecologists that you can't really have an ecological science, in the objective sense of that word, if you don't have, for example, an ecological epistemology, an ecological worldview, even an ecological spirituality. That is, there is no way to understand the intricately rich connections in nature with a disconnected Cartesian epistemology. You cannot take the old objectified form of scientific knowing and come up with an image of the world, of the web, the gaia, because that very way of knowing fragments the world, atomizes it, deals with it as disconnected data bits. But the new epistemologies say that "knowing" is itself a richly interconnected activity—interconnected between mind and heart, between intuition and cognition, between various knowers situated in various places with different viewpoints. In that sense these ecological epistemologies yield a deeper knowledge of the rich interconnections in the natural world. So even if scientists aren't talking about spirituality, they're getting very close when they talk about epistemology. The way I have learned to open what I think of as the spiritual issues in education is through the door of epistemology. If you can get people to talk about the revolution in *ways of knowing* in their disciplines—whether it's biology or literature or physics or social science—you're into those inner issues that have to do with how we are connected as knowers with that which is known. Ultimately that drives toward spiritual ground, I think. Not spiritual in the sense of anybody's creed or propositional belief system, but spiritual in terms of the nature of this reality in which we are embedded, and of which we are one of the knowing agents.

BW: So when you inquire about shifting epistemologies, people will let you know that they are up against old, confining limits and are in the process of breaking through them.

PJP: Exactly. The old epistemology was driven by an objectivism that held us at arm's length from the world so that the world could be known truly and well, which meant that none of our subjectivity would slop over onto it.

BW: Instead of being connected to it?

PJP: Instead of *recognizing* your connection with it. The fantasy of the old objectivism was always that the farther away the knower could stand from the known, the more objectively one would know it. But as far as I can tell from reading the biographies of great scientists, that does not describe with any accuracy at all how great science gets done. Great science gets done in a dance of intimacy and distance. Great scientists move close to things because they love them, and they move back to check their perception, and then they move close again. They hold together a paradox of intimacy and distance. So what's that one-sided objectivism all about? That "cut flower" way of knowing? I think it's about the fear of getting too close to the world that it might make a claim on your life. It might make you not only into the changer but the changed. It might look back at you and say something about how you are living if you get too close. If you talk to great ecologists, I think you're talking to people who have gotten so close to the world that it's had a chance to look back at them and say something about how we all ought to be living. This is not an objectivism that stands back and says, I am the master of nature, I rule over all, I can do anything I want. This ecological epistemology is a way of knowing that draws you so close that you can no longer throw your beer cans in the street and pollute the streams and mow down the mountains at will, because you've heard the voice of the world speaking back to you. But you hear that voice only in an engaged way of knowing which draws you close in subjective passion, even as it requires you to move back for the sake of precision. It requires both. Knowledge is about both passion and precision. Read the biography or autobiography of any great knower—like Barbara McClintock—and you will find that paradox of passion and precision. And those are ultimately spiritual issues.

BW: So while it's only natural to put the arm out and resist the changes, you're saying there is also a willingness among educators to enter into new ways of knowing and practice in their craft.

PJP: Well I like to live with hope, so I probably try to see more of that than the other side. But social change is very interesting. If I read history right, it has never taken a majority to create significant change. It's just taken a critical mass, a minority that has tipped the balance because their energies have consolidated in the form that I think we normally call a social movement. I've been doing some study of movements in recent years because I think it's very important to think clearly about how movements happen if we want to encourage and be part of one in this area of reform.

What impresses me about how social movements create change is that they are often symbolized by one person who makes a deeply inward decision to "live divided no more." This person is usually representative of a lot of other people who are trying to make that same decision at the same time. But somebody rises to prominence to become the icon of a movement that is much more widespread than one person, that somehow needs to get catalyzed by that iconic or emblematic act. I've come to call this the Rosa Parks decision, because she is the icon of the modern civil rights movement. If you think about her decision to sit at the front of the bus that day, it was a decision to live divided no more. It was a decision that said, I am no longer going to be living on the outside in a way that contradicts a truth I hold on the inside. I'm no longer going to sit at the back of the bus when inside I know that I'm a full human being worthy of sitting anywhere I want. And in that simple act she catalyzed a movement that many others were already engaged in, who had basically decided they were no longer going to collaborate with an evil system that denies them externally the full human status they know they have internally.

And every movement that I've been able to study—whether it's the movement for liberation in Czechoslovakia or parts of eastern Europe, in South Africa or in Latin America or here at home in the civil rights movement, or the gay and lesbian liberation movement, even the historic labor movement—all of these were catalyzed by that decision to live divided no more. That's another way of talking about the power of our inner lives. If we claim our inner truth and act on it, we're doing what Gandhi called the most powerful act we can take, which is not an instrumental act calculated to reach a certain end, but what he called an expressive end that expresses our deepest truth. An inner truth. A spiritual truth. And the power of expressing my deepest truth in outward behavior is a power we're not taught much about in school. In school we're taught about the power of armies and governments and guns and money. We don't learn much about the power that people have achieved by manifesting and expressing their deepest inner truth. And yet in every crucial moment in history, that is what is happening. And that's what's happening in the world of ecology.

BW: How would you assess the direction and health of the environmental movement?

PJP: My sense is that the movement has in fact been animated by people who have said, "Inwardly, I understand myself to be part of a community of creation or of nature," however they may image it, "and I'm going to act out of the truth I know, which is that I am part of it." One of the interesting things about people who start movements and who engage in movements is that they tend to incur the wrath of institutions that would really like us to keep our inner truths to ourselves. We live in a society in which the divided life comes highly recommended.

BW: It's very profitable.

PJP: Very profitable, and it makes things a lot easier. So don't make a federal case out of it. If you have a feeling or a belief, just tuck it away, take it to church on Sunday maybe, but don't stand on it the rest of the week. I've often asked myself where these people who start movements find the courage to take a stand to live divided no more—like sitting at the front of the bus—which they know will bring down the wrath of institutions on their heads? The answer that I've come up with on the basis of their lives is one that really fascinates me. I think these are people who suddenly realize that no punishment anyone could lay on them could possibly be greater than the punishment that they have laid on themselves for conspiring in their own diminishment. Because if you fail to act on the truth you know, you are conspiring in your own diminishment. If you know you're a full human being, but you keep sitting in the back of the bus every day of your life, you're punishing yourself more than the Montgomery, Alabama, police could possibly punish you.

BW: The voices just scream within you until you give voice to them.

PJP: Yes. It goes back to where we started this conversation. Once you know your inner truth, you've got two choices. You either act on it or you become unwell. These are people who have made a choice for wholeness in their own lives—Rosa Parks is a brilliant example—which then contributes to the wholeness of their society. Not without pain. Not without struggle. Not without threat. Because wholeness, unfortunately in our world, is painful, is a struggle, and is threatening.

BW: So it's a matter of being willing to walk through the fears and the fires that invariably come our way.

PJP: Very much so. And none of us does that gladly or willingly. For most of us, it's a journey we take reluctantly. It's a journey we need to support each other on. It's a journey I certainly have needed a lot of help with. And it's a journey we probably take because we can't *not* take it. We just get to a point in life where it's not something we want to do; it's something we can't *not*. Whether that's because of a crisis in our life, or a nagging sense of unfulfillment, or whatever. We find ourselves having to take that journey through the fears and the fires.

BW: We'll be needing to support each other in that.

PJP: That's right. That's where community becomes really important.

PART 2

PRACTICAL LINKS BETWEEN RELIGIOUS AND ENVIRONMENTAL SENSIBILITIES

Reconnecting to What Sustains Us Physically and Spiritually

STEVEN C. ROCKEFELLER

Steven C. Rockefeller is a Professor of Religion at Middlebury College in Vermont where he formerly served as Dean of the College. He received his Master of Divinity from Union Theological Seminary in New York City and his Ph.D. in the philosophy of religion from Columbia University. Professor Rockefeller is the author of John Dewey: Religious Faith and Democratic Humanism *and the co-editor of* The Christ and the Bodhisattva *and* Spirit and Nature: Why the Environment is a Religious Issue. *His essays appear in a number of books and journals. In his recent work, he has given special attention to the subject of environmental and global ethics and is coordinating the drafting of an Earth Charter for the Earth Charter Commission and Earth Council in Costa Rica.*

BW: The subtitle of *Spirit and Nature* is "Why the Environment Is a Religious Issue." There are lots of issues we can point to as religious concerns, but is there something of overriding and crucial importance about the convergence of religious and environmental sensibilities?

SR: Our environmental problems will not be fully addressed until we come to terms with the moral and spiritual dimensions of these problems, and we will not find ourselves religiously until we fully address our environmental problems. On the one hand, human behavior is controlled to a significant degree by the values and attitudes that people adopt, and this is certainly true regarding the way people treat the environment. Furthermore, a good argument can be made that on the deepest level a solution to our environmental problems requires adoption of a new set of ethical and spiritual values that will transform how we think about and relate to nature. The world's religions have a critical role to play in this matter. However, in many cases the religions must undergo an ecological reconstruction of their worldviews before they can be helpful.

This is the issue when one looks at it from the side of the environment.

On the other hand, looking at the situation from a religious point of view, it is my strong belief that humanity will only find its spiritual center in the next century by committing itself to realize the spiritual meaning and value to be found in everyday life including relations with the natural world. There has been a tendency, certainly in religion in the West, to look for God outside the world, as though God's being were in some sense separate from everything else. However, modern culture over the past 200 years has increasingly turned attention away from the other world and focused it on this world, shifting its attention from the supernatural to the natural. From the religious point of view, this can be interpreted as a great loss, because it seems that people have turned their attention away from God and have become wholly absorbed in the natural world and secular concerns. What is needed, however, is not a return to the quest for God outside the world or apart from the world, but rather a more profound exploration of this world, the natural world, reaching the point where we can see the divine as the deeper center of this world.

In this regard, our environmental problems and the science of ecology have a spiritual significance. They call us to focus fresh attention on the living Earth and the most basic aspects of our everyday life—the biodiversity and the natural systems that sustain us. Further, they challenge us to wake up to the truth that we are interdependent members of, not only the human community, but the larger community of life as well and that with this membership goes a moral responsibility to respect and care for the community of life as a whole. They challenge us to become aware of and respect the intrinsic value of other life forms quite apart from whatever utilitarian value they may have for humans. There will be no lasting solution to our environmental problems without this kind of spiritual transformation in our attitudes toward nature, and contemporary men and women will only find their spiritual center by responding to the spiritual and ethical challenges implicit in our environmental problems and ecology. To use the theological language of a mystic, our urgent religious need is to seek and find the Beyond in the midst—the divine in and through our relations with people and the larger world of nature.

BW: To discover that the transcendent is also immanent, and to find we are immersed in the transcendent.

SR: Yes. Another way of expressing this is the way Martin Buber put it. You won't find God if you seek God outside the world. You won't find God if you seek God as a particular being in the world separate from everything else. You will only find God by entering into relationship with persons and the natural world, in the spirit of "I-Thou."

BW: You've suggested that our quest for a spiritual center and our search for ecological sustainability is converging today, as though it were a result of our religious evolution as a species. Why is it that we can no longer effectively address one without the other? Why do you say that the challenge before us, the challenge in every religious tradition, is this integration of the moral and religious life with an ecological worldview?

SR: The environmental movement needs to be reinforced by a spiritual sense of the intrinsic value of the natural world and the sacredness of all life. At the same time, an ecological understanding of the interdependence of humanity and nature reinforces the growing religious awareness that ultimate meaning is found in and through relationship and building an inclusive community that embraces all life and ecosystems as well as people. In this way the ecological and the religious converge and are interrelated.

BW: Some of our religious traditions, as you've indicated in your work, have much to offer us in terms of stretching our sense of the sacred, finding inherent value in nature, and deepening our reverence for life. But we've also heard much about the understandable critique of our religious traditions. In most of the religious traditions you've explored as a scholar, does there exist the potential for this broader reverence, this wider sense of sacramentality? Despite institutional tendencies to resist change, do our religious traditions have the self-revising, self-renewing potential that is needed to reinforce what the environmental movement is grasping for?

SR: All of the great religions of the world, and many indigenous religious traditions, have this potential. The seeds of a deep respect and appreciation of nature and a reverence for life lie within all these traditions. In some it is much more fully developed than in others, but the potentiality is certainly there. So I think one can be optimistic. The critical issue in developing this potential is that the leadership within these traditions recognize the urgency of the challenge posed by the environmental crisis. Perhaps more work has been done in the Christian tradition on this subject than in any other. During the past twenty-five years literally hundreds of books and essays have been written by Christian scholars in an effort to address this problem.

BW: Some of which I presume comes in response to Lynn White's provocative essay which considered the Judeo-Christian role in the environmental crisis.

SR: That's correct. However it is also sadly the case that the majority of theologians and ethical thinkers in the Christian tradition have not yet fully integrated the environmental concern into their work. In the Jewish tradition a significant movement in the area of ecological theology and ethics has also slowly taken form in recent decades, and important work is now being done.

BW: Both theological and ethical?

SR: Yes, and practical. There is a coalition within the Jewish community which includes representatives from the Orthodox, Conservative, Reform, and Reconstructionist movements which is jointly sponsoring this environmental program.

BW: Are they organized under the rubric of the National Religious Partnership for the Environment?

SR: They have been instrumental in supporting the Partnership, but there is a separate Jewish group, the Coalition on the Environment and Jewish Life (COEJL), that works with the National Religious Partnership.

BW: With this example you're demonstrating that our religious traditions are indeed capable of engaging new environmental realities. We don't have to feel confined by seemingly inflexible religious institutions. We are actually part of living religious traditions, each of them subject to change and reinterpretation by those who participate and engage in them. Is this self-revising work going on in all the world's religious traditions?

SR: It certainly is. There are Islamic thinkers and Buddhist thinkers and Hindu thinkers, all of whom are engaging this issue. Furthermore, they are now beginning to work together. This collaboration began with the Assisi conference in 1985, sponsored by the World Wildlife Fund. Each of the religious leaders who attended that meeting identified their tradition as one with strong environmental concerns and respect for nature. Since then there have been many interfaith conversations around the issue of religion and ecology just as there have been many meetings devoted to, for example, the Christian or Jewish or Buddhist discussion of this issue. So there is now much work being done within the framework of each religious tradition, along with interfaith dialogue on the issue.

BW: As this spiritual and theological and scholarly reflection proceeds and becomes more widely available to lay and ordained leaders, we're beginning to see this changing worldview take root in local faith communities. Which puts me in mind of the address Secretary of Interior Bruce Babbitt delivered to the National Religious Partnership for the Environment on the occasion of congressional threats to the Endangered Species Act. This was the first time, I believe, that we have heard public officials in America justify environmental protection and biological diversity not only on scientific grounds but on scriptural grounds. In a nation where biblical language is still a second language for many Americans, Babbitt justified public action on behalf of species diversity and protection by drawing on biblical stories—in this case the Noah story and the Covenant with the Rainbow—in essence using scriptural language as a moral language that can help guide public policy.

SR: And what's particularly significant about the Noah Covenant is that it is God's covenant with all creation, including all humanity, not just one particular group, and all species. It is all-embracing.

BW: Bringing it closer to home, you've been a professor of religious studies at Middlebury College in Vermont for twenty-six years. During this time we've witnessed the emergence of the interdisciplinary field of environmental studies at both the undergraduate and graduate levels in America, which is increasingly becoming mainstreamed in the college curriculum. Schools like Tufts have begun to integrate the ecological worldview throughout the disciplines, the social and natural sciences as well as the arts and humanities. More and more, it also appears that environmental ethics is drawing on a religious dimension to inform and guide our ethical understanding. If the educational challenge, as Parker Palmer has suggested, is to put back together the world we have taken apart, what response do we see at liberal arts colleges like Middlebury in this regard? Specifically, what is the contribution of religious studies to environmental studies?

SR: Middlebury College has a well-developed environmental studies program that is interdisciplinary, and students are required to take courses in both the humanities and the sciences. Among the courses students can take to fulfill their requirements for the program are two or three religion courses that deal with religion, ethics, and the environment. In addition, the environmental studies program has created an ethics concentration for majors. In that regard we draw on courses from religion, philosophy, political science, and other disciplines. So here at Middlebury the religious dimension of environmental studies has an important place in the larger program.

BW: How long has that been so?

SR: Since the late 1980s. However, the first time that the college community as a whole became aware that there was a significant interconnection between religious and environmental issues was the occasion of the Spirit and Nature Symposium in 1990. This was a dramatic statement within the college community of this convergence. There were between 300-500 students at each lecture, and when the Dalai Lama spoke there were 3,500 people present, including the majority of the student body. So the awareness here is significant. Each year we have at Middlebury somewhere between 75-100 students taking courses in the area of religion, ethics and the environment. But like most people in colleges, universities, and seminaries who teach courses in this area, we are still fighting an uphill battle in trying to get all of our colleagues to make environmental issues a priority in appropriate courses. The subject is recognized and respected here, and people are slowly beginning to integrate it into their teaching. Middlebury has a very strong environmental studies program which today has the second highest number of majors in the college. So it is a strong presence in the college community. However, there are many faculty members who still remain uninterested in integrating environmental studies into what they are teaching. This is also largely true in our seminaries across the United States. I was at a meeting in Stony Point, New York, a few years ago that was a gathering of academics who teach the subject of religion and the environment in colleges, universities, and seminaries. All of them agreed that they felt relatively isolated within their institutions given the lack of widespread interest in what they were doing. This is slowly changing.

BW: How are our academic communities—be they liberal arts colleges or universities or theological centers—going about this change? Is there some kind of network or association that is attempting to raise these issues of curriculum and context?

SR: It is important to view this question with some historical perspective. Since the 1960s theological seminaries and universities have been through a series of major intellectual transformations related to social and political events, such as the Civil Rights Movement, the Vietnam War, and the feminist movement. In addition, there have been various currents of postmodern thought that have challenged traditional ways of thinking. It has been a time of tremendous intellectual ferment and change. The challenge of our environmental problems has arisen during this period, and many faculty have no training in this area and find it difficult to adjust to all the demands upon them to integrate new knowledge and fresh methods of analysis.

Nevertheless, environmental studies programs are being established, and environmental issues are gradually being more fully addressed in the curriculum outside these programs as well. There are several reasons for this. First, there is growing popular concern about the environment as the science on the subject is expanded and given media attention. A new generation of students is being introduced to ecology and related topics in elementary and high school, and these students are keenly interested and want college courses to address the critical issues. Second, it is increasingly clear that there are significant connections between environmental problems and issues involving race, gender, and social justice as well as economic well-being. Third, some institutions—Tufts University is a prime example—are trying to provide the financial and teaching resources that faculty need to get themselves further educated and prepared to teach in this area.

BW: So this is a very understandable process of internal change. And there are some college administrations that are taking proactive steps in this direction.

SR: Middlebury College has a one-semester term called Winter Term in which each faculty member teaches one course. A few years ago the college made it possible for a group of interested faculty to work together during Winter Term on how to integrate feminist studies into their teaching. The same thing could be done with environmental studies. The book which I gave you, *Greening the College Curriculum*, has a chapter on how to teach the environment from the point of view of many disciplines: anthropology, biology, history, philosophy, literature, religion, and so forth. With its good bibliography and suggestions on course curricula, a book like that becomes a valuable resource.

BW: As you scan the horizon of higher education, especially your colleagues in religious studies, do you see others contributing to the ethical, theological and spiritual dimensions of environmental studies?

SR: One initiative that has tried to promote the greening of seminary education is Theological Education to Meet the Environmental Challenge (TEMEC), which was launched by Richard Clugston, Dieter Hessel, and J. Ronald Engel in the early 1990s. Much of the funding has come from the MacArthur Foundation and the Pew Charitable Trusts, and its secretariat today is at the Center for Respect of Life and Environment in Washington, DC. TEMEC has helped to build a nationwide network of teachers and scholars concerned about these issues.

Another very important initiative is being led by Professors Mary Evelyn Tucker and John Grim in collaboration with The Center for the Study of World Religions at Harvard Divinity School. They have organized a series of nine conferences on religion and ecology, each of which focuses on one of the major religions of the world. These gatherings and the publications that will follow are setting forth an invaluable overview of the state of religion/environmental studies at the end of the century, and they lay out the agenda for the future. What you can say about environmental studies in general is this. Programs of environmental studies are successfully being established, and some are interdisciplinary. Students are very enthusiastic and flocking to them. There is a slow moving process underway of integrating environmental studies into the larger curriculum. We are at the very beginning of that process. One issue here is convincing college and university presidents that this is an issue—

BW: And boards of trustees?

SR: And boards of trustees, many of whom are not particularly well informed about the environmental issue. The Talloires Declaration was issued by a group of about twenty university presidents in 1990. It's an important statement that calls upon university and college presidents and faculties to take seriously the issue of sustainable development and to integrate teaching on this subject throughout the curriculum. Middlebury's president was one of the early signers of that document. The declaration is an important step forward.

There is another important thing happening. In addition to the effort to develop environmental studies programs, many colleges, universities, and seminaries are taking seriously the challenge of greening the operations of the institution. This is both an issue of social responsibility and good citizenship on the one hand, and a way of promoting environmental awareness throughout the whole institution and community or the other. This movement is going forward with considerable energy and is gaining momentum. In 1993, with funding from the Heinz Foundation, there was a Campus Earth Summit at Yale University. The purpose of that meeting was to set forth a blueprint for greening the college and university campus. It was a very productive gathering with representatives from schools all over the United States, and they produced a fine document, which is titled *Blueprint for a Green Campus*. It also created a national network that involves thousands of students and faculty and staff as well.

BW: Is that coordinated between our "secular" institutions and theological institutions, or are they separate networks?

SR: The issue of greening the campus is moving forward in theological seminaries, and they are part of this network. The group that has been promoting this in the theological world is the Center for the Respect of Life and Environment, headed up by Rick Clugston. Here at Middlebury, this movement is well advanced. For over twenty years Middlebury has had an environmental council which both Professor John Elder and I have chaired at different times in the past. Originally called the Energy Council, it was created in the 1970s in response to the energy crisis. In the beginning, its task was to promote energy conservation and help the college adjust to the energy crisis. It has now expanded its role and is concerned with the issues of environmental awareness on campus, energy conservation, waste reduction, recycling, and so forth. The environmental council issued a major report in 1994 which was essentially an environmental audit of the campus. Each of its eleven chapters reports on a distinct aspect of the college, such as recycling, hazardous waste management, or dining services. Each chapter identifies the relevant federal, state, and local legislation, describes the problems the college faces, what it has done and has not done, and then goes on to make recommendations about what the college needs to do in order to get itself fully on the path of sustainable development. This report was presented to the president as a set of recommendations, many of which have been implemented. Right now there seems to be in the college's administration a real openness and a spirit of cooperation in this area. This kind of initiative is going on in many schools and colleges all over the country and is gaining momentum.

BW: For those not so far along as Middlebury, it's good to know there are schools like Middlebury that others can consult with and learn from as they contemplate how best to move forward with the change process.

SR: There's a very good network available today.

BW: I'm interested in Middlebury's response, in part, because this is a wonderful example of how every institution has moral purposes, of how we can expand these moral purposes to include the environment, and how the institutions through which we live require our involvement to help reshape them.

SR: Middlebury has very strong student leadership in this area. They have an Environmental Quality organization, an environmental house, and a number of different organizations in addition that are concerned with the outdoors, like the Mountain Club, etc. But there are some students who see the environmentalists as a pressure group that is trying to tell everybody how they ought to live and what they ought to eat, and this provokes some reaction.

BW: And so the community is also learning something about a civil society and moral discourse, how to talk with one another across our differences. Even how to live with unresolved tensions. It sounds like a healthy place to grow and mature.

SR: It is. The ethical issues raised by the environment are hotly debated on campus. Right now Middlebury is in the midst of a heated debate over a ten- or fifteen-acre plot of land that some people would like to develop for a new set of social houses and others would like to preserve as a woods, a retreat, and a resource for faculty teaching in the fields of biology and ecology. This places the whole question about college responsibility for preserving natural habitat and the beauty of the local environment in tension with the college's need to expand and develop. The debate provides a very good way for students to get into the complexities of life. They're getting some good training on how to resolve very complicated social and ecological problems.

BW: So the intellectual enterprise here is by no means divorced from the moral enterprise and questions of the common good, of immediate ends versus ultimate purposes.

SR: Absolutely not. And a number of college courses today use this problem in their actual course curriculum as an example of these issues.

BW: I'd like to return to something we were talking about earlier. When we look at religious traditions, stories, myths, images, symbols and rituals, what is it about these religious qualities that are so important in addressing the environmental crisis and our hope for an enduring human culture?

SR: Myths, symbols and rituals that are spiritually alive for people express and strengthen commitment to the values and ideals that they hold sacred. Music, drama, poetry—all of the arts when they become part of religious life—have a special power to inspire and move people. I think it is fair to say that we will not see full religious support for the environment until environmental values are integrated into the symbols and rituals of these different religious traditions. The arts and religion in this sense have a crucial role to play. When we held our 1990 symposium on Spirit and Nature at Middlebury, we were very careful to include music—with Paul Winter in this case—and a substantial art exhibition which drew on art from many different religious traditions.

BW: When you talk to people engaged in these changes, do you sense that they're drawing on some kind of religious tradition, on living symbols and images? Or is it sufficient motivation that we are just deeply concerned about our environmental future, with the plight of the living Earth?

SR: Some environmentalists have deep roots in a religious tradition and find inspiration in its stories and symbols, but others follow a more secular approach. However, quite apart from organized religion, the environmental movement is developing symbols and rituals that have spiritual meaning for many people. I am thinking, for example, of the image of Earth photographed by the astronauts and celebrations like Earth Day. During the Spirit and Nature symposium, we tried to introduce some explicitly environmental symbolism and ritual. We created, for example, a set of handsome large banners to hang in the college chapel where both lectures and religious services were held during the symposium. These banners included symbols of many of the world's major religious traditions and also a symbol of the planet Earth.

BW: This strikes me as significant in itself, that you chose to host most of the sessions on Spirit and Nature in the chapel, which most Americans would identify as sacred space.

SR: Yes. Holding all those lectures in a sacred space, in the center of the campus, was powerful symbolism in its own right. In addition to the banners, a photograph of planet Earth was placed on the altar during the big interfaith service at the end of the symposium. After the service, there was a common meal. It occurred in a big meadow below the chapel. The space was designed like a large mandala. In the center was a platform with a huge table on it. On the table were baskets of bread and fruit. The bread and fruit symbolized the goodness of the Earth with which all beings are nourished and sustained, and in which all people and life forms have a right to share. Everybody was invited to come forward and receive this bread as a kind of communion with the Earth and with each other and all other beings in the community of life. They were seated around this space which was decorated with flowers and so forth. We called this the common meal, and it was seen as a participation in the larger community of life, in the form of a ritual with rich symbolism. This same ceremony was repeated last year during Earth Week, and the students have chosen to do it again this year. So this is a kind of ritual celebration in a fairly light-hearted spirit that may become a new tradition here.

BW: This particular community of faculty, students, and staff is, of course, a highly diverse community in cultural and religious terms. In working with those realities, you are nonetheless consciously drawing on all kinds of symbols and images that we traditionally call religious.

SR: We're at least experimenting here with things of this nature. In terms of ritual in American culture, it is very important to keep in mind the new interest that is emerging in American Indian ritual. Many Americans find that the American Indian traditions have a special power to awaken a sense of interdependence with Earth and a sense of communion with the larger world of nature. We had a very powerful voice from the American Indian community at Middlebury in 1990, Audrey Shenandoah, who is an elder from the Iroquois tradition. In New York City, at the Cathedral of St. John the Divine, some especially imaginative ritual and ceremony have taken place that integrates environmental, American Indian, and Christian values.

BW: There is so much creative work underway in the areas of ritual and liturgy that can put us in touch with the transcendent that surrounds us everywhere. But nature, like ritual, also has the power to connect us to something much larger than ourselves. One of its powers is its role in our spiritual formation. As a scholar you've been immersed in books and the study of religious traditions and scriptures. But can you say anything about nature's influence on you in terms of your own spiritual formation, your own spiritual journey?

SR: As a boy, the most powerful religious experiences I had were in the outdoors rather than in churches. From very early in my life, I was deeply moved by the beauty of the natural world and felt a very powerful pull to enter into deeper communion with the mystery and wonder of nature. There were three places in my childhood that were especially influential, perhaps most importantly the Teton Mountains of Wyoming where I worked on my grandfather's ranch and on trail crews in the national park. The Tetons worked a wonderful magic that has stayed with me all these years.

BW: The Wind River range nearby did the same to me. If these indelible experiences are so important to us in childhood and continue to form us as adults, why do many of us still need more than that? We can affirm that nature is an indispensable teacher, but what is it that we find so valuable in religious traditions?

SR: Religious traditions have struggled over the centuries to find a language, symbols and rituals that express the meaning and value of the human encounter with the sacred. In addition, the religious traditions—and I'm thinking here in particular of Judaism and Christianity—have put heavy emphasis on our moral responsibility to care for each other, to build just communities and societies, and to care for the natural world. What I personally believe is the most promising route to pursue today in terms of religious thinking is the one that I was describing at the beginning of our conversation. The quest for God needs to be focused on the ideal possibilities in the relations between human beings and between humans and nature. God will be found in and through these relationships. We need the language and the stories and the vision that come from these traditions to help us talk about this and to shape our actions, for example, the work of some of the great mystics like Meister Eckhart, who developed ways of talking about the deeper meaning of these kinds of relationships. But the challenge today is not just to repeat what has been articulated in the past; it is to reconstruct these traditions in the light of our own living experience and the changed intellectual, social, and ecological situation.

BW: Though we seek out religious experience that may involve no words, we are still a people of language. The stories we receive through one another and the written tradition help us immerse ourselves in the needs and concerns and life of the world, help us embrace it and live without fear despite the changes that may be required.

SR: Yes. And people need opportunities to come together to celebrate and share what they treasure and value. They need to come together to renew their commitment to their shared ethical values. The challenge to institutional religion is to provide this kind of opportunity in a way that is connected with what people are experiencing and thinking in contemporary life. It is very difficult because the predominant forms of institutional religion, and I'm thinking here of the ritual and liturgy, were formed in the ancient and medieval world. We live in a totally different social and intellectual environment, and the struggle has been to preserve continuity with the past while recasting these traditions in a way that makes them genuinely meaningful vehicles of religious expression today. This is very difficult. My own feeling is that the environmental crisis can help the religious institutions of America meet this challenge if they will only take it seriously.

Building Bridges

PAUL GORMAN

After two years of preparatory meetings, strategic planning, diplomacy, and fundraising, America's major faith groups launched the National Religious Partnership for the Environment in 1993 at the Cathedral of St. John the Divine in New York City. Under the direction of Paul Gorman, this coalition of Jews, Catholics, Protestants, and Evangelicals represents a broad new force for moral consensus on the environment at the highest levels of institutional governance, but it also signals the formation of a new and very large grassroots constituency for environmental and social action in America's local congregations. Never before has there been such a concerted effort among the religious communities in the United States to address the moral—and practical—dimensions of the environmental crisis. Together they are building bridges of understanding and action that could have a lasting effect on the moral integrity of the environmental movement and communities of faith, as both discover how much they need each other. As Gorman said, "For me, this is about how religious life understands itself and its purpose."

BW: What is the National Religious Partnership for the Environment trying to communicate to the one hundred million Americans who comprise its membership?

PG: It's a multiple message to multiple audiences. For the religious community itself, it is that care for creation and the work of environmental sustainability and justice must become central to what it means now and henceforth to be religious. Such a priority suggests that these concerns have not been sufficiently at the heart of people's active religious lives. Yet these are inescapably and intrinsically religious issues. To be faithful to God, scripture, teaching and tradition, these concerns have to be addressed more systematically across the fabric of religious life: in theology, in scholarship, in worship, in education, in public policy, in community engagement. That's the first message. The second is that there really is, and needs to be, a distinctively religious response to these issues. This is not just something that we ought to do, but clearly something we can do.

BW: What is that distinctive religious response?

PG: Religious thought has a great deal to offer environmentalism. It offers a scale of vision, cosmology, a kind of encompassing narrative, which is equal to the dimensions of the problem itself. I think we have moral perspective and witness to offer. I think we have a history of social teaching about the common good which can assist in facilitating arrangements of the greatest benefit to the greatest number. I think we have a tradition of social justice and equity, as well as spiritual resources, that can be helpful to people as individuals. We have a long history of engagement in social struggles that give meaning to sacrifice and endurance amidst setbacks. We know something about how to deal with defeat, and the value of struggle over the long run.

BW: A living tradition with moral capital that can be usefully drawn upon?

PG: To the extent it's living, it's an asset. But it's up to us to make it real, to bear the fruit. Our third message is that part of what we have to contribute comes from within religious life itself, and part of it comes from how religious life engages other sectors of society that are relating to this issue.

BW: You're talking about the public nature of religious life.

PG: Yes, and its interface with the humanities, the arts, the sciences. We have something to say to people of faith, but we also have something to say to the other disciplines that are addressing this. The fourth message is that a deep engagement with these issues offers a profound source of religious and spiritual renewal. This isn't something we're doing to burn ourselves out on. Those are our main messages and goals.

BW: How do you gauge the response so far from America's faith communities?

PG: I think the response has been thoughtful, enthusiastic, focused, and irreversibly positive. There is the phrase in Psalm 46, "There is a river; we can track it down." And this is a river; we can track it down. The American religious community is already set on the course of bringing these issues into the heart of religious life, and determined to make a daily contribution to public education that invokes a human response. The deepest currents of this river are irreversible for religious life and human civilization.

BW: So each of these religious traditions is now engaged in a recovery and renewal process.

PG: I don't quite accept the model that religion used to be one pure way because of Hildegard or St. Francis, and then it got messed up by Francis Bacon and the Enlightenment, and now we've discovered this suppressed legacy of religious teachings on the natural world which we are attempting to recover. I suppose in some sense we are all recovering certain teachings, but in another sense it's just a healthy and spontaneous response to what is biblically called the "signs of the times," to what is being revealed about the condition of the planet itself. And in that way I think the religious community is about where every other major community or discipline is with respect to its complicity and response to the consequences of human behavior. I don't know that religious people and religious leaders are any different than scientists, artists, or entrepreneurs on this one. We've all been blind to the consequences of who we are and what we've done. But what I see happening in religious life in response to this crisis is deep, spontaneous, natural. It resonates with people, even though it's part of a crowded plate of problems that beset religious institutions in our society. The religious community in America at century's end has profound responsibilities to human well-being in the more narrowly human sphere, with poverty, injustice, war, racism, and sexism. And so part of the problem for us has been what you might call an "agenda-glut," which is simply the growing list of tasks that fall to the religious community, especially in the United States where the social role of government is shrinking.

BW: All these human needs are real, but I can't imagine you're saying that with the environmental crisis we're merely adding one more issue to an already crowded agenda.

PG: For some people it is. But other particularly passionate advocates, including myself, would say we're doing something far more than adding an issue. We're proposing a new way of looking at the world, and a new way of incorporating all these issues. But when it comes to the daily struggle of conflicting needs in organizational life, the environment can sometimes become just another issue without a comprehensive context.

BW: Is there any real doubt in your mind that the concerns and worldview you're advocating will become central to our sense of religious being in the future?

PG: If it's possible to say this, I have no doubt, yet plenty of doubt, that these concerns will be central to religious life and activity. I have no doubt because I think the recognition of their intrinsically religious character is irresistible once that question is brought to the human heart, spirit, and mind. It will become as irresistible as the central religious duty to care for children and for one's elders. Yet I have plenty of doubt when I look at how we're actually caring for our children and our elders. And, frankly, I have some doubt about how capable organized religion will be in appreciating the full dimensions and causes of this crisis which are so profound and long term. I have some doubt when I think how society is generally such a prisoner of the present tense. In certain respects, this engagement is irreversible. In other respects it's still an open question. And we're all living in the middle of that paradox.

BW: So you're not sure if organized religion can evolve rapidly enough to meet the environmental crisis?

PG: You're dealing here with ancient traditions and large and complex institutions, both of which make rapid change in any direction difficult. I think we're seeing an increasing recognition, among both religious scholars and religious community leaders, of the richness and potential of this encounter between religion and the environment. But the people in the pews are often ahead of them in this recognition—and in fact, it is voices from these pews which have, in many instances, convinced leaders and scholars to more urgently address environmental concerns.

BW: And why is that?

PG: Because there are too many pundits and too few prophets. There's an understandable fascination with the dynamics of religious life as it has been and is presently being experienced, at the expense of a prophetic perspective which would allow scholars and commentators to understand how much is at stake with the environment and what more is possible here. Of course, it's a lot harder to be a prophet than a pundit. Prophets have always been few and far between, no matter what the issue.

BW: Where, if anywhere, do you see that prophetic voice or some recognition of it? In our poets? Our writers?

PG: The great stream of American naturalists is still a very rich source of prophetic inspiration and imagination, as it has been all along. Around issues of human poverty and social justice the prophetic tradition emerged within the organized fabric of American religious life, from its pulpits and congregations, its church basements, and its activists. But if you want to talk about the reasons this enterprise is flourishing across so broad a spectrum of religious life these days, you needn't look further than a newspaper. I have an article in front of me from Colorado Springs, a major center for Evangelical Christian organizations. Entitled "Conservative Christians Embrace the Environment," it leads off, "The religious right brings all sorts of issues to mind: abortion, homosexuality, school prayer, family values. Now an unlikely new element is joining the mix, environmentalists. Sparked by the growing concern of scientists, average conservative Christian leaders and scholars are shaking up their religious colleagues and Republican politicians, urging them to take a more active role in saving the earth. They are Evangelical, Southern Baptist, Catholic and other right-wing groups. They are re-reading the Bible, taking a closer look at its verses and seeing a message they say has been overlooked.

One of the remarkable developments within the National Religious Partnership has been the breadth of engagement among conservative Catholic bishops, Baptists, Evangelical Christians, and Eastern Orthodox. The reason that's true is that each of these traditions—these faith groups or denominations—has been going back to fundamental teachings in scripture and finding powerful prophetic vision and normative thoughts and behaviors that apply to the present situation. This deep orientation overrides more narrow traditional political predispositions, and it overrides inertia. And it's coming from the heart of the tradition itself. One of the single most exciting experiences for me in this Partnership has been the frequency with which these ancient teachings are coming freshly to life in particular situations, with the full power of venerable prophecy. I attended a meeting of all Eastern Orthodox churches in Baltimore, and I saw them experience the full relevance and power of a form of theology in which they see Christ redeeming all creation, the entire cosmos. The significance of that at this particular moment, when suddenly all of creation and the whole cosmos means more to us than ever before, is extraordinary! In a moment like this you really experience how these teachings live for us, here and now.

BW: And this same experience is occurring simultaneously, though differently, in other faith communities with which you're working.

PG: Unquestionably. I've seen it happen among Jewish scholars exploring the Torah, the rabbinical tradition. I've seen it happen among Evangelicals who went to Colorado Springs and prayed for two days about how to engage this issue. Their prayer led them to the issue of biodiversity and endangered species, and two months later they were holding a press conference in Washington, DC and calling for preservation of the Endangered Species Act. It was on network news, in the *New York Times*, all over the wire services, and had Republican congressmen scratching their heads, wondering, "How did Evangelical Christians and the Endangered Species Act get in the same sentence?" I mean, look at this. A group of several hundred leading Evangelicals went to the mountain, prayed about this issue, and within a matter of months were having an impact on the U.S. Congress. They were on network television saying, "The earth is the Lord's, and this means we are called to be stewards of God's gorgeous garden." That journey took two months. It started in prayer, and it ended on the floor of the United States Congress.

BW: The same thing is happening simultaneously among Catholic land-based religious orders. They're drawing enormous meaning from re-examining scripture in light of the signs of the times and their particular "charism," or spiritual identity. But the result comes down to the same thing.

PG: Including those functioning in the midst of ancient traditions and large institutions. This issue is more powerful than even religious bureaucracy. This is really interesting. I'll tell you a couple of anecdotes. One senior staff person for the U.S. Catholic Bishops said to me at the beginning of this Partnership, "I've got good news and bad news for you about the environment and the Catholic church. The good news is that the environment is very important. The bad news is that when the bishops accuse us of trying to tackle every issue, the environment is the one thing I point to as one thing we don't do." This was in 1991. At the same time a Catholic bishop said to me, "How come I never see people on calendars for environmental organizations?" A year and a half later there was a pastoral letter from the Catholic bishops. For three successive years, starting in 1993, materials were sent out to every Catholic parish. Environmental justice is now one of the issues that the Catholic bishops have singled out and given priority status in the political responsibility statement to every parish which briefs people on how to look at elections and judge candidates. The video that they produced, which was brilliant, is one of the best-selling videos. That has happened at the center of organized Catholic life. All because of this issue's prophetic power, its inherent spirituality, the excitement of applying Catholic social teachings to a new issue, its resonance among parishes, and its ability to be so seamlessly integrated into traditional Catholic concerns. This isn't out on the periphery, the margins. This is now front and center.

BW: So this is coming from grassroots people in the community.

PG: Yes. We have documented 2000 congregations that are very active on environmental issues in one way or another, and there have got to be 5 or 10 that we don't know about for every one we've documented. So this is clearly beginning to come to life congregationally. But there are two other things that are just as, or more, important. It is just as important that these issues are being embraced by leadership, and, more importantly, that they are weaving their way through the existing agenda and priorities of religious life.

It's being integrated into religious life more pervasively every day. You know, there is a strategy of prophecy and a strategy of integration, and they must feed and nourish one another in order to take root. The strategy of prophecy calls us to really envision and embrace the full dimensions of this issue, its power and its promise for human imagination and the human spirit. The strategy of integration involves finding a way to weave "environmental concerns" into the existing rubric of religious life, so that the people working with Catholic relief services or Evangelical development projects overseas can talk about the environment in addition to everything else they've been talking about. For instance, when Catholics talk about the culture of violence and the culture of death, mindful of everything from abortion, to violence against women and children, to pornography and crime—they now also talk about violence against the natural world. So it's now part of the full religious vocabulary and agenda.

BW: Despite the tendency to think of ourselves as an increasingly secular society, anyone looking at America from the outside would say we certainly look like a religious culture, and most of our polls confirm that. Can we effectively engage American culture as a whole in environmental justice issues without the use of scriptural language and religious worldviews, given the reality that scriptural language is a second language for so many Americans?

PG: Most Americans understand how religious this nation still is. But there is a particular sector of society you're talking about—politicians and environmentalists in the secularized, liberal culture—that don't understand what scripture and its cultural perspective means in peoples' lives. But let's not forget that there are also people of the Book who often don't recognize the power of the Book. So I am very grateful to environmentalists for their prophetic voice in the past. It's just too bad that the prophetic imagination in the naturalist and agrarian traditions didn't find its way into earlier and deeper conversations with the religious community. And it is profoundly unfortunate that the religious community has taken so long to awaken to this. Without the National Religious Partnership for the Environment, it would have been a lot slower in coming. It has required a concerted and well-resourced effort.

BW: The fact that the Partnership is now possible attests to the growing community of people in this country who care about this connection.

PG: Yes. It was bound to happen. But it is still taking work to convince the secular environmental community that the religious voice needs to be part of it. They're still not sure how to relate to us.

BW: So what are the growing edges? As you talk things over together, do you find environmentalists backing off and saying, "Hey, this guy's talking about a much bigger agenda coming from the religious community than the shock troops for the Green Party that I'm prepared to embrace!"

PG: No. My overriding experience is that there is almost as much enthusiasm in the secular environmental community as there is in the religious community itself for the work of the Partnership at its deepest level. Enthusiasm not just for the political power we bring, but the perspective, the comprehensiveness that the religious community has to offer these issues. Pete Myers, one of the authors of *Our Stolen Future*, a book about the pervasive presence of endocrine-disrupting compounds in our environment, was speaking at the National Cathedral in Washington. We had lunch together and he was eager to learn what religious texts might say about health and risk. Ever since that lunch, he has been quoting ancient rabbinic commentaries. I also met recently with people who are working with the Endangered Species Act who wanted to know about the religious messages concerning biodiversity. There's a tremendous response to religious perspective and language around these questions. It gives these people permission to think more broadly than their immediate policy world usually permits.

BW: And are they surprised to see the religious attention and perspective given to environmental issues?

PG: They're surprised, grateful, intrigued, and nourished. Advocates of biodiversity make their case to the public based on utilitarian arguments about the pharmaceutical benefits of yet undiscovered species. That's a utilitarian argument, and it has its place. But when we say that we must protect endangered species because God made them and beheld them as good, millions of people resonate deeply with that message. You don't have to shrink your vision of life in the name of protecting life. You don't have to be utilitarian in order to prevent the weakening of the Endangered Species Act. You can say that life is grand and God made it so, and people will care. That's a very affirming experience for people, because people are being given permission to think as fully as they want to about life itself. The fullness of life, the mystery of life, the purpose of life. People who are working on behalf of biological life are profoundly grateful for the opportunity to do so with an expansive and sacred view of what life itself really is.

BW: So by drawing on these sacred texts we can raise the level of debate by investing it with intrinsic value that otherwise has to be described in more utilitarian terms.

PG: You know what it is? The religious contribution to secular environmentalism is that it often allows our impulses to be as full and expansive and comprehensive as we really want them to be. That's what religious experience is supposed to do! To magnify life! And that's what's happening. I know that sounds abstract. But we're talking about a bunch of scientists, foundation executives, advocates of biodiversity, politicians, policy leaders; people like Tim Wirth, Undersecretary of State. All of a sudden those people feel the magnification of their own perspective. Willingly, gratefully.

BW: What's ahead for the Partnership when we consider politics as a search for the good society, the good community, the good life?

PG: Most immediately for the Partnership, the real issue is whether this vision and work will become sufficiently rooted in the organizational structures of religious life, permanently present beyond the life of the Partnership itself. Have we pollinated a sufficient number of flowers to assure their perennial presence?

BW: How are you feeling about the prospects?

PG: I don't doubt that these concerns will become a permanent part of religious life. I do have real concerns about whether they will become sufficiently important and powerful enough to re-prioritize religious life. For me this is not just another issue. For me this is about how religious life understands itself and its purpose. So there's reason to be concerned about myopia, short-sightedness, bureaucracy, timidity. There's reason for caution.

BW: The tendency to resist change is in every individual and every institution. Yet if our religious leaders shrink from this task, it will cause a break of trust in people that will further erode our religious institutions, damaging their potential to serve as local centers for spiritual, environmental, and cultural renewal.

PG: I repeat myself. At this moment, I am poised between the conviction that engagement is powerful and irreversible, and simultaneously fragile. Fragile because it is insufficiently perceived as urgent. That is where we are living and working right now. It's not a bad place to be.

The Oneness of Biblical and Ecological Teaching

CALVIN DeWITT

Calvin DeWitt has been a professor at the University of Wisconsin's Institute for Environmental Studies since 1972, the same year he led a successful campaign addressing the rapid urbanization of rural land and natural ecosystems in the town of Dunn, Wisconsin, by implementing a land stewardship plan. A fellow of the Calvin Center for Christian Scholarship, DeWitt also directs the Au Sable Institute of Environmental Studies in Mancelona, Michigan, which conducts academic programs and field research with over 40 Evangelical colleges throughout the U.S. In this dual role, DeWitt has helped shape the scientific and biblical response to the environmental crisis within the Christian Evangelical community for the last twenty years, out of which has emerged an important grassroots movement in the churches called the Evangelical Environmental Network. EEN, with DeWitt and Ron Sider as its spokespersons, together with the National Religious Partnership for the Environment, sought to turn back Congressional assaults on the Endangered Species Act. As DeWitt charged, "Congress and special interests were trying to sink the Noah's Ark of our day." DeWitt thinks Congress is slowly waking up to the fact that the number of Christians involved in this movement is growing exponentially. "We have a movement, and it can't be stopped."

BW: On a personal note, at what point in your life did issues of the environment become inseparable from issues of faith? What was this process like for you, and when did things crystalize and come together?

CD: It really goes back to when I was three years old. I had my first turtle in a tank in the backyard, and that grew into a backyard zoo, which I developed and maintained throughout my youth and on through college.

BW: You were a budding herpetologist?

CD: That's right. In fact, when I was in my teens, I built a little shack in the back yard with my neighborhood friend, Al. The label above was "A & C Herpetological Society." But coupled with that in my upbringing, I was taught, and still believe, that the testimony of God in this world comes both in the creation and through the scriptures. I was taught that these two books, as they were called—the Book of the Creation, and the Book of the Bible or the Book of the Scriptures—have the same author, and so they cannot be in conflict by definition. So I wasn't taken off into all these debates that really distracted so many other people who might have emphasized one to the exclusion of the other. I was taught, and again I still believe this, that wherever there is apparent conflict, it is only apparent. And it's up to us as scholars, as students, as scientists, as theologians, to work to resolve those conflicts, but not to see those conflicts as things that put everything into question. Instead, each book provides us the opportunity to investigate things that we otherwise might not have investigated. So wherever you have these challenges, they're heuristic opportunities, but that you never had a worry about where these things would lead because there was one author of all. That was the reason everything was wholistic, everything was integrated. Nature and the whole of creation was perhaps difficult to comprehend, difficult to figure out, but everything was consistent. There was a thorough consistency to everything. You could study it, and as you explored things as a whole, you would come to some understanding of the mind of God. It was not until my very late teens or early twenties that I realized that this kind of approach was quite rare.

BW: What a gift your parents gave you! Did your local faith community and its leaders also teach this understanding about the authorship of both books?

CD: It was all of those. My family believed this and lived it out. We lived a very devotional life with a lot of reading of scripture and taking theology seriously, but also taking the world very seriously. I was taught that to be a scientist or an artist or a poet or a politician would be wonderful, because this was consistent with a worldview and life view which was whole. We were not supposed to separate ourselves from the world but work in it as transforming agents. Not arrogantly, but very humbly, acknowledging that we don't know everything that needs to be known. Yet also accepting that, if we put our minds and our bodies to it, we can really make a contribution toward human understanding of wholeness and integrity, which really is God's design for the world.

BW: When did you come into an understanding of our environmental problems?

CD: The deeper issues of humans and the environment really arose when I was doing my Ph.D. in the late 1950s and early 1960s. I worked on the desert iguana in the Coachella Valley in southern California, where Palm Desert is now located. It was not then a city; it was just a point in the desert. I was very

interested in understanding this lizard physiologically, behaviorally, and in relationship to its micro-climate. In the course of my studies, I began to realize
that some of the habitat of other desert creatures was being threatened by people
moving out from cities to live in the desert. But what overwhelmed me even
more was that this was not a livable environment for people, yet it was being
steadily transformed into something that had the illusion of supporting human
life, by importing electrical energy to run air conditioners, water to create lawns,
etc. This occurred in the context of my study of animals and plants that were
remarkably adapted to living and thriving without these amenities.

Curiously, when I went back to that site just a couple years ago, to what is
now a city called Palm Desert, I went to the gates of what was once called the
Desert Lodge, a motel now right in the middle of the city. I asked the proprietor
whether she had seen any lizards. Her response was, "Lizards?" For she hadn't
seen any lizards at all, having been the proprietor there for 14 years. The oldest
person I could find in that city who had been there the longest, had been there
only 20 years, and I had been there 30 years before, when it was desert. Virtually no one realizes where they actually live. Not in a city, but on the alluvial fan
of a deep canyon, which is a delta of a river that flows only once in a hundred or
more years during torrential floods. They live in the mouth of that canyon, on
that flat, sloping delta because it gives a good view of the desert. As the city
builds and builds, the reality of their setting is obscured by the busy-ness of the
urban world and by the false security that its restaurants and banks brings them.
But they've unknowingly set themselves up for immense tragedy. In fact, my
study site is now the approach to a drive-in bank. It's paved in asphalt. My
desert iguana is now represented by a single animal in the Palm Desert Zoo.

So I saw that process starting there and in the desert dunes back in the early
1960s, and when I took my first teaching position at the University of Michi-
gan-Dearborn, I saw it again. The campus there is located on Henry Ford's
estate. Henry had maintained the estate lands as a kind of nature preserve where
he and Thomas Edison and Henry Firestone and John Burrows would all watch
birds together. In fact some of his business partners complained that they couldn't
get him to talk business when he was there because he was so much into the
study of the natural world. But as a faculty member there, I was walking one
day through that forest along the Rouge River in Dearborn, and I saw that a line
of trees had just been cut in order to get a survey sight-line. They were going to
extend a divided highway right through it to the river valley. It was at that point,
in the mid-1960s, that I actually learned how to take action, in this case through
the Women's Garden Club of Dearborn. I'd advised the club earlier on scholar-
ships, and I decided to take them for a walk through this forest to see the natural
gardens there which were, and still are, abundant in springtime. After that wonderful tour was over, I informed them that this place was going to be destroyed
by their husbands and others. Well, that started a chain of events which taught
me politics, and ultimately the road project was abandoned. It's a large preserve
now, part of the university.

BW: What is it that Evangelicals find in their serious study of scriptural texts that is in deep accord with ecological principles, that perhaps even challenges the presently destructive tendencies in our economy?

CD: At the core is belief in a single Creator of all that we see and all that has been and all that will be, and believing that the Creator is just and right, not because everything is done by committee, but by one great mind. So that no matter what you see or find in the marsh behind my house, which may at first look like a big bunch of mush, you can come to nature with the assurance that it has great integrity. And as you come to it with that theocentric and wholistic view, what becomes shockingly apparent is that it does have integrity. The way it manages water, the way the plants interact with the chemistry of the soil, the way the animals and plants relate to each other. It is all one grand symphony of interaction. Everything works together. The way atoms work and the way ecosystems work are all in accord. What's beautiful about this as I study it as a scientist, is that it in fact turns out to be this way. So in my work, I have been continually reaffirmed in my faith. The faith allows you to proceed as if the world truly were whole. Then, as a scientist, you work to make these discoveries and learn from everyone else's discoveries and it comes back to say, Yes, it is whole. That affirms one's faith again.

BW: So one of the solid ecological foundations in scripture for you is this idea of wholeness, this integrity and inherent value in the created world. But you've enunciated other ecological principles that can be found in reading biblical texts through an ecological lens, such as our responsibility as earthkeepers.

CD: Yes. But it's important to recognize that Genesis is actually recorded in writing at a time when we were confused about whether there is one God or many gods, whether the world is run by a committee or by one mind. So already in Genesis 1, instead of referring to the sun and to the moon, it refers to these as the greater light and the lesser light. The reason being that to use the word sun or moon in Hebrew would be to use the name of gods. And Genesis 1:28, where human beings are told to "subdue" the earth, is really saying that every one of these things is a creature, and not a god, and you can be in charge of that. Not that you should destroy or pervert or distort these things, because the Hebrew rabbinical perspective says that if you exercise dominion by destroying what is subject to you, you make a fool of yourself. No king is proud of destroying his subjects to prove he is king. So you don't destroy that for which you are responsible.

But when we come to Genesis 2, Adam is clearly expected to till and keep the Garden. *Adam*, in Hebrew, is also the same name for the whole human race. And *Adaama* is also the word for earth. So we have the whole human race, which is of the earth, being told to till and keep the Garden. But when you look at the word "till," it's the Hebrew word *'abad*, which means "to serve." So the human race is asked to serve the Garden, God's Earth. The idea here is that since the Earth serves us with oxygen, food, etc., we also need to serve the Garden by taking care of it and protecting it. This calls for reciprocal service, con-service, conservancy, conservation—a service that runs in both directions.

Then we come to the next critical word in this request and expectation of Adam. We come to the word "keep." The human race is asked to serve God's Earth and keep it. The word "keep" is transliterated from the Hebrew word *shamr* which means "to preserve." Shamr is best known in the blessing of Aaron found in Numbers 6:24: "The Lord bless you and keep you." The word there means to "keep in all integrity." So when this blessing, "The Lord bless you and keep you," is invoked at the end of a Jewish or Christian service, it really asks and expects God to keep us physically and spiritually, to keep us psychologically well-balanced in thought and perspective, to keep us in good relationship with family members and friends and community, to keep us in right relationship to the Garden we serve, to the whole of creation, to the animals and plants under our care, and all the other creatures. This same kind of keeping is expected of the human race, which is the only kind of keeping that will really sustain life in its fullest integrity. It's not like keeping animals in a zoo or prisoners in a cell, although keeping animals in a zoo may be one kind of Noah's Ark rescue strategy that enables greater preservation and integrity in another generation. But it's not the final solution to keeping God's Earth.

BW: Do Evangelical Christians take these stories to heart?

CD: My definition of an Evangelical is that they take the Bible very seriously, including the biblical stories of those who undo the things of integrity that we're supposed to preserve. So when we humans mess up in our generation, degrading the very creation that sustains us, Evangelicals see that we have in the biblical tradition a means to clean up our act. It's called repentance. And our repentance should show in the amendment of our lives. Now amendment of life often requires deep forgiveness. To be forgiven, or to forgive those who have destroyed things you love, is absolutely critical to get on with the work of putting things back together. It's not a willy-nilly or passive forgiveness. Forgiveness not only puts things behind us, but seeks to get beyond it. Forgiveness says, please join me in putting things to rights.

BW: In keeping with that, can you tell me about your role in shaping the Evangelical response to the environmental crisis? I think many people are still surprised to learn that Evangelicals have been organizing around the environmental movement for a long time. Where did it all begin? And what have been the major developments along the way, such as your work with Au Sable, the Evangelical Environmental Network with its Declaration on Creation, and the Noah Covenant churches.

CD: The main thread for me is this post-modern movement the *Washington Post* calls "The Noah Movement." In my case, I trace that back to 1977 when my alma mater, Calvin College, started the Calvin Center for Christian Scholarship (CCCS). The topic chosen by the board was Christian Stewardship and Natural Resources, and I was one of five professors contacted who eventually joined the Center. I initially spent one year at their expense thinking about and studying a project we were calling Christian Stewardship *and* Natural Resources. Together with a physicist, an economist, a biologist, a philosopher, and a writer/theologian, we produced a book published in 1980 called *Earthkeeping* which reflected a critical change in the title of our project, Christian Stewardship *of* Natural Resources. That book was seminal. It was used as a textbook which covered all the issues using models of theology and history and philosophy and science.

BW: Did that spark an awakening in the Evangelical community?

CD: I think this was particularly key. But then I was called to consult at Au Sable, originally a youth camp whose resources had suddenly grown, whose board now wanted to create an institute for environmental studies. I suggested that they link up initially with twenty Christian colleges and universities across the United States, because there was emerging at that point in the Christian world in America a fairly strong movement, most of it related to the Moral Majority, in which there was little identification with care and stewardship of Creation. I felt it was really pretty critical to acknowledge God as Creator in whatever Christians did, and to provide an opportunity for students and faculty to refresh and renew themselves, to learn about Christian stewardship, and to teach every course, regardless of subject, from a biblical Christian stewardship perspective.

We have had many hundreds of students come through our doors, some of them now pastors who are working to transform their communities and their churches. But many of our students have gone on to earn advanced degrees and return here to teach. We now have 40 colleges participating, with two or three more joining us every year. Faculty come to teach at Au Sable, and as they teach there they learn a new way of teaching. Not that they violate anything from their disciplines, because we try to find the best people in their disciplines' preparation, but they now teach in stewardship perspective. For instance, every Thursday we have an integrative session where professors and students all come together to focus on a common environmental problem. We explore its biblical and scientific basis, and then we couple that with actual work at a field site that's experiencing this problem. This is where we teach each other as professors and students. Everyone's on a first-name basis so that no one has the illusion of authority or knowledge; we're all mutually exploring these issues. When you conduct yourselves in this interdisciplinary mode, you don't want to have titles intervene and have someone defer to some doctor or professor, because that person may have only a small part of the total picture, while students and other professors may illuminate another part, so we work as a team. That teaches us how to teach, and we always teach in the field. We do have lectures, but we make a very important point of teaching things as they really can be seen, felt, heard, and observed firsthand, to avoid a sterile academic relationship to Creation.

At the same time we bring a devotional sense to it. I remember joining one professor on his student field trip up the Jordan River in northern Michigan. They had been studying for some time and we were all standing in the river just letting this wonderful, beautiful place soak in; the log gardens with 18 different species of flowers growing on one log; the clear, cold, spring water flowing by our feet. Then everyone fell silent for a long time. Then the professor said, "Let us pray." I'd never seen that happen before in the field. But out of the experience of that moment he just released this tremendous psalm of praise to the Creator for this magnificent creation. It wasn't contrived, but spontaneous.

BW: With everyone experiencing the beauty and wonder of the place, it's also easy to imagine the silence as prayer.

CD: That's true. It was. There is a lot that happens as you do these things together. Our professors are responsible for nurturing the students' devotional life, recreational life, and academic life, and so we learn how to be an integrated people. As the students get together for meals each day, they share these experiences and they grow in community. We've also shifted our class times in order to meet from Tuesday through Saturday. We call Monday "preparation day." What has happened is that Sunday has become a genuine functional Sabbath, not just a legalistic Sabbath. People have learned how to contemplate by experiencing situations where meditation and reflection, where the reading of scripture, and where prayer come as a natural consequence of finally experiencing Sabbath. Many students have said this is the first time they knew what Sabbath was about. We don't have to make a big deal out of what Sabbath is, because of the experience of real Sabbath for itself. So we now have had 42 different faculty members from 40 Evangelical colleges teaching at Au Sable, 18 teaching in any one year. They have influenced their colleagues, and the Au Sable students who return to these colleges influence their teachers, and the result is that the stewardship programs and reflective experiential learning that we do at Au Sable is emerging all across the continent.

BW: So the Au Sable model is penetrating Christian colleges and educational institutions, as well as Evangelical churches. Did the Evangelical Environmental Network just arise organically because there was so much going on that now required some intentional shaping?

CD: Let me explain that. Almost every summer at Au Sable, we have held what's called the Au Sable Forum. We bring together people who are already professionals in their various fields—theologians, scientists, practitioners—and they share papers from which are produced books. In 1992, a forum was jointly sponsored by Au Sable and the World Evangelical Fellowship, which produced a book and a special issue of their journal. The participants in that forum were Evangelicals from five different continents. During the business meeting it was decided to form the International Evangelical Environmental Network (IEEN). I, on this side of the waters, and Chris Sugdan at the Oxford Center for Mission Studies, were voted as the Secretariat, and a fellow by the name of Reverend Mastrah from Bali in Indonesia was the President. Along the way came the Joint Appeal by Religion and Science for the Environment which later gave rise to the National Religious Partnership for the Environment. Simultaneously, the Evangelical Environmental Network (EEN) was developed as the domestic counterpart of the IEEN through Evangelicals for Social Action, under Ron Sider, to solidify the U.S. movement.

BW: What's been happening with the Evangelical Environmental Network in its efforts to galvanize congregations and in focusing on the Endangered Species Act? And was it difficult to get support within EEN to stave off Congressional threats to the Endangered Species Act?

CD: No. There was immediate support for this at a meeting of the Christian Environmental Council held at Bear Tramp Ranch in Colorado. Joseph Sheldon, a professor of biology and Au Sable instructor, made the proposal that we should get right into issues that had currency. So Susan Drake and I drafted a resolution and put it before the whole council for a vote, which then elicited a chain of events that brought the proposal before the EEN. The Center for Environmental Information, a major lobbying group that helps the National Wildlife Federation, the World Wildlife Fund, and other environmental causes negotiate issues with Congress, was planning to launch a one million dollar campaign to prevent the weakening of the Endangered Species Act. They heard of our efforts and decided they should launch this campaign together with the Evangelicals. They were the ones who organized the news conference, and they went way beyond what we had expected anyone would do, so we were all rather surprised and overwhelmed by it.

BW: But not displeased?

CD: Not displeased at all. They were really on target.

BW: And what was your message at the news conference?

CD: My primary message was that the Endangered Species Act is our Noah's Ark, and Congress and special interests are trying to sink it. The subsidiary message to that overriding one was that this is God's creation, and we all have a responsibility to take care of the creatures. We're curators of creation, much like a curator of an art gallery is of Rembrandt paintings. To honor Rembrandt without taking care of Rembrandt's paintings doesn't make sense, and similarly, honoring God as creator without taking care of creation doesn't make sense.

BW: What has been the response?

CD: The response is immense and widespread, and not only among those who take the Bible seriously, but everyone. As this began to unfold, I began to get responses from everywhere. At one point I checked Books in Print on my computer and found 18 current publications on Noah's Ark. I got two congratulatory calls from rabbis. And I got one call from a woman who said, "I'm a card-carrying atheist, but I think what you're doing is absolutely wonderful."

BW: What are you hearing from conservative Evangelicals?

CD: That's where the fan mail is just pouring in.

BW: That's surprising, given how unhelpful conservative Evangelical groups have been to environmental legislation.

CD: Many of them have been unhelpful, but they haven't confronted the issue that you have to confront as soon as you say the word, Noah. The more conservative one is, the more powerful this is. Because Noah is an example of obedience. Noah brings up the question, Do we answer to Bill or to Newt or to the Creator? For conservative Evangelicals, there's only one correct answer concerning ultimate authority. Now the Noah story is one that everyone learns as a child. So we know the story superficially, yet we usually never unpack it. Why? Because if you take scripture seriously it grips you, and if you take Noah seriously the message is there. Is the ark the solution? The answer to that is right there. No, the ark isn't the solution; it's the means to get to the solution. Are people more important than saving species? The answer is there. Apparently bad people are less important than saving species; that's an embarrassing discovery you make when you unpack this story. But if you're a good person and obedient, yeah, you're really worth something. Does God care for creation? There's a covenant made by God in Genesis 9 with all life, with all creatures, with all animals, with the earth, and it's repeated over and over.

BW: What's your sense? Are we on the edge of a series of new initiatives from the worldwide Christian family on environmental issues that will make a practical difference?

CD: I think we are, and I think it's an exponentially growing factor. We're now coming to the point where the curve really turns up sharply. There's also going to be a lot of resistance yet by those who refuse to think of the story, but the story will break through, and it's going to get broader and broader. All good stories, as we reflect on them, ultimately transform us.

BW: As this continues to happen, and as we come closer and closer to the central nervous system of what is wrong and misguided about our culture and economy, do you think the resistance will also grow substantially?

CD: Yes. We'll have strong resistance. But what's different here is the undeniable power of belief, which I think will supersede the resistance. What's also interesting is this. When you lead from the top and people don't follow, you don't have a movement. But when you stir things from the bottom and it rises to the top, you have a movement. I think we have that, and it can't be stopped.

Belonging to Community:
Earth Household and God Household

DAVID STEINDL-RAST

Brother David Steindl-Rast has been a Benedictine monk for forty years, twelve of those at New Comaldoli in Big Sur, California. A native of Austria, Brother David said, "I grew up at a time when we still had sacred springs and sacred trees and every day of the year was a feast of some kind, and we were just living in this religious atmosphere." From that blessed experience he went on to study philosophy and theology, and ultimately acquired a doctorate in child psychology from the University of Vienna. Over the years, his devotion to prayer and to dialogue between religion and science and between Buddhism and Christianity has made him a respected bridge builder, spiritual leader, and teacher around the world. Brother David has published many articles and is the author of The Listening Heart *(1982),* Gratefulness, the Heart of Prayer *(1984), the co-author of* Belonging to the Universe *(1992) with physicist Fritjof Capra, and most recently,* The Ground We Share *(1994), with Robert Aitken Roshi. What is religion? "Religion . . . always has to do with belonging, with community, and that is the decisive interface between ecology and religion. Ecology seems to be our contemporary form of expressing this belonging, this belonging to the whole universe, this being at home in the world, in the earth household, in the God household." And what do we have to offer each other? "I think people who are open to nature and ecology are long on religious experience and short on religious vocabulary. The ones in church may be long on religious vocabulary and short on religious experience." In this life, it is always good to laugh. Brother David was interviewed at Esalen Institute along the Big Sur coastline on a glorious day in which the grey whales could be seen migrating north in the waters of the Pacific.*

BW: You have spent many years in dialogue between Buddhist and Christian religious traditions and between religion and science. What is there about the edge of things that you find fruitful?

DSR: Well, I've been studying chaos theory lately, and its application to biology, and I am interested in the fact that life occurs at the edge, between chaos and order. If it's only order, it's not alive; it's dead. If it's only chaos, it's not alive; it's dead. So the interesting things are happening on the interface areas, and I've experienced it that way. I'm also interested in pulling things together, because when you connect two points or two realms, you do so only by going deeper or higher—whichever metaphor you want to use—to a deeper level on which the two are already one. Then whatever you find there you can connect with something else on that level by again going deeper and finding some entity that connects these two, because on the deepest level everything is connected to everything. So one of the aspects that I like about the edge and the bridge building and the connecting is that it forces you to go deeper and deeper.

BW: To constantly reexamine things. And there's fruit in that?

DSR: Yes. Questioning is very important to me. When I teach I always want people to ask questions. I learn that way. There are teachers who feel that questions are disrespectful. I feel I learn from questions.

BW: In thinking about the interface between ecology and religion, are there some parallels?

DSR: Well, this question is a bit ambiguous because of what we may mean by the word "religion." Religion is not a clear term. It means, on the one hand, our religiousness or our spirituality. On the other hand, it means sociological and historical religions which are separate entities. If you take it as religiousness, I find it difficult to even conceive of an edge between religiousness and ecology because our embeddedness in the world, our feeling at home in nature, is an integral part of our religiousness. Think of the "Kingdom of God," this all-inclusive term which Jesus speaks about that is so central to his teaching. Nowadays we wouldn't call it "Kingdom," because the king doesn't mean much to us. But a fairly good translation for the Kingdom of God in our contemporary language is "earth household," or "God household." Gary Snyder's term, earth household, could be widened to God household. That means not only humans, certainly not any one group of humans, but all humans—along with all animals, plants, and the whole household, even its furniture understood as the lifeless forms in the universe. In other words, this God household is the whole universe.

And from that perspective of religiousness, we cannot speak of an edge between ecology and religion. If you speak of religion as the various churches or religious groups, then I guess you could speak of an interface between ecology groups or people whose religiosity or spirituality finds expression through ecology or nature. There are many people for whom this is the main area of their being religious. And there are those whose religiosity finds expression in a church or synagogue or some religious group. It seems very important to me to help the ones who are in church understand that for the others, nature and their concern for nature is their church, and they should not be looked upon as some sort of heathens, as though we are the only ones who are religious. On the other hand, I would encourage people who are ecologically alert and so forth to realize that there is this similarity, that in both cases we are dealing with deep religious impulses, and to make every effort to help all those whose religiosity is expressed in church to see that their own concept of belonging and community must, nowadays, include the animals and the plants and the whole cosmos, because otherwise it is very impoverished. Religion in any sense, and in both senses that I have used the word, always has to do with belonging, with community, and that is the decisive interface between ecology and religion. Ecology seems to be our contemporary form of expressing this belonging, this belonging to the whole universe, this being at home in the world, in the earth household, in the God household.

BW: So when we speak of religion as religiousness, we cannot speak of an edge with ecology because it is—or rather we are—embedded in the world, in the earth community.

DSR: Of course under the aspect of religiousness, or of being religious, it is an aliveness not only to the world of animals and plants and the cosmos, but also to the horizon of the cosmos, and that is the divine horizon. So when we speak of religion, it is not just an inner-worldly affair, it is a transcendent affair. From a real openness to nature, one is also led to transcendence. I cannot very well imagine any human standing under the starry sky and not being religiously moved, not being open to something that transcends this universe. On the other hand, I know of people who are open to this religiosity but have no vocabulary for it, have no map for it. That is what the traditional religions provide: a map and a vocabulary to speak about this experience. I think people who are open to nature and ecology are long on religious experience and short on religious vocabulary. The ones in church may be long on religious vocabulary and short on religious experience.

BW: So do they have something to offer each other?

DSR: Absolutely. Just that. The cosmic Christ, for instance, is a very traditional concept in the Christian tradition and, whenever I speak about this to any groups that are unchurched but open to nature and ecology, they are fascinated. So there are valuable and beautiful concepts in the various traditions that could help people who are completely impoverished when it comes to religious language and images.

BW: Why is such language and imagery important for those who are having direct kinds of spiritual experience through nature?

DSR: Because our experience is enriched by being able to speak about it, and our lives gain meaning only when we tell our story. What the various religious traditions have done over the millennia is to tell the universe story. And one of the reasons why the Christian tradition has been in turmoil the last two or three centuries is that the cosmology that it carried with it was no longer applicable in the particular form in which it was expressed and told. As a kind of defensive posture, Christians closed themselves off to a new cosmology, and every religion without a cosmology is dead. It just doesn't work. And now, through the efforts of people like Matthew Fox, Tom Berry, Brian Swimme, and others, we have a new cosmology coming out of a Christian understanding of the universe that can also enrich other people. It enriches our experience if we can tell the story, for which you need to have the vocabulary and the framework, because the scientific cosmology is not enough for human beings. We need meaning, and science, by its own definition, doesn't give us meaning. It just provides us with facts.

BW: But does it have meaning and value in its ability to amplify the story? For instance, the Genesis story is but a few lines long. Unless we read these passages of scripture poetically, looking for meaning in the largest sense, we may not be able to reconcile what we read there with what we know of the universe today. So perhaps science amplifies our reading of scriptures, especially when we read them poetically, and in that way it gives meaning.

DSR: That is right. The biblical cosmology is an old cosmology, even though intelligent and alert people who were Christians have, over the millennia, been able to stretch and adapt it to their particular time and worldview. But as such, the biblical cosmology is a three-story universe with heaven above, the earth in the middle, and hell below, and the pillars of earth can be shaken. It's just a stone age or, at best, an iron age cosmology. And that's perfectly all right because we read myths from other traditions and we can look through them, seeing they are mythic expressions, and we can appreciate the poetry even though we would not express ourselves in that way. But when it comes to our own tradition, we often take it literally, or it has been hammered into us literally. This literalism is our problem. So we have to break out of that and look first at the scientific facts of our world and how we can, in the context of our religious beliefs, express this in a new way. So today, to speak of the divine force that drives everything, the creative force, is quite compatible with the biblical tradition. The Spirit of the Lord fills the whole universe, holds everything together and knows every language. It is the life-giving spirit. It's all there. Only when we have made the connection between our scientific picture of the universe and this traditional religious view, is the religious view viable today and the scientific view meaningful.

BW: What has your role been in this conversation, in this convergence of religion or religiousness and ecology, this movement that some people call the earth and spirit movement?

DSR: I just happen to be a monk who by now has been in this monking business for more than forty years, and I feel perfectly at home in it. And I've had the opportunity of exposure to many different things, many different experiences that most monks normally don't have in their lifetimes. Yet I didn't look for it; I didn't even want it. It was sort of my fate, for better or worse.

BW: So it found you.

DSR: It found me. I just respond to the given situation. And I'm always amazed why this should be so relevant to people, but apparently what is happening is that people who are rooted in the tradition in which I feel firmly rooted, or in any spiritual tradition, often stay within their own walls and speak only to one another but not to those outside, and so an exchange never takes place. I happen to be one that was in some way thrown into that opportunity to dialogue. That is all. By nature I am just not defensive, because I feel so completely secure. I have nothing to fear. I want the truth, so I don't mind if I have to change. I've changed my opinions many times. That will not shake me to my roots. I grew up in Austria at a time when we still had sacred springs and sacred trees and every day of the year was a feast of some kind, and we were just living in this religious atmosphere. This is so life-giving. It is not in your head. It's not just something you learn in religion class. It is your life. And I'm not afraid of losing that. But precisely because I have a firm stand I can enjoy going way out. When you have a firm stand you can enjoy swaying, but if you cannot stand firmly, you start swaying and fall over. So I enjoy stretching and discussing these things with people, enjoy changing and also learning. I also like language, a good expression, and a good story that really comes across to people. For that reason I try not to use any religious jargon words that just alienate other people. I try to say it in my own words that other people can understand. That's how you dialogue.

BW: I am reminded of something Wallace Stevens once said, "We don't live in a place but a description of it."

DSR: Yes, that's very good. It's the same thing about stories. We don't live events; we live a story.

BW: And we live out of those stories, and it makes a difference.

DSR: You can revise your story. That's another thing. Over the course of your life, you can revise your story. That does not change the events, but it may make them clearer, more meaningful. That is also true of a religious tradition. You have to retell and revise your story. And you are not changing it or falsifying it. You're making it clearer.

BW: Is there, in your estimation, some healthy revision occurring in the religious story or stories that is being influenced by the environmental movement with all its concerns?

DSR: Absolutely! You see, up to now, I was mostly speaking about these new insights from the scientific field, cosmology and so forth. But when I answer your present question about the influence of ecology, we are really concerned with something else. We are concerned not so much with facts, for we are now talking about an attitude, our attitude toward nature, this feeling at one with nature. We've heard it so many times that we have to take it seriously, that we are a very young species. We are just coming down off the trees and out of the caves to this day. It cost us a great deal to rise to our challenge, the challenge that our particular place in nature gives us, of freedom and responsibility. We have freedom and responsibility in a way that is unprecedented, given our recent journey from the cave and our reflective thinking. It cost us much to rise to this challenge. We did it by distinguishing ourselves from the rest of nature, which was necessary. We have to distinguish ourselves because otherwise we cannot rise to our stature. We are doing what people do when they are in puberty, finding out who we really are as human beings. That means we have to distinguish ourselves from nature just like a young person has to distinguish him or herself from all others. But you can push this too far, as we have done. We have pushed it so far that we not only distinguished, but also separated, ourselves from nature. And now we are waking up and saying, "Well, we have achieved it and we have gone a little overboard." Now comes the next movement where we have to recover a new innocence, a new naiveté. First we were simply part of nature. Then we distinguished ourselves and separated ourselves. Now we have to retain the distinctiveness and recover the oneness, and that's our great task right now. What is characteristic about people who are in the ecology movement is that they have learned this, at least they seem further ahead in this particular attitude and change. The rest of us still have to learn it. This is a very important task.

BW: That sounds like an important perspective to impart to the religious community as it revises its story. But what about the environmental community. Is there also something the environmental community needs to hear or stands to gain from religious communities and traditions?

DSR: Well, if you stay with this rough sketch . . .

BW: . . . of maintaining the distinctiveness while recovering the oneness?

DSR: Yes, in terms of recovering the oneness, we could point out that there is of course a danger—and we have seen it in some people—that through their rediscovery that we are really a part of nature, they might tend to throw out the distinctiveness. For instance, I believe that deep ecology is correct, that we are not the goal of nature, nor is everything subject to us. We are members of nature and we have to respect other creatures. To believe otherwise, that they were all created for us, is a very myopic perspective. But when you discover how wrong that perspective is, you have to resist the tendency to throw it all out.

Yet I have also heard frightening statements saying essentially that we have nothing over any other creatures, and that would be wrong because that would mean that we are not rising to our responsibility. This cosmos has given us a particular responsibility and we have abused it. But the biblical image in the second chapter of Genesis, where we humans are put into this world as in a garden to keep and tend it, that is still valid. We have abused and exploited it, but our task is to keep and tend it. The danger is that we neglect this, or forget it, or overlook it in our effort to blend with everything. And the religious traditions are the ones that uphold this distinctiveness, although they tend to push it too far, as I've said.

The process by which we humans rose to our stature was largely connected to religion. It was not primarily a philosophical or a psychological effort. Philosophy and psychology are so young in this process. For a hundred thousand years we have religiously raised ourselves to where we now are humans. Philosophy and psychology are just icing on the cake. It has been a religious effort, and that is why the religious traditions still emphasize human distinctiveness. That is true even of Taoism, and of the religious traditions that we are familiar with today in this culture, and of Native American nature religion where the distinctiveness is quite clear. This distinctiveness is quite clearly there, particularly in the Taoist tradition because it is more philosophical and more explicit that we are different, we are distinct, we have our freedom and responsibility. But at the same time, we are part of it all, not above and against it.

BW: This puts me in mind of a trip I made to Asia in 1991, and how struck I was by the extent of environmental destruction in some of those countries that are principally Buddhist in their religious and cultural orientation. And then I think about these same destructive patterns in ostensibly Christian cultures. This raises not only the question about whether all of our religions have something fundamental to teach us about our relationship to the earth and to nature, but also why they fail to impart that more effectively. Has the message become subverted? What is the problem?

DSR: It suggests we are not religious enough. We are not spiritual enough. And the deeper and more gripping spirituality and religiousness now emerging in the ecological movement is, for many people today, the real place for religion, not the churches. But on the other hand, precisely an experience like that— of Buddhists who abuse the environment despite Buddhism's respectful sense of our embeddedness in nature—helps us see that they are not exploiting the environment because they are Buddhists, but that the better Buddhists they are, the less they will harm it. Then we can turn around and say, "Ah, now we understand. The Christians who have been harming nature did so not because they were Christians, but in spite of it." But if this is easier to see in Buddhists, it is equally true in Christians. It reminds me of how we sometimes hear people say that Buddhists are such peace-loving people and are not fighting one another like those Christians. Someone once voiced this to the Dalai Lama when I was present and he replied, "Well, wait a moment, it is not that easy. Look at history with an unbiased eye and you will see that all religions—Christianity, Buddhism, Judaism, and the others—teach peace. But members of all religions wage wars, not because they are Buddhists, Christians, or whatever, but because they are fallible humans."

BW: So we need to pay a little more attention to our own texts.

DSR: Yes, and more attention to our being humans. This is again what the ecological movement does. It makes us pay attention to our human experience, our human stance, our human embeddedness in nature, rather than some doctrines. There are people who put the religious or confessional aspects above their humanness. They act as if you could become a better Christian at the expense of being a human being. But Buddhism, Christianity, Islam, and Judaism are all given to us as the means to become better humans. The goal is the same for all of us, never in the end to become great Christians, great Buddhists, or great Moslems, but great human beings. We have gotten it wrong, because it is easy for us to see that there are Moslems who think they can become better Moslems at the expense of being good humans. We don't see that this can happen in our own Christian religion as well.

BW: You once said, in effect, that all religious traditions respond to a sense that things are out of order, that human life is grinding against the axle, that something needs to be put right, that we are in some sense lost and looking for our way home. In the Judeo-Christian tradition, for instance, there are the prophets who can frequently be heard to call the people to return and live. What might that mean for us now?

DSR: In every age there is this call to return, this notion of turning, of conversion. The key word I would use for us today is "common sense." The world we have created is not based on common sense. I give to this term deeper meaning than we usually give to it, but nothing that is not implied in the words—common sense. We have created a world that is not run by common sense, but by very destructive conventions and agreements. Conventional society doesn't run by common sense. It is run by a dog-eat-dog mentality, a legalism. Things like prestige and power are the great things to achieve. Whoever has power can lord it over others. What we need to come back to, or return to, is common sense, which is the force, if you want to use that term, or the Holy Spirit, or the life stream or bliss within us that carries us. It is what we all have in common, and the only thing that makes sense. It is the Tao, the Logos. Those were words that Lao Tzu or Heraclitus would respectively use. Tao meant "a road," so we took this word "road" and turned it into something that now the whole world uses for this specific thing. And to Heraclitus, logos meant "thought" or "word," and he used it in a very specific sense, as that principle of understanding, or understandability. Heraclitus asked himself, like Einstein, "How come I've been so amazed that everything makes sense mathematically? How come we can understand the universe at all?" It is because we have the Logos within us, and that which is within us is the same thing that makes the outside world. It's the same thing that moves our thoughts and makes the trees grow and makes us understand that clearly.

BW: You make it sound very ordinary and accessible.

DSR: It used to be very accessible. So we have to do something similar today and use a similar word, like "common sense," and just give it a little more depth and sweet reasonableness, and say it's what we all have in common, that which makes sense, the only thing that makes sense. The word "sense" is a good word because it is connected with the senses. It is not disembodied up there in your mind. But it has a much deeper meaning, and I think we could use it as that Logos, that Tao, that force that makes all of nature move and also moves us in the right way if we attune ourselves to it. That is the one great thing that makes a difference between the world we have made, this demented society in which you have to be crazy in order to get along, and the common sense reality. The next time you go to a meeting, any meeting, try to use common sense, and you will see how you clash. In almost all circumstances, we have been trained not to use common sense because we get in trouble.

BW: This does make sense to me, and yet I sit here thinking about the structures of power, and whether common sense is compelling enough in the face of such power.

DSR: Well, it is not compelling enough to promise success on that level. The story of common sense is, of course, the story of Jesus. In the end, the authoritarian power structures, both the reigning religious and civil powers, put him away. And it is the story of Socrates, who followed common sense. The deaths of Socrates and Jesus have often been compared. If you follow common sense, you may well run into danger. But ultimately you must ask yourself, "Would you rather be on the side of those who killed Jesus and condemned Socrates, or would you rather be in their shoes." And that says, "Do I want to side with Socrates and Jesus or with those who condemned and killed them." And if you side with those who live by common sense, as did Socrates and Jesus, you will be alive in a way that cannot be destroyed, not even by death. That is what religion is about and what we all long for in our hearts.

BW: What strikes me is that death cannot keep common sense down.

DSR: You can oppress and repress and silence common sense, but you cannot refute it. And since what we call common sense here is not just intellectual argument but a whole way of living, common sense stands here also for that life which cannot be wiped out even though you are being killed. That's what stands behind this notion of the resurrection. It's not that he was killed and zap, here he is again, but, as is said so poetically in the Apocalypse, the book of Revelation,

"The lamb that was slain, and behold, he lives." It doesn't mean that he is no longer slain. He is slain, yet he lives. In all the ancient hero stories, you have the hero who is dead, really dead, killed and dismembered, and behold, he lives. And he not only lives but is the lifeblood of the community.

BW: Well, if common sense has so much to do with how we live out our daily lives, our spirituality, our religiousness, our relationship to one another and the earth, then perhaps the environmental movement is bringing that resurrection message—that common sense message—back to the religious tradition which is searching for more effective ways to practice its faith in the world. Could this be so?

DSR: That's right. This is overgeneralized and so not entirely applicable, but one can say that religions have become very ritualistic, dogmatic, doctrinaire. When this happens, the real spirituality, the real religiousness always springs up in another form, in another way. Like common sense, it cannot be kept down. In this transition from the age of Pisces into the age of Aquarius, there are some rather earth-shaking changes taking place, and among them is this common sense attitude, this aliveness, this common sense aliveness that is springing up outside the customary religious channels and boxes. And the more you really move this aliveness into religious tradition, regardless of which one, the more you will recognize it. And the more you are not moving and growing but just clinging to the forms, the more you will be threatened by this aliveness, because what you are serving are the forms, the structures, and not the Spirit.

BW: Yes, indeed. This puts me in mind of spiritual fruits, spiritual practices, and spiritual vigor, and whether they require spiritual roots.

DSR: But how do you get spiritual roots? I think this is one of those questions, "What comes first, the chicken or the egg, the practices or the roots?" You have little roots when you are born, otherwise you wouldn't be alive, and you strengthen them by practice with the roots becoming stronger as you strengthen your practice. But it is the practice that roots you in your spiritual life. If you practice, you will be at home there.

BW: Is it important for most of us, to some extent, to develop those spiritual roots within a tradition, to go deeper within it before we spread out? Or can we pick and choose all the time?

DSR: Well, it is a great help to be able to live deeply out of one particular tradition. It is also a gift for a child to be so brought up, but, of course, with great openness for the others. Otherwise, we tend to be attracted to a tradition and follow it for awhile until we come to some aspect of it which does not appeal to us, when we may turn to another and start over again. This simply does not work. It scatters your energies. But if you persist in one and take it very seriously, study it and live it, you will ultimately reach that center where all religious traditions are connected with one another. There is no competition there. Of course, there is competition between the institutions because an institution is something that is in competition with others. This does not apply to religious institutions only. Personally, I have great respect for the people who carry the institution. Life always creates structures, and these people are needed to support and refine the structures. However, while life creates structures, structures don't create life. So we have to keep the spirit going, the life strong, and then we will create the structures we need at a given time.

BW: So the structures are important but they always need to be open to the life-giving sources that renew and revive them. What, then, is your counsel to the religious structures today, Christian or otherwise, in terms of what the environmental movement can bring to them in the way of new life?

DSR: Well, it's easy for me to sit here and give advice, but my counsel to any sort of religious structure would be, "Don't focus so much on the institution. The institutional structure serves life; it is not life that serves the structure. So look at the life." If that life happens to occur somewhere else, not inside the structure but outside the structure, then be open to it. And if that life is so strong and so new that it bursts the existing structure, allow that to happen. The structure will renew itself. Life does that all the time. Every Spring, all the protective structures that are around the little leaves burst and fall off. If we pay attention, we will see these little brown things lying under the tree, and the little leaves overhead. And in the middle of the new leaves, the structure which will protect next year's growth is already forming. So let it happen.

BW: You mean, trust the resurrection potential?

DSR: Yes. And don't take yourself so seriously. Take seriously that for which you are created as a structure, and that is the life. That is very difficult advice to take because institutions have a built-in tendency to perpetuate themselves. We know that.

BW: Even in the interest of perpetuating themselves, and recognizing that some of the mainline churches are declining in membership, you would think they would want to be open to this new life. Well, what counsel would you have to offer the environmental movement, for the people who may be frustrated by the resistance to this new life which they perceive within the structures of religion, and who may therefore feel like rebelling or turning away from those structures?

DSR: From a strictly political point of view, I would say, "Realize that these structures are potentially dangerous enemies if you alienate them, and potentially helpful allies if you get them on your side." This should not be difficult today because ecological consciousness has become a big issue in the public mind and in the media, and is now penetrating organizations previously indifferent to these concerns. On a somewhat deeper level I would say, "Realize that in the different religious groups and traditions, there are many genuinely religious people." We may be disappointed that there are not more, but there are still many in there and they are potentially very strong allies. They are the people who are best prepared for an awakening to environmental issues. You have a whole reservoir of people who are potentially ready, but may be somewhat shielded by their institutions.

BW: You're saying they need each other.

DSR: Yes, they absolutely need each other. We all need each other. Nobody can be left out. This is an absolute emergency situation, and we cannot afford to leave anybody out. We are in this little boat that is going over the waterfall and we need to do anything we can. It is very serious.

Let me say this, because people are always asking me, "What can I do?" Every one of us can start where we are. Each of us has to realize that this is my world, not somebody else's. I live here. I'm at home here. And if I'm at home, I do what I would for my home. When I go on my morning walk, I take along a bag and pick up the garbage, just as I would in my living room, for this world is my living room. I'm at home here. You see, it is not "they," but "us," all of us. And every day it gets a little better. The first day you might bring home five pounds, the next day two pounds, and after awhile you'll notice a difference. Robert Miller did that in New York City. He walked a mile to his office in the United Nations building and every day picked up the garbage along the way. He said that after a while, the old garbage was gone and there wasn't that much new garbage. Also, when it's cleaner, people are a little more reluctant to discard things so irresponsibly. If everybody did that, can you imagine what it would look like? Just this one little gesture.

BW: This puts me in mind of environmentalist friends of mine who have been working in this movement a long time, some of them committing much of their lives to the cause these last twenty years. They're now at mid-life and discouraged with how little progress they see, and some of them are succumbing to cynicism and despair. Is this one of the antidotes, to simply continue doing the right thing that is within your power to do, even though you don't necessarily expect the outcome you're hoping for?

DSR: I think so. Any activity is good. It's like talking to somebody who is inclined to get depressed, and this is a form of depression. When you're depressed, you can't think anymore, you can't talk anymore, you can't do anything anymore. What shall you do? Well, brush your hair. It helps. You do something for yourself. Well, I belong to this world. The world is the border of your body, so do something. Brush it. Clean it up.

BW: What do you do on those days?

DSR: Take a walk. I should say I give myself to a walk. Movement is very helpful. It is also very helpful to remember that we have come some way. As Robert Miller says, "When you are pushing a car uphill, it may be very, very hard, but don't always look ahead at how much further you have to push. Put a rock under the wheel and look back at how far you have come." So remember that we have come some ways. There are incomparably more people nowadays who are aware. Don't look ahead and say, "Yes, but it's too late." It may be too late or not too late. That doesn't make any difference. I still want to go in this direction even if it is too late because, in the last moment, at least I will know that I have put my weight where I wanted to put it and am not totally part of the problem.

BW: Keeping a sense of perspective is important, isn't it?

DSR: Yes. And to remember the other people who have done so much. We don't want to let them down. A person who was a model for common sense, for instance, was Diane Fossey who studied and lived with the gorillas and was shot for trying to save their habitat. I remind myself when I just want to give up, "Look, you don't want to let Diane Fossey down," or somebody of that sort. These people are really our saints. And it's not only that you want to honor them, but they are here. They are very powerful and they are right here. They haven't dissolved into thin air; they are here at our side.

BW: So our memory of their common sense, their spiritual power, is available to us. That makes me wonder. If there is a practical link between spiritual and ecological renewal, what would the local church or any local faith community look like if it began to make those connections?

DSR: What would it look like? I know, for instance, a Benedictine community in Minnesota where they are collecting and recycling cans, and that is really part of their spirituality as a religious community. How could we possibly not do it? And so I could imagine that to a really healthy and alive parish, this sort of activity would be part of it. Just as it is quite common that we gather money and food for redistribution to the poor, by integrating that into the service at the offertory, along with the bread and wine we bring. By extending our concern for the Earth and its creatures, we could also integrate recycling into the service of the church. That is profoundly religious. If you're approaching the Kingdom of God, the God household, then keep it clean, keep it going. It's so obvious. This is not just a practice we bring into liturgy! It *is* liturgy! Because liturgy literally means the service of the people, the work of the people. The original notion of liturgy was that somebody, a wealthy citizen, would build a water fountain as a legacy for the community. That was liturgy. It was doing something for the community. One of the most important aspects of religious services is to open our eyes to the world community, not just this little community, but the world community. Not only in space with all that live today but in time with all who went before and all who will come after. Think ahead, plan not only for our children but for seven generations ahead, as Native Americans say. Turn the service, the so-called religious service, into real service. If it's only in service to "God up there," you can kid yourself by making your God anything that you like, and then your idea of service will follow from that. But if you take seriously these words, "Whatever you have done to the least of my brothers, you have done to me," or their parallel in other traditions, then your service to God becomes a service to everyone, to every creature.

BW: So my hour-long experience of Sunday worship is inseparable from the daily liturgy that is life, and the real work of the people is to serve life.

DSR: Liturgy is a Christian word with Greek origins, one that probably has its parallels in other traditions. But in the Christian context it is truly the worship of God as father or mother, as head of this earth household, as parent figure that is head of the household. Since that is so, the best worship, the best service to the deity is to show love and respect and care for all the other members of the household whenever it is needed. You see, it is all one piece. I can't even take it apart. I wouldn't know how to express it any other way.

BW: But don't you think there is this tendency, for many, to walk into a worship service and experience it as though this was all there was to sacred time and space and actions, and so fail to see the wider sacredness of life because we fail to connect liturgy to life?

DSR: Yes. Well, there was a very good little film put out by Franciscan Communications where you see someone walking down a street in the city, and this person sees a homeless person. To avoid contact, he steps to the other side of the sidewalk where he sees someone of another race, so he slinks by—just a few little things that we do in daily life. Then this person walks up some steps and opens the door to a church. At that point the image freezes and a voice says, "If you didn't find God outside, you won't find God inside."

BW: What could help us notice this wider presence of the sacred in life?

DSR: Well, I think poetry helps. Poetry is another link between the religious tradition and the ecological movement. Religious language is poetic language, and people who really live in their religious tradition continue to feed that poetic element in their lives. There is also a poetic quality in nature, in environmental concerns, that links it to the religious. But you can see, in both cases, a danger that this can all become too abstract and ideological. This is always the danger, but it can be avoided when what remains between them— between religious language and the language of nature—is a deep poetic sense that really serves as a bridge. It is just something that the two areas have in common. And that is why a poet like Gerard Manley Hopkins, whose poetry is deeply religious, wrote "Binsey Poplars," a poem about a row of poplars that was cut down. It was one of the really early ecological or environmental poems, written around 1879. It's a powerful requiem for this sweet, special, rural place whose loss he bemoans.

BW: I think of other contemporary figures in these terms too, such as Wendell Berry, whose poetry for me and I think for many others is just imbued with religious significance and meaning, rich with what you earlier called "religiousness."

DSR: Yes! Absolutely! Hopkins' poetry is more explicitly religious, but clearly environmental in many cases. Wendell Berry's is more environmental, but clearly religious in many respects.

BW: So poetry and a poetic approach to one's reading is a way to see more deeply into the truth of things and, perhaps, offers us a more common language with which to converse with others?

DSR: Exactly. And that brings us back to our being human. You see, if we are just human, that is all we need to be. Don't ask about being an environmentalist or being a Christian or a Buddhist or whatever. Just be a human. And then all these other things help you be more human. According to the image in the Hebrew scriptures, you have Adam in the garden—he's a gardener and thus an environmentalist—and he gives names to all the animals, which makes him a poet. Adam is the human. As we become more human, we become gardeners and poets.

BW: In keeping with that, what kinds of virtues are appropriate for us now? There are people who bemoan the fact that we don't have the sort of strong moral voice that we once had, say, in Martin Luther King, Jr., which some believe is needed again today. Yet others say that we don't need heroic virtues so much as we need humble virtues and qualities that allow us to make small changes in our everyday lives.

DSR: The two are not opposed to one another. I very strongly believe that we need patience and humility, which means down-to-earthness. But I think the most important virtue would be obedience.

BW: Obedience?

DSR: Usually, when we say obedience, we mean the thing that dogs learn in obedience school. But literally, obedience means to listen thoroughly, to listen with the heart. And if we listen moment to moment, we will know whether this is the time to be patient or impatient. There are moments when it is right and good to speak up, to say "This is enough." We will know this from heartfelt listening, from this openness of the heart, from listening with the ears of our heart. That's what we need most, to listen—to one another, to the institutions, to nature, to what the whales and the waves have to say, to what the peregrine falcons have to say, to the rainforests. Just listen, and you will know when it is time to stand up and protest. It is easy to say that this is not the time for it. But listen to see whether it's the time for it. Maybe it is not yet time, but maybe it is.

BW: If we are listening carefully enough, we may find that this capacity to stand up and express resistance or moral outrage may be in all of us?

DSR: Well, it has been hammered out of many of us through fear. That is why courage is one of the real virtues that we need, because fear demoralizes us, while authoritarian power deliberately instills fear in us so that we won't speak up. So we need to listen for courage.

BW: What is your hope for our culture?

DSR: Survival. Creative survival.

BW: Through common sense?

DSR: Yes, through that endangered common sense.

PART 3

RESTORING AND RE-STORYING

Ecstatic Rootedness

JOHN ELDER

For nearly twenty-five years, John Elder has taught at Middlebury College in Middlebury, Vermont, where he now has a split appointment in both Environmental Studies and English. Middlebury has the oldest Environmental Studies major in the country, founded in 1965, and in the last decade it has become fully interdisciplinary. John has served as director of that program and has been instrumental in advancing experiential "place-based environmental education," incorporating his love for poetry, nature writing, and the literature of place. John is the author of a book of poetry, Imagining the Earth, *and co-author with Steven Rockefeller, his colleague in Religious Studies, of* Nature and Spirit. *He speaks here, among other things, about the inseparability of our deep dilemmas that we have brought upon ourselves and the "creative grieving that is going on in our world now as people try to refigure nature and the spirit." In this light he discusses the importance of literature that is "rooted in attentiveness to the more-than-human world . . . spiritually open, but also scientifically attentive, and personally grounded." Elder says these authors are analogous to the Victorian sages in the way readers seek them out for sane guidance and wisdom about living with "ecstatic rootedness."*

BW: How has your unusual role here at Middlebury evolved over the years?

JE: I came here straight from graduate school as a teacher of English literature. For ten years I taught the modern British novel course which was my focus in graduate school. I loved teaching that. At the same time I was growing more and more interested in environmental issues because I was living in a place where my family did so much hiking and camping. In the process, the American literature of nature, which began with Thoreau and continues through writers like Terry Tempest Williams today, began to speak to me personally, as did the English Romantics, and eventually the East Asian literature of nature—of Basho and the Haiku tradition—as well as the classical Chinese poets. So I began veering in this new direction. At the same time, Middlebury's Environmental Studies major was growing. But it was always the stepchild of the biology department. Then Steven Trabulack of biology took it over about a decade ago. He was deeply committed to making it fully interdisciplinary. He graciously invited me to become more involved in it. Several years later I was teaching one of their core courses, called "Visions of Nature," on the art of literature and its relationship to contemporary attitudes toward nature.

BW: What role has nature played in your own religious experience and spiritual formation?

JE: It's had a strong role in my spiritual formation. I spent my early childhood in the South, but from the third grade on lived in northern California. I went through high school in Marin County. My parents were devout Southern Baptists and I was raised in the Baptist church. So I had a very Bible-centered upbringing, hearing the Bible read at meals and at church services several times each week. That's actually been an important context for me to draw on in evaluating arguments by people like Lynn White who claimed the Genesis accounts are inherently anti-environmental. My experience in a fundamentalist biblical family was certainly not that way. I probably read the Bible as much as any other child of my generation, and I was always struck by the Genesis parables, stories of the kingdom, and the psalms. As a result, when I discovered the environmental movement in high school through the Sierra Club, John Muir, and outdoor expeditions to Yosemite and Muir Woods, it seemed to me quite compatible. I never felt a tension. And when I discovered Darwin, I just never felt a tension with the Genesis accounts. I always thought, What a great way for God to create the world. But the Bible gave us some latitude there. We weren't left with any blueprints, and Darwin was one good way to understand it. So I have never experienced in my personal life the conflicts that some people find between biblical Christianity and the environmental movement, or between the spectacle of evolution and the biblical accounts.

BW: Your experience has been so similar and yet your conditions so different from those of other environmentalists. A lot of them have jettisoned their religious traditions and are no longer exploring those intersections.

JE: That's true, though Bill McKibben is an exception. He didn't feel that he had a particularly intense religious experience through high school, but a good one just the same. Yet the Bible, and especially the book of Job, are now very important to his spirituality, so the biblical model is there. A lot of environmentalists have sublimated their religious experience into a non-traditional form. In a way, I have too, but I feel very affectionate toward my religious background. Sometimes we look at our tradition and evaluate it in a very ahistorical way, as though it were all this urban, post-World War II, religious sectarian experience. But my parents were country people from the South. They weren't shaped by today's T.V. evangelists and their model of fundamentalism. My mother grew up on a farm. They lived close to animals, wasted nothing, were intensely in tune with the weather, and were very thankful for their food. That fundamentalist Protestant biblical experience was a lot closer to Native American wavelengths than contemporary upper-middle-class Americans who are interested in Native American culture. It was a land-based spirituality. Non-consumerist, modest, and frugal. I'm not in that faith community anymore, but I have enormous respect for what it meant in the lives of my parents.

BW: And yet your own upbringing has shared much in common with many urban environmentalists.

JE: That's true. I was living in Mill Valley, California, in the '60s, at a time of tremendous ferment in the environmental movement. I still remember those first grand format books produced by the Sierra Club under David Brower's leadership. The photography of Ansel Adams and Elliot Porter thrilled me. I was just overwhelmed by them.

BW: Tell me why.

JE: They were the most beautiful books I had ever seen. Look at this photo on my wall. It's called, "Clearing Winter Storm in Yosemite Valley, 1944." The books were a sublime experience, in the same way that Yosemite is sublime. So I began going on pilgrimage up there. That's the right word for it, too. The experience of the "mountain sublime," as it goes through John Muir and Ansel Adams, is closely associated with a particular strain of Protestantism. It's an experience of something so vast that our humanity is both dwarfed by it, yet also embraced by a much bigger world. The danger is that it becomes an experience of wilderness versus civilization. Though I was unusual in coming from a fundamentalist biblical background, it's a background shared by influential environmentalists like John Muir, David Brower, Edward Abbey, and David Foreman.

BW: David Foreman, too?

JE: Yes, I talked to him about that one night at some length. Protestantism and romanticism are very closely associated. Romanticism is an outgrowth of Germany, England, and northern France. And clearly, there's a certain sense of the unmediated priesthood of all believers that's related to going to places like Yosemite Valley and climbing a mountain. So I think I was prepared for that, and I was ripe for that. People from many different backgrounds experience it. There's an interesting religious resonance there. It is my sense that the wilderness movement, and the Wilderness Act, grew out of that experience of spirituality, that sublime mountain vision. I love these great figures, and the wilderness movement has provided deep insights missing in the rest of our culture. At the same time, I think it is susceptible to genuine criticism as being a little monolithic, a little stark, a little abstract. This is hard to talk about, because when you're in the mountains nothing needs an apology. On the other hand, the wilderness movement has often had a hard time building bridges from that wilderness experience to the experience of our cities. I've simply tried to account for my personal experience, and being in the mountains was for me the most powerful spiritual experience of my youth, and I'm very grateful for it. It's not where I am now spiritually, or as a teacher, or as an environmentalist, just as I'm no longer a Southern Baptist, though I feel really grateful for the experience and very respectful of people for whom that's their main focus.

BW: It's not too difficult to think of Muir and Brower and Wendell Berry and others in our generation as standing in some way in the prophetic tradition.

JE: Absolutely. Aldo Leopold, too. In fact, John Muir compared himself many times to John the Baptist. Just as John the Baptist's function was to point at Jesus, in effect, John Muir's job was to point to the mountains and say, "There's the saving power. Don't just read my books. Go to the mountain, and then you will be saved." He said that over and over in many different ways.

BW: That's interesting. Just last week Bill McKibben and I and thousands of other Americans, using the same cycle of lectionary readings, heard the text from the prophet Micah. He talks about how God has a controversy with his people and says, "Plead your case before the mountains, the hills, the very foundations of the earth."

JE: That's wonderful. There is a land ethic embedded in the Bible, not in all of it, but embedded in it. I was just talking with some folks from Fremont College about this. One of them was saying basically what the "Wild Earth" folks say, that we have got to go back to the hunter-gatherer stage, pre-agriculture, to get a nature spirituality. I feel the force of what they're saying. Gary Snyder also speaks to that in ways. But tradition is not something that can be traded in like a car. Since we're already living in our tradition, what we can do is identify the parts of it that help us to live most vividly. We can only reconstruct it from within, since we can't shove it aside or stand outside of it. To find these biblical figures like Micah, who speak to our current situation, is wonderful, even though not all biblical figures will speak equally to us.

BW: You're saying the task of reconstructing our religious traditions is primarily up to those of us who are willing to live by these traditions. We are the ones best situated to reinterpret the meaning of its stories given new terms and conditions of life.

JE: Yes. That's one of many things that impresses me about Terry Tempest Williams. In many of her beliefs and actions she's not a conventional Mormon woman. But she deeply identifies with her Mormon community and is in transaction with it. She brings her feminism and interest in Native American culture

and ecology into dialogue with the strong emphasis on family that character-
izes Mormonism. That's a great challenge and a great service.

BW: So if the prophets of our day are pointing to the mountains and saying
that the natural ecosystem is our standard, that the God of nature is an indispensable teacher and inescapable judge, then how important are these religious
traditions in sustaining us?

JE: We're at a point of culture where so much diversity is available to us,
yet most people have been born into a life. Most people in the world have been
born into a particular religion, into a place to live, into a marriage, into work, in
ways that really never rise to the level of much conscious choice. But in America
these days we ask ourselves, "What religion will I be? Where will I live? What
work will I do? Will I draw on Asian culture, African culture, European culture?" So it's an unusual time in human history. Your question about drawing on
these traditions is interesting. In the sense of a wheel turning, there is a kind of
revolution underway in environmental thinking and ethics. I've heard David
Brower and Dave Foreman, both of whom I really like, speak a number of times
with fire and brimstone, like fierce prophets.

BW: Like Jeremiah!

JE: And like Jonathan Edwards—"Sinners in the Hands of an Angry God."
I'm an admirer of Edwards, and I think I know what he was up to. He wasn't a
sadistic, hell-bent puritan. He was a psychologist who knew that without experience there is no new idea. So he was interested in giving his congregation an
experience of their own sinful hell so that they would have a saving experience
of their own conversion. Brower and Foreman try to do the same thing. They try
to scare the hell out of their listeners so that we will change our ways. The
Jeremiah and Edwards lineage is traceable to that form of environmentalism,
and it's been very powerful and effective.

BW: Are we needing something more now?

JE: I think we are. My sense is that environmental thought has come to a
new stage. I feel it moving in my own life and in the culture. For instance, when
Bill McKibben goes to the book of Job, and reads those lines about the os-
triches and the lions and the antelopes, he's not only making an ethical point.
He's making a theological point, that providence extends beyond the human
circle, and the ways of the world are mysterious. What's more, he's saying that
we should be humbler parts of a more integral world. That has lots of ethical
implications. I view the high peaks of the Adirondacks in upstate New York and
the Green Mountains of Vermont as part of the same bioregion. I like having
Bill here because I think his message is very compatible with this place on
earth. Unlike the Sierra, which is the ultimate landscape for me, that I will
always love, this bioregion is a very different landscape. It has definitely formed

my spiritual experiences as an adult householder. It's a cut-over, recovering, ironic, inter-folded, non-sublime landscape. It feels like a really good place to be a grown-up. That's been my experience.

BW: As a grown-up.

JE: A grown-up, a householder. It's the black and white—high mountains versus corrupt city—that you got in a lot of wilderness literature from the '60s and '70s. "Civilization as cancer" was such a dominant strain in a lot of writing at that time. But in New England and the Adirondacks, you don't see a civilization that always encroaches on wilderness. That may have been the western story, but out here, as Bill's written, the woods have been coming back spectacularly. It's still precarious in lots of ways, but Vermont and the Adirondacks are so much wilder now than they were a hundred years ago. Really, a lot wilder. And that has just turned my thinking on its head.

BW: I'm still thinking about what Bill is saying that is different from the Jeremiahs of our day. In paying attention to this character of Job who has lost so much, we must face our losses and the grief that goes with it. Enormous loss, enormous grief. But with Job, Bill is suggesting that we can come down off our high horse of excessive material pleasures and insatiable material appetites to a better place. We can come through the loss to renewal. We can come through the tragedy of it all to redemption. That's a very powerful theme, a comforting whirlwind, as he puts it.

JE: Very powerful.

BW: When our way of living leads us into the darkness of a dead end, a light woos us out.

JE: I think that's wonderfully put. It helps me indicate the balance I feel. Because I appreciate these Jeremiahs, and I appreciate the sublime experience of nature. But Bill and Terry are helpful to me now, exactly because I feel we're called upon to do grief work. And that's the center of my spirituality right now, creative grieving. That's how I'm working with it in my own writing, and in my own teaching. This is undoubtedly stimulated in part by the fact that both my parents have died in the last two years. They were both very ill for several years, so that's brought it all very close to home. But I think the way you put it is good.

We're in the shadow. I'm not a scientific expert, but as I read the recent intergovernmental panel's report on climate control and as I look at the recent studies about the oceans and human population, and so forth, I feel that we have already set in motion certain harrowing forms of damage to the biosphere, and that we will not escape suffering the consequences. I don't think there will be a technological solution that will prevent the enormous loss of habitat and the enormous human suffering that are both coming our way. So the question becomes: how do we respond to that? We might blame our western tradition but that would be an evasion and finally fruitless, though tempting. We might also try to solve this problem with new technology, but as I said, that's not going to happen either. This won't submit to a techno-fix.

But what happens when we put this in the context of grief work, in the context of death and dying? Elisabeth Kübler-Ross has helped a lot of us to think about grief as productive work. Before you can get to grief you pass through a stage of denial. I think that the politics of growth in America is the politics of denial. We're denying that there's any limit to our ability to continue getting more and more prosperous and using more and more natural resources. That's denial. It's like being an overly assertive adolescent who won't accept any limits, who refuses to grow up. The other thing Kübler-Ross associates with the evasion of grief work is transaction, like the techno-fix. We say, "Oh, this isn't a real problem. I don't really have a person in my family who's dying of cancer. We'll find a way to fix it." The transaction is just another form of denial. And then there is anger. "Somebody's going to pay for this." I think that explains in part our castigation of western tradition, or the book of Genesis. It's very odd that an author in an ancient pastoral kingdom is to blame for our own abuses of our own technology. Very strange.

But once we've worked through all those stages, as I hope we're doing, then we're left with the fact that there's a grave problem, and it's you and me. We are ourselves identified with everything that besets us environmentally. Everything about our way of life is an inseparable and inescapable part of the problem. In a way, everything about our humanity has brought us to this point of technology and population. It's not an accident that we have these problems. It's not even a scandal. It's just the end result of a lot of things coming together which are a massive problem. So then the mature question is, how do we deal with it? And my sense about grief work is that it's always a creative challenge. We're called upon to affirm a world of loss that could overwhelm us. To do so we have to widen the circle. We have to move to a bigger context. We have to understand, for instance, that the opposition between civilization and nature is a false one. That our notions about the present are much too constricted.

This is where Gary Snyder helps. He says the whole Holocene period is our present, and some of the things we think are essential to being a human are just a little blip on the post-World War II screen. Our larger human perspective in the modern era is very different, but it can give us strength. We can snap back into a healthier balance. As a college teacher this may sound abstract, but this is my spiritual experience. This is what New England has offered me: To be in a recovering landscape, where there's no pristine wilderness, as you find in the western high mountains, where you're never far from the noises of civilization, but where it's much wilder than it used to be. Bill McKibben spoke to a local ministers group here recently. He said something that I thought was helpful, "Grace still lives in the world and it's always willing to meet us halfway." That was a wonderful thing to say, and it says something about New England. I would never say anything disrespectful of the wilderness tradition. I deeply love it, and am myself of the Jeremiah prophetic tradition. But it has its limits, its monolithic nature, in that it tended toward a patriarchal experience of the spirit. Men going up into the mountains by themselves and coming back to make their reports. But check out the family of someone like John Muir. Again, I don't mean to be disrespectful, I just notice that we're all limited in our ways of being in the world. New England has been, for me, a way to live with my family. Though I can never get to a state of pristine wilderness anywhere in Vermont, I can literally walk out my back door with my kids and enter mountains where there are bear tracks. Bears and moose surround our family, and that's valuable. They're coming back. You can suffer from a kind of environmental fatalism in the West that I think the East helps you to recover from. I'm sure this has something to do with my confused spirituality, a confusion in the sense of many things being poured together in New England. I've welcomed that.

BW: Confusion, in my own experience, is of course dreadful when you're in the midst of it. It's bewildering. But in retrospect, it always proves to have been a very fruitful time. It tends to make one re-evaluate where one goes for sources of wisdom. How to be open to new patterns of grace that can teach and instruct.

JE: That's right. Grace, for me, is one of the aspects of Christian belief that remains most valuable. My sense of grace is that you can't earn it, you can't even arrange to have it, but without it you can't live. And when you receive it you say thanks. That's where the word "grace" comes from. It's always a surprise. A necessary surprise. It goes along with the sense of an idea in the science of ecology that I find meaningful. The "edge effect" or the "ecotone," is that zone along the border of two more or less discrete ecosystems within which you find species from each ecosystem, as well as some species that live only along the edge. In the ecotone you also find a greater density of organisms within each species than exists in either ecosystem. But the edge is always moving. So it's a risky place to live, but very rich and fruitful. In lots of ways I think that becomes a metaphor for a moment like ours in the world.

BW: Where we're living between chaos and order?

JE: That's right, between different paradigms. I think there are lots of ways to understand edges. Creative grieving has an edge effect that we associate with darkness. But for me the question is: how can we affirm what overtakes us in ways we would not choose? How can we affirm that as our opportunity for growth—without denying the pain or loss or confusion. It is my sense that all the creative grieving that is going on in our world now, as people try to refigure nature and the spirit, is related to our deep dilemmas. They're inseparable.

BW: Considering creativity from another angle, through the current renaissance in nature writing, what can you say about the attention that's being given these days to nature, place, and spirit by poets, literary regionalists, and other writers? Is it just a reaction to the losses we see in nature, or is there more going on here?

JE: There are lots of terms and none of them altogether adequate. Nature writing is the one that tended to be applied to that Thoreauvian tradition of the personal essay. And then there's also the wonderful poetry happening now; some people use the word "eco-fiction" to describe some of the novels. Take nature writing as one area I've worked in as a teacher and also as a writer: that term sort of collapses under us. It is literature rooted in attentiveness to the more-than-human world. Sort of spiritually open, but also scientifically attentive, and personally grounded narrative essays. People like Terry Tempest Williams or Gretel Erhlich or Barry Lopez or Scott Sanders are all working in that mode. If you also look at poets like Mary Oliver, I think that they are in some ways in reaction. They're in reaction to a society of insufficient rootedness and excessive consumerism. They're also in reaction to literature that has itself become disconnected, to the sorts of short stories and poems often mastered in writers workshops and printed in *The New Yorker* which tend toward disconnected people.

There are an awful lot of people who have a hard time maintaining relationships with each other, who never even consider having a relationship with the physical world. These are indoor stories with few glances out the window. Scott Sanders has written very well about this. If you compare it with American fiction before about 1950, you see there's been a great erasure of the landscape. A solipsistic tendency, this folding back onto ourselves that's not very rewarding. So these "nature" writers are popular in part because they're suggesting it's still possible to have a spiritual adventure in the physical world. That life can still be a quest for meaning. That science and poetry can speak to each other. There's a tremendous affirmation here and many people respond to it. These writers are not only literary figures; they are leading the way in terms of education and spiritual practice. When you listen to Terry Tempest Williams, you realize she is both a religious figure and a literary figure. A lot of boundaries are blurred. The wholeness of personhood and culture becomes evident again.

BW: So their writing is by no means just about nature in the narrow sense, but about reconnections on lots of different levels.

JE: That's right.

BW: What do you think these writers offer that people are searching for, that can't readily be found in other settings? What social roles are they playing?

JE: They play a lot of different roles. I've sometimes thought of these figures, like Lopez and the rest of them, as analogous to what used to be called the "Victorian sages." A writer like George Eliot was obviously a very important author, but people also looked to her for wisdom. They wanted to know what she thought about how to be a person in their day. And I think that nature writers too, like Snyder, Lopez, Williams, Scott Sanders, and Wendell Berry provide some sane guidance and wisdom for a lot of the people who read them. And that can be tricky. For instance, sometimes people call this environmental non-fiction, though the problem with the word "non-fiction" is that these people are definitely not journalistic. They're as alert to metaphor and use as powerful a voice as any poet. In fact, they're closer to lyrical poets than any kind of writer, certainly more than most novelists. Furthermore they often fictionalize their persona, the better to wield it with power. So they're not simply transcribing their experience, or anybody else's experience. Nonetheless, because their voice tends to be a first person voice, and tends to relate to some of the things we think we know about their experience, we read them as though a person were telling us about her life or his life. And that's the kind of experience we take in without much distancing, because it's so valuable to us.

BW: And especially valuable in a time when, as you said, we live in an adolescent culture striving for moral and spiritual maturity. The valid and lively question is still, Where do we go in search of wisdom?

JE: That's right.

BW: And these figures, whether transitional or primary, are themselves living within various traditions.

JE: They are indeed. I think about a distinction Barry Lopez makes. He says that just as traditional indigenous cultures always have, we need stories to live by. But stories, he says, are not all equal. There are valid stories and invalid stories. A valid story is one that helps you live in balance in a sustainable way on the earth. I think these are writers who try to tell us valid stories. Living stories.

BW: Stories that tell us about loss and renewal.

JE: Yes. They may not be as coy as a lot of contemporary writers, but they're very sophisticated.

BW: Barry's comment is similar to one that Wendell has made about literary regionalists, that they are "essential to a decent civilization and its survival because they amplify and shape our capacity to belong to each other and our places in the world."

JE: I think that's right! I feel so personally grateful to all these figures we've mentioned, which might strike some teachers of literature as an unprofessional thing to say. But I really feel that Williams and Snyder and Lopez and Berry have helped me live my life as a father and husband and teacher, in place. They've helped me stay where I am and not run off to new fields, to new professional advancements, which is such normative behavior in American post-war culture. They've pointed out the possibilities of ecstatic rootedness. And that goes along too with creative grieving. If you're not connected with anybody or anything you don't really have to grieve.

BW: That's right. It's only through the investment of love toward others around us and places we care about that we ever reach that depth of grief we may now feel over the loss of parents, or siblings, or places that have been destroyed.

JE: And I think the experience of people everywhere over the last half-century has been one of growing up in a world in which the places you have loved are damaged. I don't mean to be morbid, and I don't feel downcast, but I do feel sorrowful, and I think this sorrow is a form of affirmation. Literature has a powerful testimonial impact. A lot of these writers are testimonial writers. Think about Williams' *Refuge* and Lopez's *Arctic Dreams*. In some way they're bearing witness; they're saying this was beautiful. But they're not just talking about loss, because the world continues and it's fresh, and there are new fields for human activity. This is a challenge for me as a teacher, which is my core vocation, to bring wonderful writers, like Basho or other contemporary writers to the attention of my students, to share with them the experience of our common community, and to acknowledge the grave reality of loss. But also to be creative and celebratory together in the face of that loss. That's what I mean by creative grieving.

BW: Some of the most joyful people I've ever known were those who went through terrible griefs. They came out the other side redeemed and full of life, remarkably transformed. That offers enormous personal hope for me.

JE: We need those figures. It's not automatic. I mean one can just be destroyed by grief. One can just give up and lie in the corner gnawing the bones, but I think it can be the beginning of a kindling.

BW: And in enough of us it might ignite the culture.

The Universe Story as Sacred Story

BRIAN SWIMME

Brian Swimme, a specialist in mathematical cosmology, has devoted more than a decade of his life to the work of synthesizing current knowledge in the sciences in order to present an integral story of the universe. He currently directs the Center for the Story of the Universe at the California Institute of Integral Studies in San Francisco. As part of its work, the Center distributes the popular twelve-part video series called "Canticle to the Cosmos," a lecture series Swimme developed to address the environmental challenge by telling the scientific story of the universe with a feeling for its sacred nature. Swimme is the author of The Universe is a Green Dragon, *co-author with Thomas Berry of* The Universe Story, *and more recently authored* The Hidden Heart of the Cosmos. *Anyone who meets Swimme is struck by his childlike sense of enthusiasm for life and his fascination with the universe in which we live and move and have our being. When he refers to the "universe story," he is not talking about the book he co-authored, but the universe itself, "this vast, amazing thing taking place around us and within us . . . and the 'new cosmology' is our present attempt to articulate through language, music, and art the vast thing that is taking place."*

BW: You're a physicist and cosmologist. What do you understand cosmology to be? What is its status and value to us today?

BS: I call myself a cosmologist because my main study is the cosmos as a whole. But cosmology would be considered a subset of physics, not something separate from it. In physics it would be the study of the origin and development of the universe. But the reason I like the word "cosmology" so much is that it also has a meaning in the humanistic traditions, as a subset of philosophy, where you're looking at the nature of the universe as a whole and the role of the human in the universe. It's one of the few words I know that actually has a clear meaning in both the sciences and in what we might call the wisdom traditions. So you can talk about Islamic cosmology, and that makes sense to a Muslim. I'm trying hard to avoid slipping into one separate and discrete discipline because I'm working toward a synthesis, and cosmology assists that process. A Muslim would know what a cosmologist is, and so would a chemist. A cosmologist is really trying to get at a sense of the whole.

BW: Which includes the human?

BS: That's right, because the sciences will just separate the human off and focus on the physical aspects of the universe. And the religious traditions will shy away from the universe because that's reserved for science. So cosmology is an attempt to deal with the whole and the nature of the human in that.

You ask about its role and value. Most of us are aware that there are major challenges and problems in our time, and everyone has a way of explaining that. As a cosmologist, it is my sense that our fundamental story about what is going on is flawed. Until we really get a story that makes sense, that we can really believe in and say, "Yes, this is what's going on," we will continue going off in the wrong direction. So the role of a cosmologist today is to tell the story of what's going on.

BW: If cosmology deals with our worldview in the largest sense, is it accurate to say that in your recent book, *The Hidden Heart of the Cosmos,* you're trying to enlarge and reconcile the religious and scientific worldviews on the one hand, while unabashedly challenging the worldview of our commercial culture on the other?

BS: Yes. And through the attempt to expand and reconcile the religious and scientific worldviews, to use that as a foundation for a critique of the consumerist worldview.

BW: I want to first discuss the limitations you see in each of the worldviews as they are normatively presented, and how you see the new cosmology responding to them and perhaps repairing what might be flawed in them. What about the religious dimension? You've spoken in this new book about what you call our great religious failing, that there is little serious contemplation about the universe, very little engagement of that as a numinous reality. At the same time, at least in the Judeo-Christian scriptures, if you read the Genesis story literally rather than metaphorically or poetically, it is irreconcilable with the truth of the scientific story.

BS: Let me just pick up on your adverb, "literally." It's sad that we can no longer believe in the literal story of Genesis, that God created the universe in seven days and so forth. To deepen our understanding we therefore approach it metaphorically, poetically.

BW: Does that imply that the literal and metaphorical are irreconcilable?

BS: There is profound truth in Genesis and in the Bible generally. So we want to know the story, to know what's going on, to get at the truth. But we can't read it scientifically anymore. If we try, we get stuck in this endless argument between science and religion which tends to collapse into one point of view, with a winner and loser. That whole way is hopeless. So we end up reading the Bible poetically or psychologically or spiritually, interpreting Genesis or some other book metaphorically to get at the truth in that way. The terrible consequence of doing so is that we then take the words of the Bible in a symbolic sense, and we lose the value of that literal interpretation. So when we talk about water in the Bible, we don't think of the rivers in our region, but instead of the grace of God flowing through our lives, as opposed to the actual, sacramental river itself. That, to me, is a terrible dualism, an intolerable separateness. We have to learn to think of the sacramental river and the grace running through our lives together.

BW: So words carry both symbolic and literal meanings that depend on each other. And if these meanings become detached, the full weight and power and usefulness of words are lost to us.

BS: Exactly. And the way educated, sophisticated leaders of our society have worked this out is that the religions have the spiritual or poetic or metaphoric truth, and the sciences have the literal facts. Separated like that we are so lost and weak. Einstein said this, too, that science without religion is lame, and religion without science is blind. You either have an enervated situation or a fanatical situation. That is why I am exploring new forms of understanding that are simultaneously nourished by the scientific and religious traditions. So we can understand that the sacramental river is not only the ecological realm of the scientist, but also the locus of all of the metaphoric and poetic truths that the Bible and other scriptures are referring to as well. That would be my criticism of religion generally, that religious people today tend to focus on the poetical and spiritual truths and interpret them in terms of the human, so that the rest of the universe is given over to science which is seen to be fact-ridden, secular, and morally neutral. Religion is great in terms of the human/divine relationship in general. But the way it disregards the universe, no matter what religious tradition we're talking about, is flawed given the needs and realities of our times. Over and over again, I end up debating people in various religious traditions as to the significance of the non-human world.

BW: So there is a pattern of religious neglect towards the non-human world.

BS: Yes, in all the great world religions.

BW: What does the new cosmology, the new universe story, offer as an antidote? Does it negate or amplify the scriptural story about human/Earth relationships and origins?

BS: When I say the "universe story," some people think I'm referring to a book I wrote with Thomas Berry. I'm not referring to that. When I refer to the universe story, I'm primarily referring to the universe itself. So if I say the story of the universe, that's a little better, but then people think I'm referring to the scientists' account of the universe, and I'm not. When I refer to the story of the universe, I'm actually talking about this vast, amazing thing taking place around us and within us. So when I say the "new cosmology," that is our present attempt to articulate, in human languages and music and art, the vast thing that is taking place. So there is a dual reference. The new story in a certain sense refers to both the vastness taking place, and also our attempt to articulate it.

BW: My question is, do you see the new universe story inherently negating or amplifying scripture?

BS: Our attempts in western culture to articulate the new cosmology are inseparably woven into the Genesis story. Science, for instance, has become a global phenomenon, but any attempt to articulate the new story also grows out of a vast cultural tradition. So I see the new cosmology as an amplification and a deepening of the religious lineage, but I also see it as an amplification and deepening of the scientific tradition. To explain that, let me get into the critique of science. The scientific accounts are for the most part based on a questionable assumption, that the human can be separated from the universe, allowing us to talk about and study the universe "out there." A few centuries ago, that was almost viable, that we were actually separate from the universe. But now, within science, we know we cannot even speak about a universe that is separate from the human, because our ways of knowing are tied up with the universe as well. We simply cannot talk about a universe that is separate from the human. One of the implications of this is that the scientific tradition has got to take into account the human and human consciousness. I would say that the new cosmology is a deepening of the scientific impulse to know. But more to the point, my criticism of science is that it has operated under the assumption that all we needed was more knowledge. We never needed to speak about the real role of the human. Now with ecology, concern for the Earth's welfare is coming out of scientific study.

BW: A concern that inherently addresses issues of human purpose.

BS: Exactly. That is a necessary maturation of the scientific tradition. The early scientific tradition foolishly eliminated deep reflection on the human. And the religious tradition, in a similar way, ignored the universe as a whole. So the new cosmology, in a sense, is an amplification and deepening of both these traditions.

BW: I know I'm treading in murky waters here, in terms of the historic origins of these patterns, but it seems that as modern scientific and philosophic rationalism was assuming a new authority over the physical world in which we live, the western religious tradition was abdicating its moral authority over that realm in favor of retaining ultimate authority over otherworldly realities.

BS: Like the human soul and so forth. I would agree. But that older form of science is now outdated and even irresponsible, and the same thing is true of any religious tradition that can ignore the realities of the non-human world. So now there's an opportunity for a much more appropriate response to our situation from the human community, coming in part from this synthesis. Not from an elimination of science or religion into this new thing, but from their mutual nourishing.

BW: I was interested to hear your description of this as a maturation process, a maturation process that is being nourished by reflection on new realities and human responsibility. Everyone is facing these new realities. Not only has science come up against the limits of its old epistemology, its old ways of approaching truth, but so are religious traditions being challenged in the same way.

BS: I think that's right. It's a new era for everyone.

BW: I wonder what this says about consumerism, which has risen to become the dominant faith in our nation, and is now vying for cultural dominance throughout much of the world. You have addressed this in your new book, in part through your concern as a father. You say that the average child is subjected to something like 10,000 ads each year, each one of which is a "cosmological sermon" in its own right, however devoid of ultimate meaning.

BS: When I was working on brochures for our university department, we would bring in advertisers, and some of them would be professionally trained psychologists. They would have brainstorming sessions with us, getting us to think about what's going on in ads. And I realized these were highly sophisticated individuals who knew exactly how to get through the first, second, and third layer of defenses to get to the heart of the human psyche, where we are not even aware of how we are being affected by this. I know this is so because we would be shown some ads, and they would question us about them afterwards. I realized I was being affected in ways I was not even aware. It's like a work of art. They know how to get to the deeper regions of the mind. It's one thing for an adult to watch some advertisements because we have a little sophistication— not much but some—and can defend ourselves against the message. But it's different with children. We're talking about 10,000 ads per year and their effect on pre-school kids.

BW: This really is a cosmology, a worldview, being presented. And it's entering children's minds in the presumably safe, protective, nurturing environment of our homes.

BS: And the message is coming from all these cultural heroes, sports and movie stars, doctors, etc. So if you're a child, what you get is the really important and believable people in the world telling you basically the same thing about what really matters in life. Somehow you've got to get money to buy stuff so your life can be improved and fulfilled. That's where a child learns to ignore the labor of others and the whole Earth community and focus solely on the object. Without even knowing it, you're suddenly grown up and out there in the world, where everything is decided according to who gets the money, the power, the possessions, the control. That basic cosmology of consumerism is what is driving the entire industrial civilization.

BW: Insatiable desire, a vice made virtue through an insidious form of manipulation that has our cultural blessing.

BS: That's right. Because if the desire isn't there already, it will be created. And if the appetite is there, it will be made insatiable. An executive of an ad firm summarized it perfectly for me. He said the whole point is to make people dissatisfied with who they are and what they've got. That's the purpose of an ad.

BW: And then to create an infatuation and craving in us for some new product that falsely promises to fulfill us.

BS: Think of that! It is the opposite of the core truth of our religious traditions. To ignite that greed and fan it. Forget about gratitude for existence! Teach ingratitude! And do this to children who have little capacity for distance and perspective! Just get right in there and warp them early!

BW: And by all means, keep the children indoors. So where does the new cosmology fit in?

BS: I think of cosmology as the nature of the universe and how the human fits into it. With the phantom cosmology of consumerism, the universe merely consists of pre-consumer items. That's all there is to Earth. And the purpose of the human is to manufacture and obtain and accumulate products. It's a real simple cosmology, but it drives all the action. Incredible, isn't it? But with a natural cosmology, we might awaken ourselves to the true ecstasies of life.

BW: You mean, discover a deeper kind of pleasure?

BS: A pleasure for the beauties that are already here, through a depth relationship with them. An awe in this amazing drama that is freely taking place all around us, in contrast to filling our lonely existence with more and more human artifacts. Every day, all across the land, people are working feverishly into the night to figure out how to get more consumer items into your home. They're working on manufacturing them, getting you interested in them, and transporting them to you. So much of America is fixed on that goal, and the economy depends on it. Our civilization today is in large part driven by that consumer cosmology.

BW: And if we allow ourselves to be reconnected with the sense of wonder in every dimension of life, then practicing sales resistance will be made easier as we discover these deeper forms of pleasures that are still freely available to us.

BS: The whole point of Dante's inferno is recognition. The problem with the people in hell is that they don't recognize where they are living. The whole journey in the first third of the *Divine Comedy* is to simply awaken to the form of misery in which we're encased. So the first step is to get an accurate picture of our true reality, how we are using so much of our intelligence and energy to make ourselves miserable. That's the first step. Then the resistance to sales pressure becomes so much easier. The perfect advertisement that captures the consumer cosmology is the car ad with the woman in the picture. It's all there. We're in a fallen state, in hell, because we don't have that car. If we could find a way to get the car, by going through the purgatorial experience of getting the money to buy the car, then we're given the promise of Beatrice, the promise of divine bliss. The ad takes the cosmology of Dante and perverts it, but it uses all of those archetypal powers. It's all done unconsciously, but the message is, "This is what's going to happen to you, all this ecstasy."

BW: But of course we make all those purchases, get a good case of post-buyer dissonance, and find we're right back in hell again. There's no real, enduring satisfaction.

BS: Right. And that's built in. So we search for satisfaction through the next product. Makes you wonder.

BW: It ought to make everyone wonder. Tom Berry, with whom you've done so much fruitful work, has said that it's all a question of story. That we're in trouble in part because we're between stories. It is my impression that you are submitting this new cosmology not only as a corrective or amplification to both scientific and religious worldviews, but in hopes of stretching our sense of the sacred. In a time when science is more and more shaping cultural consciousness in societies all around the world, I suppose it's impossible to think of ourselves living with a sacred Earth if we don't also live in a sacred universe. Is that right? Is that part of why this new story, this new cosmology, is so critically important?

BS: For me, if people have a sense of living on a sacred Earth, that's just very natural. The first thing is for people to see that the non-human world is sacred. The sacred community includes the non-human world. Some people make the shift to a sacred Earth and never get to the stars and galaxies, and that's fine with me. If you can get outside of the tight human world and see that we're just swallowed up by this immense experience, I don't have any problem with that. It's easy to get involved in the soil outside your door, with the earthworms, and then realize how the earthworms themselves came out of a six hundred million year evolutionary development, and know you're working with materials that came out of the stars. The Earth itself is a way of seeing the universe. I don't see the Earth here and the universe up there.

BW: It's all one continuous, multitudinous reality.

BS: Definitely. And that, to me, is part of the thrilling thing. For a little kid to just feel an earthworm, and to realize that wiggle comes from the sun. All that energy comes from the sun. Everything is somehow present, and it's right there in the soil.

BW: You're already talking about this, but can you highlight some of the main features of this new narrative that you find most compelling and astonishing and transformative?

BS: One would be, in a word, communion. The communion experience in the universe, by which I mean to echo John Muir, that everything is hitched to everything else. If you grab onto one thing and look at it carefully, you realize that everything is there. Think again of the worm. The mistake in consciousness is to somehow think of the worm in your hand as separate. What we're learning now, after a lot of hard scientific work the last few centuries, is that there is, to use this one example, at least six hundred million years of information and intelligence invested in the worm. Throughout this immense amount of time the worm has persisted and developed and adapted. The new cosmology helps us alter our understanding about these realities, so that a person can really feel the deep roots of another being. It is overwhelming just to feel those great chasms of time concentrated there in your hand, because the materials of the worm, and our entire Earth, came out of the explosion of a star eons ago.

BW: It is astonishing. I'm reminded that with recent photos taken from the Hubble Space Telescope we have been enabled to take our deepest look yet into a slice of the universe, and the number of galaxies we found there far exceeded our wildest dreams.

BS: All this is pouring into us just now, and it is almost too much to hold. But if you can hold onto it, what it ends up doing is deepening your sense of this communion experience. That even the energy from the beginning of time is present there with the worm. So I would say that the more a person enters into the new story, the more deeply one enters into an intimacy with the whole community. And it doesn't just go back in time—six hundred million years with the worm, and five billion years to the exploding star—but also forward to all the future beings that are going to be influenced by our decisions now. Let's stay with the worm. If you go back six hundred million years ago when the first worms were coming along, those worms developed, over the ages, the spinal cord and brain, so that our brains actually developed out of the worms' brains.

BW: Our ancestors, the worms.

BS: Our ancestors. If you were there back in time with those worms, you'd say they were not that impressive, yet all the human future depended upon their activity then. Well, the same thing is true for us. We're making these immense decisions about our community and the future of all these vast creatures. We can't imagine them, but somehow we must take them into account. So this sense of intercommunion would be one of the major discoveries of the new story.

Another central feature of the new cosmology would be the notion that the universe is a developing reality going through a series of irreversible changes. At one time the universe was all plasma, and then it developed into galaxies, and then there were solar systems and planets, then life, then advanced life, then human life. All of these are major irreversible moments in the ongoing development of the universe, as opposed to a universe that is always there and constant. This is actually something that no other culture knew, but now we actually have some of the details for how this whole vast reality developed. That is an amazing, enduring truth of the new cosmology.

BW: I was in part fascinated by the new story's sense of origin, of a cataclysmic birthplace, a sacred birthplace from which all energy and matter has flared forth with amazing fecundity, of what you describe as the "all-nourishing abyss." But I was also fascinated by this idea of "omnicentricity," which changes my notions about center and periphery as two things opposed to each other. Is that right?

BS: Absolutely right. Isn't that wonderful?

BW: So, though the birthplace of our universe occurred fifteen billion light years away, it's almost irrelevant, because at this very moment, everything is not only expanding from the center where we are, but from every other center. So that every place is special.

BS: That's right. Think of it in terms of cultural evolution. In the Middle Ages we had the Ptolemaic worldview in Europe, this idea that the Earth was the center of the universe. And it was so obvious because you had the sun coming up and going down, and the Earth was solid.

BW: An up/down reality.

BS: Yes. And that worldview was subsequently adopted all around the globe. And then Copernicus comes along and says, No, the Earth is going around the sun. So we went from a geocentric to a heliocentric cosmology.

BW: From an Earth-centered to a sun-centered orientation. And that threw us.

BS: That threw us. That was one of the major splits between science and religion right there. Because the Bible seemed to talk about a geocentric world and now science was talking about a sun-centered universe. And then the worldview advanced again, to the idea that the sun itself is also moving around the Milky Way galaxy. So you went from a geocentric to a heliocentric to a galactocentric universe—though people don't use that phrase—where the Milky Way galaxy was the center of the universe, and the sun was just two-thirds of the way out there. But then in this century they discovered that there were all these other galaxies. So the Milky Way seemed not to be the center. Then came this amazing discovery, made by Hubble, that the universe is expanding. And it's not a typical expansion. It's a strange kind of expansion. It's an expansion where every place in the universe is at the center of the expansion. So we went from an Earth-centered, to a sun-centered, to a galaxy-centered, and now to an omnicentric or a poly-centered universe. We have deepened our understanding of the universe again. Now when we look out into the universe, we see that all the other galaxies appear to be moving away from us. But if you were situated on another galaxy far away and you looked out, it would all be moving away from you there. The image scientists use to talk about this is a loaf of raisin bread that is rising. If you're on any one raisin and you look around, all the raisins are moving away from you.

BW: So if we're on raisin Earth . . .

BS: Or raisin Milky Way, everything is expanding away. And what's so exciting, as you say, is the idea of periphery and center, which become much more interesting. Because from where we're situated, we are at the center of the expansion, but we're also at the periphery from someone else's point of view. Think of the application of that cosmology to civilization. In a certain sense, every civilization has important central truths about it, but in other ways they are peripheral. There are certain things we really understand centrally, but other things we don't understand, so we need the help of other civilizations. Where I especially like it is in terms of species. Before, and too often still, we think of the human as the "be all" and "end all." But we must think now of every species as being at the very center of the action. If you removed one species there would be a major crippling of the whole Earth community. So every species is at the center. The phytoplankton, compared to our highly developed brains, may seem so simple, but they are providing the oxygen on which our brains depend.

BW: This new cosmological view reinforces both ecological and religious worldviews that support the intrinsic value of all forms of life. This new view of an expanding universe, of center and periphery, retains a sense of humankind's own importance at the center, while making room for others. There's a tension in the balance. We may be at the center, but . . .

BS: Yes. A healthy tension. We're making decisions that are absolutely central. But in some ways we are peripheral to the whole life community. They would do just fine without us. So there is a kind of humility built into this, as well as responsibility.

BW: Do you mean that simpler forms are more basic and necessary to life processes, to subsequent forms, than the other way around?

BS: Yes. Because phytoplankton would do fine without humans. They did fine without us for billions of years. But if you took out the phytoplankton, the humans would evaporate right away. So we're more delicate and complex.

BW: But what a beauty in complexity. I mean, here we are, as Tom Berry is so fond of saying, the creatures who have such fine sensory perceptions. We are the ones who are looking into the universe with this sense of wonderment for the mysteries around us. We are the ones who are celebrating that.

BS: At least we could be celebrating that. We could be providing that.

BW: Yes. If commercial society weren't determining our patterns of life so much we could be involved in a marvelous celebration of life!

BS: And all the other species would clap with us! Clapping because we finally figured out our role.

BW: In your book, you're not only trying to help people learn to appreciate these things, but to actually experience these realities. You talk about dawn and dusk being the great gateways for this celebration of the cosmos. As times of the day when we can best experience the immensity of the Earth rolling on its axis, seemingly into or away from its orientation toward the sun. I'm reminded that other creatures already do that quite nicely. The crepuscular birds are up at dawn and actively singing, and at dusk are singing again. In our own species we have a monastic tradition with its daily cycles of prayer, especially morning and evening prayer, which has carried over into the traditions of some of our churches through the Book of Common Prayer, with its morning and evening liturgies. As you say in your book, one way or another we need to experience it, to actually feel ourselves a part of the immensity of life, and give thanks. What are some of your spiritual practices?

BS: Well, one is greeting the dawn. I describe that in detail in my book, but it's to actually feel in your body the reality we know in our minds about the Earth and the sun. I really do feel and experience it. It comes in waves, sort of jerking into my mind, when I'll enter this larger realm of feeling, but then inevitably drop out of it again. But it's a thrill, and it comes at different times of the day, in particular at dawn and dusk, or with the moon. What's so wonderful about the sun is when you're reflecting on the fact that it's a million times larger than the Earth. When we box ourselves up in human artifact, we end up domesticating everything. We live surrounded by a domesticated world, and that sense of the wild is lost on us, that sense of terror as well as delight. Since we can't go live in wilderness because there is so little left and we'd just ruin it, the question is, how can we get a sense of the wild? Well, one of the ways is with the sun. Simply to feel this explosion taking place, a million times the size of the Earth, whipping us around it and basking us with energy.

BW: Holding our planet and others in their courses. Whipping us around, but also holding us.

BS: In an embrace. Yes. To actually feel that bond. Not just to know it, but to feel that bond, and even to feel, as night falls, a sense of loss as the Earth turns away.

BW: I suspect that all of us have felt, at one time or another, that sense of loss at dusk. Even grieving. Along with the hope and trust we will meet the dawn again.

BS: Yes. What a drama.

BW: To really experience that. I am remembering our return to Iowa from California. One evening my wife and I went to visit friends who live in the country. In Iowa at night there is the awesome reality of starlight undiminished by the glow of city lights. After dinner the four of us went outside and lay down on a blanket on the grass beneath the night stars. It wasn't our intention, but we all just fell silent for long periods of time beholding the magnificent presence of celestial light as it entered our eyesight and consciousness and souls. It felt like a long, sustained meditation triggered by that vast bowl of delicate lights overhead. It is so good to enter the immensity of this mystery, to let it penetrate our bodies and expand our being.

BS: That by far is one of the deepest experiences. As I tried to say in my book, this sense of feeling the stars below you.

BW: I was probably using "above" language, wasn't I? I just didn't realize at the time that I was looking into stars below me. I only knew they were out there beyond me, and yet somehow within me.

BS: Up and down is something we have to learn as primates just to function. But beneath you, and without and within, is something we have to learn as humans. One of the things we feel is the vastness of the chasm, but also the bond with the Earth. Not letting us go.

BW: This is a lot of learning for a culture to go through in a short time, isn't it?

BS: Yes. That's why a lot of people are needed.

BW: Well, who do you think is listening to the new story? The scientific community, educational institutions, religious communities? Just who is paying the most attention right now? Where do you see the most hope, and what are the greatest challenges at this stage of things?

BS: Everywhere I go to lecture and teach, people move into this understanding with a sense of adventure. After all, people invite me to do this. Even if I go to a conference, people have a sense of what I'm going to talk about and they're coming to hear this on their own volition. Even in my classes. So I'm not getting a cross-section of society. But everywhere I have gone to talk and teach in the United States and Europe, I find very receptive people. It goes back to your initial comment about the sense of wonder. We really have this natural sense of wonder! We really want to know about ourselves and the universe!

I live on the thrill and the hope that I sense among people for this. Because I'm a teacher, the way I explain the world is that we have to teach more because ignorance is the problem. Not malevolence, just ignorance. So I think the biggest challenge is extricating ourselves from a consumer cosmology, this cosmology of self as you called it, and teaching this embedded understanding about the world. I talk to and work with scientists, religious people, and educational institutions, all three. And I've had nothing but a sense of excitement in response to this picture of the world. I spoke to the American Association for the Advancement of Science, in Boston. A room full of scientists. When I was done there was complete silence. Scientists recognize just how tremendously exciting this all is, but we haven't had the time or the motivation to put it together.

BW: That's good to hear. You know, I can imagine someone looking outside their window, or standing in a garden, deeply appreciating the beauty and wonder before them and saying, "The view from where I sit looks pretty good. Pretty satisfying. I don't see how a photo of Earth from space, or photos of the universe from the Hubble Space Telescope, can improve on this or enlarge my appreciation for the place where I live." What do you say to that?

BS: Some people are living wonderful lives and doing very purposeful and meaningful work with very little understanding for the new story. They have a sense of significance about their lives and work. There are many people doing fine work in this world. But there are some people living very local lives who are not being helpful. They're either living lives that are unconsciously destructive, or they're sort of neutral and don't appreciate what's taking place around them. In the way the universe works, the creativity of the universe is one time and that's all. It's bizarre. In the early universe, the hydrogen atoms were created. There were no hydrogen atoms in the first half million years and then suddenly, the whole universe created hydrogen atoms everywhere, but never again would they be created. Then later, another billion years, the moment came, and only then, for creating galaxies. Some of the material was swept up in galaxies, and some wasn't. But the material that wasn't would never be swept up in a new galaxy. That's sort of the way the universe works.

Right now, we are also involved in a one-time event, the creation of what Thomas Berry and I call the ecozoic era. It's another phase of planetary development, not because we are naming it but because it is really an emergent process. When you start to understand what this means, you realize we are drawing on fifteen billion years of creativity, and all the unborn generations of beings will be influenced by the decisions we make at this juncture. In other words, there is a tremendous source of creative energy a person can get by going forward with this understanding that we might not have otherwise. We might make the terrible mistake of thinking that this little local scene here doesn't have a significance that goes beyond the local. That would be a terrible mistake, a product of false consciousness. There really is a way in which the decisions we are making on this little local scene right here are going to influence people for hundreds and thousands, even millions of years. I don't mean that to sound paralyzing or farfetched, I just think it is accurate. The new story demonstrates the significance of the local and the importance of our thinking and actions now that we might not appreciate otherwise. Even if we had, say, an aesthetic appreciation for a garden, it's good to have a cosmological appreciation that affirms just how important it is to carry on with this work.

BW: So with the new cosmology, an enlargement of perspective is possible, a perspective that doesn't diminish but increases our sense of value for the present moment and for local efforts. Because with it we see our place and part in something much larger that is full of wonders and mystery, and with this comes a greater appreciation for both part and whole and our role in it.

BS: The sense of wonder and responsibility both grow. So I don't insist that everyone knows this, of course, yet it contains a tremendous reservoir of energy and insight for people to draw upon.

BW: You've obviously been around plenty of people who are absorbing this and drawing a lot of creative energy and excitement from it. Because of some of the work I'm doing, I'm reminded of a number of fascinating land-based religious communities, who are embracing this new story with enormous enthusiasm today. Furthermore, they are using this new narrative, along with new insights into the religious metanarratives they inherit, to motivate and sustain a process of institutional change that will guide their common life together toward just and sustainable community.

BS: That's great to hear. So they feel some new excitement about their lives and work?

BW: Yes, indeed. This gets at something I find interesting. Here we live in a world full of religious traditions. Yet we also see emerging within all these cultures the scientific paradigm, and yet the scientific tradition is itself evolving along the lines of the new cosmology. Why is this new cosmological story so vital in human transformation and cultural change and institutional reform, especially human transformation, which usually precedes cultural and institutional change?

BS: This is the way I think about it. Every species is unique. Each has a central role and each has defining characteristics. One way to define the human is to say that we are the species that requires a transgenetic wisdom. Other species develop a little bit of culture, but for the most part humans need culture as much as we need our biological genes, both of which link us to the past. As far back as we know anything about humans, we've developed wisdom traditions, and without them we really can't become fully human. One way of talking about that is the second birth. We have a second birth. To our genetic birth and genetic power is added a cultural birth. We're born again culturally. That's one way of interpreting these initiation rites and so forth. That's something to think about, that we can't rely upon DNA alone. As vast as that genetic structure is, we still need cultural guidance, this transgenetic dimension. And that cultural guidance changes. The cultural guidance that was helpful for perhaps twenty thousand years is still important, but it misses the crucial challenges of our time, and that is amazing to think about.

One example. The Earth system can process two billion tons of carbon a year. But now we have released over 300 percent more than can be processed into the air. This is a catastrophe because we can't upset these ancient patterns in our Earth system. And yet we have no information for how to deal with that in our cultural traditions. So I would say that the understanding of the new cosmology is absolutely necessary in order for the cultural tradition to give us the kind of guidance we need to move forward. You can look through the Bible or the Sutras or the Koran for information about genetic engineering and you'll find nothing. And yet those questions are of central importance.

BW: Let me ask the question another way. Is the human transformation that seemingly has to occur for us to address these enormous global issues on a local basis and otherwise, is this transformation possible when there is a jarring discontinuity, in the minds of many, between the religious story and the scientific story? Aren't you trying to reconcile these narratives in a way that makes sense in our age, so that we can proceed with this task?

BS: The difficulty isn't so much the jarring or the dissonance between the scientific and the religious traditions. The primary difficulty is the way in which we have committed ourselves to a consumer culture. That is the primary difficulty. One of the reasons it is so difficult is because it's more invisible. Religion is all around us and we can all talk about it, yet we just continue to embrace all these ads without comment. If there were 10,000 little sermons on Lutheranism given to pre-schoolers or public school children every year, we would know how to deal with that. We would say they have to stop! Don't do that! But when those sermons are on consumerism, we don't say a thing. So that's the primary problem. The synthesis of science and religion is a lot easier because they are not that far apart. When the power of science and the power of religion come together in this new cosmology, then we will have a potent means to deal with the consumer culture.

BW: That's an interesting way of putting it. That we need the full powers of those stories reconnected and working together as a corrective to things.

BS: If we have a story that really does synthesize science and religion, then we'll have the proper cultural tradition we need for guidance. The tragedy of our time is that neither religion nor science, taken by themselves, can effectively guide the human species. We've talked about how they've been broken apart, and so here we are and we don't really know what to do because our wisdom traditions haven't really come forward with power. So we're victimized by the consumer answer.

BW: We want a religious tradition that has more ecological focus at the very least, to say nothing of the cosmological. And we want a scientific tradition that will offer us more in the way of values and purpose for human guidance. And we're not getting it sufficiently from either at the moment.

BS: That's right. So we're vulnerable and easily victimized.

BW: How can this new narrative, this new cosmology, be integrated into the life of local churches and religious communities? What have you seen going on that has impressed you in this regard, whether it's an incorporation of the story into ritual and liturgy, or whether it's being embodied in new spiritual practices with a practical dimension? I have the same question with regard to educational institutions, for instance, whether you see the new story being incorporated into the scientific curriculum?

BS: I've thought about your first question, but I don't have much to say that would be very helpful at the moment. It requires a longer answer. But let me give you an example from educational institutions. At the University of Chicago, they now have a full-year course that starts with the big bang and goes up to the human. It's fantastic. They've brought together their scientists and they tell the whole story. Unfortunately they stop when they get to human culture. They haven't drawn in the humanities scholars and the religious scholars. But they're moving in exactly the right direction. They're telling the whole scientific story at one of our major educational institutions. Likewise at Harvard University a few years ago, Eric Chaseman taught a course incorporating the whole story. Believe it or not, it was the most popular course on campus. Unfortunately the university shut him down because they heard various criticisms and they couldn't deal with it. Mainly, they wanted to break it apart into specialties again. They didn't really understand what an amazing opportunity they had. And I hear from other people at different colleges. It's exciting to see how they are trying to get the big picture across. Within that larger picture you can teach anything. You obviously have physics and astronomy and chemistry, but you can also teach literature and history. You can even teach economics, real economics in terms of the new story. I'm very excited about this.

BW: So the new story is obviously another way to cross boundaries in our educational enterprise.

BS: That's right, and it's happening.

BW: You once said that Einstein "burned to know what the Old One thinks." What drives you?

BS: I share that faith, but I would say it a little differently. I burn to know what the Old One *is* thinking. Because one way to think about the universe is that it is the thinking or the acting of the Old One, the ancient mystery. You can say it's matter and energy and information. You can also say it's all a process of intelligence, of genius, which is the way I think of it. So I want to deepen my understanding, but it is ultimately for the kind of joy that flows from that search. In celebrating and teaching those understandings in community, I really want to know, but it comes to fruition in learning communities in which I participate. There is no greater life than the life of a teacher. That's my ecstasy.

Writers and Geographers

WILLIAM KITTREDGE

Bill Kittredge grew up on the MC Ranch in south-eastern Oregon where he lived until he was thirty-five. He now teaches English at the University of Montana and directs its Creative Writing Program. His books include Who Owns the West?, Hole in the Sky, Owning It All, *and* We Are Not in This Together. *As Terry Tempest Williams said with reference to* Who Owns the West?, *"When I think about our beloved American West and the challenges we face as a people, I hear Bill Kittredge's voice. Within these pages we find both our instructions and inspiration on how to proceed." Bill and his colleagues have had a large influence on a new generation of poets, nature writers, and literary regionalists who are themselves acquiring quite a following. Together they are contributing to a cultural renewal through new stories that help us conserve both community and nature as we build a decentralized system of enduring local economies. As Thomas Berry once wrote in* Dream of the Earth, *"It's all a question of story. We are in trouble just now because we do not have a good story. We are in between stories. The old story, the account of how the world came to be and how we fit into it, is no longer effective. Yet we have not learned the new story." In Bill Kittredge and in the West, people are revising their story and living into it.*

BW: Your new book, *Who Owns the West?*, continues a process of interwoven meditations begun in your earlier memoir, *Hole in the Sky*, which Wallace Stegner praised as "one of the few thoroughly honest accounts of a western upbringing . . . the kind of book I have been hoping to see come out of the West in greater and greater profusion, as the West at large discovers the sort of honesty that Kittredge has discovered in himself."

WK: What Wally said about the West is true. There is a whole spate of good books coming out of the West. I just read Kim Barnes' new book about a western upbringing. She was a student in the writing program here at the University of Montana. This whole business of western writing is self-invented in a way.

Stegner called for it and called for it, and various others including myself began to say, "Look it's happening, it's happening." The self-fulfilling prophecy we hoped for has arrived. It is happening. The West is a different place now than it was fifteen or twenty years ago. It has filled up with writers, and it has a real sense of itself. Not just a literary sense, but a real regional sense of itself that is independent and not derivative from the East in ways it was even as recently as twenty or twenty-five years ago.

BW: What kind of role do you think Wallace Stegner has played in these developments?

WK: For me he was an example of possibility. When I was on the ranch years ago and feeling very isolated, very out of the loop, there was always Stegner over there who had, by the evidence of his writing, a somewhat similar upbringing in the deep West, in the boondocks. Yet he somehow figured out a way to have a career of saying things that were paid attention to, about the place where he grew up and the things he valued and the things he held sacred. And as a result of his example, I always told myself that it was possible to do that. I think a great many writers of my generation in particular hung onto that, so the example of his life was one thing he gave us. But perhaps the more important thing he gave us was a sense of moral guidance. That you should take a stand for the things you care about, should stand up and be somebody, which over the years he proved increasingly willing to do as the West became its own self. He had moral integrity, that willingness to go out on a limb and just say what you think, to hang with the consequences. So Stegner gave heart and hope to all of us.

BW: So his life and work have been exemplary and instructive for everybody?

WK: Yes! I would probably have been too timid in the same circumstances. And not just me, but people like Ed Abbey and others. We all had Wally as a model in front of us, and so we were inspired to just go for it.

BW: Your own books certainly demonstrate that. In fact, your description of growing up in Oregon's Warner Valley is poignant in part because it seems like a microcosm of western history, if not human history, a story of how humans transformed paradise. You describe the valley as a wondrously beautiful place, and it was there that your family owned one of the great ranches in the American West, an empire the size of Delaware.

WK: Yes. We had 21,000 irrigated acres there in the valley, and we leased another 10,000 acres for grazing land. That land had never been broken out at all. A lot of it was tule swamp and there were a lot of feral hogs down there that the men gathered up. The land was only roughly fenced and that was about it. But when my dad came in '36 he built a long drainage canal around the east side of the valley, from Twenty Mile Creek on north, and began to break out those swamps so they could be plowed and farmed. We had huge oat crops at first.

BW: Were you using teams of draft horses for that work?

WK: At that time, no. You see the draft horses were then being used only for the lighter work of haying the high meadows and swamps and such. Because in '36 dad began to farm with powerful Caterpillar tractors, running them day and night.

BW: So the coming of the tractor to Warner Valley was the beginning of the end, the beginning of an enormous change to the landscape, like it was all over America?

WK: Especially as the tractors came to farms and ranches at the end of World War II and more and more replaced the horses altogether. But in '36 we were still using both, tractors for farming and horses for haying. Since most of the valley was still in grass, there were still a lot of horses around. The end really came in 1945, when my grandfather traded off 200 matched work teams to buy a bunch of John Deere tractors, and the harnesses rotted in the barns until the barns were torn down.

BW: I was struck by two things you said about that in your book, Bill. One was the way in which your own flesh was magnified through horse flesh. The love you felt for the horses, you said, was enough reason to revere everything in sight for another morning.

WK: It's astonishing. I wrote about my memories of going down every morning to herd the work teams into the corrals so everybody could harness their teams. And those horses seemed to love where they were, as the sun came up and the mist rose off the valley floor, and they were snorting mist themselves. You couldn't help but love the world on those days.

BW: I can understand that emotion, having had some draft horse experience of my own. I suppose that's why I was also struck by another comment you made expressing bewilderment with your elders who, in selling off the horses, acted as though they didn't care about giving up what gave them the most joy.

WK: That's absolutely true, because all they talked about was horses and deer hunting and animal presence of one sort or another that pervaded their life. Yet here they were actively trading them off and wanting mechanization. Of course their only use for the deer was to shoot them. And the astonishing array of birds! One of the things we're losing, that we don't even know we've lost for the most part, is the presence of those huge accumulations of animals in our midst which we've lost over the past hundred years. The passenger pigeon. The buffalo. There were millions and millions of those water birds in Warner Valley and places like Thule Lake along the western flyway. And in my lifetime they've disappeared.

BW: Not only the wild creatures but all too many of the domesticated ones are in jeopardy, the draft horse among them, and of course a pattern of rural life they make possible. It sounds like mechanization was the beginning of a big change on the ranch toward agribusiness that brought enormous damage to the valley.

WK: Yes. My grandfather was a very orderly man, and we came to the idea, though I don't know how we came to it, that we could remake this place. The success of my father's enterprises, of building these canals and drainage ditches and head gates and such, was like bringing order to the world. Everything is going to be just the way it is supposed to be because we planned it that way. It was intricate, and it worked for a long time, and we felt enormously proud of ourselves and successful. And then it began to come unraveled, and there were lots of signs of unraveling around us. The work became very mechanical, repetitive, and dominated by machines. You were a servant of the machine rather than vice versa. People weren't as eager to do the work. Soils began to decline and erode from the winds. Suddenly we had to fertilize and use chemical pesticides. So we got into industrial chemical agriculture very rapidly because we had to for some reason. I've always said that the big industrial practices that we adopted in agriculture, which seemed so like making the world work in a human way, just didn't pan out. We did more damage in thirty or forty years in that valley than I see in European valleys that have been farmed by hand and with animals for 3,000 years. They're better preserved.

BW: Seeing this industrial pattern play itself out in so many places, in Montana where you now live and elsewhere, prompts you to make a statement I found to be full of wisdom born of painful learning. You wrote, "We have taken the West for about all it has to give. We have lived like children, taking and taking for generations, and now that childhood is over. . . . Now it's time to give something back to the natural systems that have supported us, some care and tenderness."

WK: That's absolutely true. I think we really have to turn our attention to that. Because there are still lots of problems in Montana, and not only in agriculture but, for instance, with gold mines and the recent experience of timber companies at Plum Creek. They're beginning to conduct themselves like magpies with what's left of a road kill, without the excuse the magpies have of being both hungry and instinctual. These are people who lack some moral sense. Because of that, among other things, the West is in the midst of a huge transformation, a transition that is going to last another couple of decades. There's going to be a lot of heartbreak and discontent, and where it will come out at the other end I'm not sure. I know where I hope it comes out. I hope we have the wisdom to bring it to some sense of taking care. The transition from "making use" to "taking care" is a big one. But we just can't go on using and using. We've got to learn how to take care of where we are. We've got to learn to stay put. We've got to learn to live in communities with our children and grandchildren. At the current rate we're going to leave them a damned mess. But with a little more sense we won't.

BW: The challenges you're facing in Montana and the West are challenges that face all of us. The problems are not just environmental, as you rightly acknowledge in your book, but also social. You've spoken a great deal about this in *Hole in the Sky* and *Who Owns the West?*, about the way some people feel disenfranchised and powerless and quite literally invaded by what they call "outlanders," many of whom have more money and different ideas about the future than those who presently think of themselves as native Montanans. You've also addressed an irony that those whose forefathers took the land from the indigenous people of the region now face the same fate themselves.

WK: That's right, because it's being taken away from them. The true natives of this land can now smile and say, "See, it's now happening to you."

I think the social costs are enormous, and they're going to be enormous until we get it through our heads that we must find a way to bring these disenfranchised people back into the loop, back into the central tasks of society. They're going to react with increasing anger and hostility, acting out like the militia groups and such, until we figure out a way to include these people. It's complex, and one of the ways we do it in our communities is to deliberately set out to foster a sense of community, a sense of taking care of each other. That's happening in a lot of places, for example in Missoula, Montana. It's a pretty good town to live in. People are pretty good to each other. One of the reasons it's happening is because a lot of people, from the mayor on down, are saying we've got to find a way to make this work.

BW: You've got a pretty remarkable mayor there in Dan Kemmis, don't you?

WK: Dan is great! You may know him as the author of the book, *The Politics of Place*. It's like having a philosopher-king in our midst. He's a good friend and a real visionary. I don't agree with him on everything, but we do agree on the basics. Bringing people back into community is enormously important. The current anger with federal and state government on the part of those who are disenfranchised is a little bit misplaced, because the people and institutions that are getting away with murder right now are the big international corporations, and everybody pretty much ignores their role in all this. The corporations are just heedless for the most part, as though they were established to be as selfish as possible. That's a terrible thing to have in the midst of our society. We really need to examine the role of corporations as institutions in a very hard light. It's not that we want to give up on corporate or communal activities of this sort, but we might want to say, "Well look, you've got to be something other than just plain selfish." The big corporations are causing enormous trouble, as they have for generations, especially in some places of the world, including Montana. A lot of the grievances that the disenfranchised have are caused by corporate activities rather than federal or state activities.

BW: You've described the tremendous need for real public discourse in our communities, and how we might move forward into a future we can all embrace. Dan Kemmis and others like him have been nurturing this possibility locally in Missoula and exercising real political leadership in Montana. But what has been the role of writers in this process of addressing social needs? Haven't you and other writers been raising these issues quite self-consciously in Montana and the West for some time?

WK: Yes, and I think it's working a bit. Slowly, these issues are coming to the forefront, because it is simply the moral responsibility of writers and artists to say these things and raise these issues. The only reason why Missoula is becoming a better community, a more generous community, if you will, is because we're beginning to understand a different story about ourselves. We're beginning to understand a story about taking care, about being generous rather than being selfish and using up. The only way we're going to begin to internalize that story is by hearing it talked about, reflecting on it, talking back and forth with others we know, forming an extended community, and slowly reinventing the story of who we think we are and what our purposes are. If writers have a job in this society, that's probably it at the moment. And I think we should have a job. We do have social responsibilities for the direction of the culture. We have pretty generous freedoms afforded by the society, and we should pay something back in return for that.

BW: That's a mature and exciting vision of the moral obligations of the writer or artist. Is it unique to the new breed of western writers in America?

WK: I think they do have a sense of mission and political intention toward society that is somewhat unique. In fact a large number of very intense, intelligent, high-powered young people are coming West, to Missoula and various other schools in the West, because they really feel the importance of the kind of storytelling that we're trying to do out here. They agree with it and they want to be a part of what is going on out here for the next twenty or thirty years. They feel the possibilities out here. I've said the West is becoming its own nation with its own set of values and rules inside the larger nation, and I think that's true in a sense. A lot of people who are coming out here agree with that and really want to partake of it. It's not just retirees from California.

BW: Tell me more about the role that storytelling plays, especially in this transition or transformation from a society that "uses up" to one that is learning how to "take care."

WK: Well, the traditional business of storytelling, as Aristotle said in *The Poetics* a long time ago, revolves around recognitions, of coming to see, of insight. That's what storytelling is all about. So we use narrative, for example, to convey a sense of ourselves that is based on an interior narrative we tell ourselves over and over all day long. These moments of recognition occur and reoccur, because just when we think we have everything figured out, something comes unraveled, and we begin to recognize something slightly different about ourselves and our world. So we are continually in the process of revising our story, of re-seeing our story, both as individuals and as a culture. That's exactly what's going on in the West right now. We're fundamentally reimagining ourselves and our role, revising our story. It was once a story of a people who came to a place, as my people did, which looked like paradise. It was there for the taking and they took it. The main objective was to use it and make it pay, and they did. Sometimes, as we know, the Native American people there were kicked off the land or murdered in the process and that was okay according to the old story told by a lot of westerners, because we had this high motive of creating a city on a hill, which now seems crazy on reexamination. Nevertheless that's how the story worked.

As it went on for a hundred years, the West really was conquered. It's a story of conquest and domination, a story of takeover. It was a racist, sexist, and imperialist story. As we settle down in the West now and don't have much left to conquer around us but ourselves and the world within us, we begin to realize that the old story may have effectively functioned as a conquest story, but it is certainly not functional anymore in contemporary society. So we have to invent a new one. We're now slowly beginning to see our way around the horn into what that new story would be. We're beginning to see it as a story of cherishing rather than destroying. Of needing to cherish and care for things and one another and the place where we live in equal measure. How to do that is not a simple process. Westerners and Americans all love stories that have simple solutions. Shane shoots Jack LaLance off the porch and the problem is over. Well, our problems are not going to be solved following that simple storyline. We are going to have to sit down and talk to each other and work with each other for decades. It's going to be a long, boring, often annoying process. But we have no choice but to do it.

BW: So this plot line looks a little more complicated in its expectations of moral maturity than we've seen in these earlier narratives from the West.

WK: It sure is. And it demands of us a lot more patience and a willingness to give and take, qualities which the dominant people who came west weren't traditionally very interested in. A lot of the people who came west over the wagon trails in the early days were wild hairs, the ones who were hell-bent on radical individualism. And that's a story we still hear a lot in our culture. But the other side of that story is that the West was settled by very communal people, by communities like the Mormons and the Hutterites. Wagon trains themselves, about three days after they headed out, became little communities that mostly took care of one another. Most of the people in the West now live in towns and cities and are very interested in participating in communal processes. So I think the actuality of life in the West is very communal already, but the story needs to catch up to the facts of our life today. Perhaps in a couple of decades we can turn the corner and begin living comfortably inside a new story which more accurately reflects the kind of society we actually live in.

BW: A couple of times you've referred to it as "the" story or the "new" story, though you don't seem to be proposing some grand new metanarrative.

WK: We're trying to find a way to understand ourselves. We say, okay, we're going to live in a narrative that leads us where? We've lived in a narrative for a long time that led us to ideas of material progress. That's a metanarrative embraced and inhabited by westerners and Americans. Ideas of progress are sacred in a way in this country, but we have to ask ourselves "progress toward what?" Progress toward simply more wealth, simply more stuff, may really not be progress after all. There are other kinds of progress. Spiritual progress. Progress toward taking better care of each other and what we've been given. Real progress versus false progress.

BW: So is this one of the narrative themes issuing from this generation of writers as they conduct their literary explorations inward, to what sustains them physically and spiritually?

WK: Varieties of it, yes. The younger writers like Rick Bass and Terry Tempest Williams and James Galvin—these and many more—are all in one way or another echoing some version of this same narrative. I don't have a lock on it. It's just that it's a compelling narrative and makes sense to a lot of us. Most every state has writers emerging who are telling their own version of this story in one way or another. There are so many more writers in the West now than there were twenty-five years ago, ten times as many good writers perhaps as there were when I started out.

BW: In as much as these voices seem to arise in moments of urgency or extremity, in times of need or crisis, isn't there a prophetic dimension to their role?

WK: Maybe. When a society seems to be settled into a mode that is working satisfactorily, literature and art go in different ways. But right at the moment the West is in an urgent time of transition, and I suppose there is a prophetic sense that a lot of writers feel about that. I think it's a sense that is quite real and workable, that if I and enough others begin to tell a certain kind of story about the place we live in, and if it's reasonable and sensible, other people will hear it, transform it to some degree, and begin to tell it in some version of their own. And that story will begin to be operative in society in practical ways, often very quickly.

BW: So there is a creative moral passion at work in many of these writers.

WK: Yes. We're trying to create something, and what we're trying to create is a whole social story. That's pretty clear, I think. A lot of people are self-consciously doing that, including myself. The West is the place I love, and I wish the West were at peace with itself. If I can find a story that seems sensible to people and encourages us all to live in more reasonable ways, I'm going to tell it, and maybe others will like it and start living it and things will change to some degree. I think that's a reasonable task and a reasonable expectation.

BW: Well, you are certainly serving as a role model to other writers in that regard. I've been impressed with how supportive this whole community of writers and artists are toward one another.

WK: One of the things about this community of people is that they're all friends. They're all basically working toward the same objectives. I've been around other groups of artists where the operative notion is that your success diminishes mine. With this community it is exactly the opposite. Everybody feels that your success encourages or increases mine, increases ours. Each of us is working at part of the same task. I don't think anybody has any sense that they're going to change the world by writing one book or one documentary film. Instead, the feeling is that if enough people do enough things, we will see a change, and for good reason.

BW: What are the directions in your current writing?

WK: I'm writing about the West, of course, and it's called *Reimagining Desire*. It's about the things we've been discussing, but attempts to carry them out on a wider stage by talking about issues of the future beyond the West. The West is obviously moving very rapidly into a world culture, and things that happen in Montana or elsewhere in the West are not isolated from what happens in Asia. A friend of mine, Bill Beavis, just wrote a book about logging in Borneo, a story just like logging in Montana to a great degree. What I'm trying to talk about in this book is our need to make the creature we are comfortable. By comfortable, I mean to honor the kind of creature we are, which is a creature that has evolved on earth among animals, insects, soil. The more we isolate ourselves from what we evolved amidst, the more we're going to become un-comfortable and increasingly crazy. It's like sensory deprivation. We see news of it in every newspaper we pick up every day. All these false constructs that we build to live in, for instance these college classrooms that are painted green with little tiny windows that block our view of the deep green. Everything very abstract, very unreal. Like the agriculture we came to practice in Warner Valley which was very unreal and abstract, a partial creation, a human creation as compared to the actual thing all around us.

BW: So the story keeps coming back around to the human, doesn't it, to the mysteries and limits and possibilities within us.

WK: I've thought about this a lot. I don't know any other way to talk about it except to say that if we're going to perpetuate ourselves and learn to live in a story that isn't a continual succession of conquest, then we're going to have to talk about what it's like and what it means to be human, what kind of animal we are, and how this animal can learn to get along with others and inhabit a place that doesn't make us crazy.

BW: We'll be examining a lot of old texts and new narratives when we get serious about that task, won't we?

WK: You bet.

In Search of Our Fugitive Faith

TERRY TEMPEST WILLIAMS

Terry Tempest Williams is from a Mormon family whose roots in Utah go back to 1847. She is Naturalist-in-Residence at the Utah Museum of Natural History, a poet, and author of several books, including Refuge: An Unnatural History of Family and Place, An Unspoken Hunger, Desert Quartet, Pieces of White Shell, *and* Coyote's Canyon. Refuge *has been praised as one of the most significant environmental essays of our time, and a modern classic in the literatures of women, nature, and grieving. In it, Terry tenderly describes her experience with the rising waters of loss associated with the flooding of the Bear River Migratory Bird Refuge and her mother's death to cancer. Writing from the center of deep love and grief over family, culture, and region comes a courageous story of consolation and renewal that spreads hope in every direction. In the Epilogue to* Refuge, *we learn that in addition to Terry's mother, both grandmothers and six aunts have had mastectomies, and all but two have died of cancer, a family history that is closely linked to atomic bomb testing in the Utah desert during the 1950s. Given her own biopsies and "borderline malignancies," Terry has become a voice not only for the growing "clan of one-breasted women" and the emerging environmental public health movement, but for people everywhere who are trying to conserve community and health in the deepest and broadest sense. I once heard Terry say that "Words matter; images heal. When the bond between heaven and earth has been broken, only stories can mend it." With the willingness to love enough to grieve, Terry Tempest Williams is using pen and passion and intelligence to reclaim "the fugitive faith we have allowed to run away from ourselves."*

BW: Your recent biopsy, along with a family history of cancer that we both share with others, brings it close to home again in very personal terms. How can we imagine that the environmental crisis we are facing is inseparable from us?

159

TTW: This whole notion of separateness may be our greatest folly in terms of our relationship as human beings to the earth. And the sooner we realize that our body is the earth and the earth is our body, then perhaps we'll be able to respond with a larger, more empathetic and compassionate intelligence.

BW: I don't understand how we have been so long immersed in the world and yet have failed to realize that any damage done to the earth is done to us as well. Why have we been so confused?

TTW: It is a complicated question, but I think if we don't raise it we will continue along an egocentric path with its short-sighted point of view. We can certainly trace this kind of philosophical thought to Descartes, to the whole notion of a mind/body split. Yet as we close the 20th century and enter the next, we are coming into a more integrated point of view that sees the world whole, even holy. We're seeing this in the writing that is emerging at this point in time in North America, and I think we're seeing it in brave community actions that are occurring on a small scale. It's incremental.

BW: Your book *Refuge* is a personal and loving meditation on your experience of loss—both human and environmental—and healing. What kind of questions were you posing for yourself and our culture in that work?

TTW: The personal question I was circling around in writing this narrative was how do we find refuge in change. The Great Salt Lake was rising, and the Bear River Migratory Bird Refuge, which was the landscape of my childhood, was being inundated by floodwaters. At the same time my mother was diagnosed with ovarian cancer. So the landscape of my childhood and the landscape of my family, both of which had been bedrock for me, now seemed to be quicksand.

The larger question is, I think, a cultural one. What is our relationship to place? What do we choose to inhabit? And how do we find solace in a world that is changing at such phenomenal rates? How do we keep an integral view, and how do we live with integrity, wherever we live? Another larger question is, of course, how do we define health: the health of the land, the health of a family, the health of a body, the health of the body politic? The shocking revelation to me as we were living this story, was that maybe this cancer wasn't random, maybe it wasn't just genetic. Maybe there was an environmental trigger or even an environmental cause that we had to look at squarely. I think that culminates in the epilogue of the "clan of one-breasted women."

BW: I was visiting earlier today with environmental activist Diane Dillon-Ridgely, who told me that about thirty percent of cancers are thought to have known causes—five percent genetic and about twenty-five percent due to personal choices and behaviors that she said involved too much of this or too little of that. But in talking to women about these issues, Diane tells them that what is missing in this picture is knowledge about what causes the other seventy percent. Very little of the billions of dollars spent on cancer research has been devoted to probing environmental triggers or causes.

TTW: I think we are in an extraordinary state of denial about this now, involving both arrogance and ignorance. We know we can poison the land and poison the waters. We watch the fish die. We have above-ground testing. We can see the effects of radiation on plant life, on livestock, but we think this does not affect us because we are not animals. I think the question, What does it mean to be a good mammal, a good animal? should be reflected not only in our public policy but in our own private lives. I just find it astonishing that we still fail to make this connection. Certainly we have a literary tradition in this country that asks these questions. Whether it's Melville and the great whale in terms of our relationship to Other. Whether it's Walt Whitman lyrically inviting us to make love to the land. Whether it's Emily Dickinson in her precision of language focusing on our relationship to nature and God, or Henry David Thoreau with *Walden*, or Emerson with the oversoul. All the way up to Aldo Leopold with *Sand County Almanac*, Rachel Carson with her revolutionary book *Silent Spring*, and Edward Abbey with *Desert Solitaire* in 1968 which, I think, is one of the great anti-war novels of our time. All these writers in the American tradition are asking the same questions. What is our relationship to Other? How do we choose to define home? What is a dignified life? We see it with Wallace Stegner in his remarkable collection of essays, *The Sound of Mountain Water*. Over and over he asks the question, "Can we create a society to match the scenery?" So these aren't new questions. These are questions we've been asking as we continue to develop North America and the world.

BW: Thinking of this tradition in which you stand, especially about *Silent Spring* and *Refuge*, I am reminded of the book *Our Stolen Future*, by Colburn, Myers, and Dumanoski. It describes the ubiquitous presence of endocrine-disrupting compounds that fill not only our environment but our bodies, making it clear again that our bodies are a concentrated expression of our water and air, our soils and food. I feel as though each of these books, especially *Refuge* and *Our Stolen Future*, carries the indelible message that environmental illness and health are inseparable from human illness and health. I heard Pete Myers discuss their book at a public gathering hosted in San Francisco by Commonweal, a health and environmental research institute that is perhaps best known for its "Cancer Help Project." Toward the end of that meeting, Commonweal president Michael Lerner said that what we badly need in this country is a large-scale environmental public health movement.

TTW: But we're so fearful of language. I know in Utah, if you say the word "wilderness," it's a combustible log. It ignites. So we talk about "home" and it's a more inclusive topic, rather than one that separates. It's the same thing with the whole idea of the environmental movement. We say "environment" and we think of something outside of ourselves. Perhaps if we were to call it "community health," and ask what that would mean to our future as citizens in this country—health in the broadest sense, of individuals, families, communities, and the land. Community in the largest sense. As Aldo Leopold reminds us, community includes rocks, plants, animals, and human beings. So I think we have to be careful with our language so that we can open hearts and minds rather than close them.

BW: That's a very good point. I'm sure you know the incendiary potential of language from your experience with these issues in Utah. This is new territory, and we still have a lot to learn from each other in terms of how best to proceed. Speaking of teachers, you have already spoken of some of the writers to whom you stand indebted. Are there others that come to mind?

TTW: Certainly my family. They have been and continue to be my greatest teachers, beginning with my parents who created an atmosphere where growth could occur. My paternal grandmother Mimi is absolutely central. When I was five years old, she gave me a Peterson's *Field Guide to Western Birds*, and that was the most subversive text she could have handed me. So I would also include as mentors American Avocets, Black-Necked Stilt, Great Blue Heron, Long-Billed Curlew. Every time I see them I feel that I am in the presence of elders. Ted Major, who started the Teton Science School in Jackson Hole, Wyoming, is a teacher of mine in a very real sense. I met him when I was 18, and he changed everything for me. He drew out our strength and humility and made us accountable for the questions we asked. We would ask him a question and so often he would say, "I don't know. What do you think?" We realized that nothing is absolute in the world, and that encouraged us to penetrate more deeply the ecological relations that were around us. He also placed natural history in a political and social context that was very important. He was the first Democrat I ever met!

BW: You had to travel a ways to find one!

TTW: Absolutely! Coming from a devout, conservative, Republican family and culture.

BW: A beloved family just the same.

TTW: A beloved family. The paradoxes are great. Florence Krall is my mentor from the University of Utah. In the early '70s, before eco-feminism was even a word, she was the one who opened the door to a feminist way of thinking in relationship to the land. There have been many writers along the way that make me feel less lonely in the world, both living and dead. Mimi fed me a sense of wonder when I was eight years old. *Silent Spring* was a metaphor that was discussed around our family, as our grandmother read that book to us.

BW: Mimi read that to the family?

TTW: You bet. I remember her underlining and reading *The New Yorker* when *Silent Spring* first came out as an excerpt. And I remember Mimi cutting out newspaper clippings when Glen Canyon Dam was being built.

BW: Back when David Brower and the Sierra Club took out full-page ads comparing the flooding of Glen Canyon to flooding the Sistine Chapel.

TTW: Yes. So there was a tremendous awareness in our grandparents' household that we absorbed as grandchildren, along with learning the names of things. I remember I must have been nine or ten years old and the winter project at my grandmother's house was identifying all the shells that she had found through the years. We had field guides, picture books, biology books, even Rachel Carson's books on intertidal life, as we catalogued and identified these hundreds of shells on the floor of her study.

BW: She knew what she was doing.

TTW: It was very, very rich. And the grandchildren were the beneficiaries. We would stay overnight and we'd almost hate to wake up in the morning because we knew around the kitchen table we would be asked about our dreams. She was a Jungian scholar, and so we were introduced to the whole notion of archetypes and symbols, of something larger going on in life than simply our linear perceptions of the world.

BW: Terry, how amazing. So it was Mimi who, as I heard you say one time, encouraged you to "go deeper, go deeper."

TTW: Absolutely. She demanded it. And she had this fierce curiosity that was infectious. Everything in the world was to be questioned and embraced at once. This was all in the context of a Mormon extended family. So it was a very strange spiritual upbringing, where the orthodoxy of Mormon religion was intertwined with the extravagance of the natural world.

BW: So here you stand in this religious tradition where family and lineage are so important, and *Refuge* just resounds with these themes. Yet you manage in that book, and every other since, to enlarge and greatly magnify the sacred meaning of community by recovering nature's place in it.

TTW: There would be a lot of people in my Mormon family and community that would disagree with you, who say that many of the concepts raised in that memoir are counter to the culture and defy it. Mormon reviews have even said that it is blasphemous for what it says about women, the heavenly Mother, and definitions of power. So I feel in a strange sort of way like I'm an edge walker. So there are tensions I carry. Home is both a blessing and a burden, especially when you have a tradition as strong as ours.

BW: Yes, I see that.

TTW: Maybe that's why I love the lake so much, because it embodies those paradoxes. And yet I think as human beings we are completely rife with paradox. That's what makes us so interesting as an animal. We can think. We can feel. We can intuit. We respond. We build defenses. We are very complicated creatures.

BW: I've heard you use a term I will never forget, and it may be a borrowed term, about our need to recover the "fugitive faith."

TTW: That comes from Eduardo Galleano from his *Book of Embraces*, where he says, "We claim the fugitive faith we have allowed to run away from ourselves." And I've never forgotten that either. I love my culture and I feel deeply tied to it. When we talk about recovering that fugitive faith, it involves a search for the roots of that faith, not merely taking it on as a piece of clothing, but rather embodying it.

BW: So what do you do when you are part of a living tradition that is flawed, that you can't escape however much you might like to, because you realize there may be something useful there worth recovering and redeeming in a time of cultural crisis and renewal?

TTW: I take great solace and strength from metaphors. In Mormon tradition the quilt is a very strong one. My husband Brook's mother, Rosemary Bradley Williams, was a master quilter. What she left us, really, was her handwork, her quilts. My favorite quilts are the ones where she takes pieces of the old and integrates it with the new. They call them crazy quilts.

Brook and I recently went down to the Mormon mission training center. As we sat down and had lunch with 3,000 missionaries, both of us once again had to face the question of what is our place in the orthodoxy. What do we hold onto and what do we let go? How, most importantly, do we embrace and support our family who is devout in this tradition? As you talk to these missionaries who are being sent out around the world, you just can't help but put your arms around them. It's always a tug at my heart. Brook and I drove home not saying much, but I know we were both holding the thought that this is one world, and it's a very safe world, and it's a very socially and spiritually prescribed world that creates a lot of happiness for those who believe in it fully. Yet once you've stepped outside, there's a freedom and an ambiguity that I could never let go of. As Joseph Campbell says, "There is a God beyond God."

BW: There is a mystery beyond the story.

TTW: That's right. And I think that perhaps our task—since we may be in a transitional time as we move from one century into the next and work through these paradigm shifts—perhaps our role right now is in bridge building. One of the most important aspects of bridge building is to embrace the mysteries. To honor what we don't know. And to find comfort in that place of ambiguity.

BW: Yes indeed.

TTW: I think about Jacob Needleman and his wonderful book, *Sense of the Cosmos*, where he says that for so long everything was answered through religion. With the Renaissance we began to enter the industrial age, the scientific age, if you will, where everything is answered through science. And he asks, At what point will we allow the pendulum to swing to the middle? At what point will we realize that we can embrace mysteries, and that we can find a stability of soul within that? I love that question. I love that idea.

I couple that with the ideas theologian John Cobb gives us, where he says that we were part of the age of nationalism. We saw the extreme of that type of thinking with the end of World War II, with Hiroshima, with Nazi Germany. What took the place of nationalism? Economism took its place, where everything was seen through the lens of economics. Cobb says we are now beginning to see the end of that strata of thinking. When asked about the next era we might move into, Cobb says he believes it is the age of earthism, which is really provocative.

BW: And deeply consistent with geologian Thomas Berry's ideas about an ecozoic era, that we must enter the future as a single sacred community or perish in the desert.

TTW: Exactly. And to me that means an era of compassion, where we begin to extend our thinking, our actions, our intentions to other beings besides simply Homo sapiens.

BW: Yes. A love for the "other," which requires spiritual humility—a grounded spirituality—and openness to mystery.

TTW: Both. And that's why I think it's so important to have a biological literacy, so that we do have a sense of the inner workings of the life around us. To think about the miracle of photosynthesis, about the power and passion of migrations, about predator/prey relations. To really think about these ecological steps of mind. It gives such richness to our lives to know who we live among, to know those natural processes, those geological processes, those cultural processes that shape us. That all begins with learning the names of things, at the age of two or five or whatever. Great Blue Heron. Long-Billed Curlew. Sage. Cedar. Spruce. It creates an intimacy of engagement.

BW: You have had the good fortune of a formal education in natural history, but your real gift was the attentiveness encouraged by your parents and grandparents and others, a priceless gift that each one of us can give to our children and grandchildren.

TTW: Absolutely. And again, it is simply being good animals. It just involves a sensory response. How can we not see, feel, taste, touch, hear the world around us? For me that is the joy, the garden of earthly delight in all its wildness.

BW: I remember your story about Wallace and Mary Stegner coming to visit. Until then I'd forgotten that they had spent some years in Utah, part of their own circlings toward settlement in California.

TTW: He's been a great mentor of mine. You talk about teachers. Wally was one of the few people who really understood the depth and breadth of Mormon culture. He admired it, but he also understood the constraints of it.

BW: He came to visit you at some point, and you were returning them to the airport. Can you tell me that story?

TTW: I'll never forget. They had come visiting because Wally had received an honor from one of the organizations here, as one of Utah's native sons. We'd been up in the Wasatch Mountains, and I was taking Wally and Mary back to the airport. On our way Wally gave this wonderfully annotated drive down South Temple saying, "Oh this is where I went on my first date," and "There's East High School which I attended," and "Here's where I played tennis with your grandfather," and "Mary, remember when we had ice cream here?" And then he said, "Oh here we have the hotel where I imagined *Recapitulation*." So it was this wonderful historic ride, hearing his own stories. And then there was the smell of sage as we were getting close to the airport. I helped them in with their baggage, and as they were getting ready to board the plane I just turned to them and said, "Thank you so much for coming." And Wally just looked at me dead eye center and said, "Thank you so much for staying." He understood.

BW: He certainly did. I was introduced to his work during college and have never been the same since. Remember his last collection of essays, *Where the Bluebird Sings to the Lemonade Springs*? In one of those essays he talks about the growing breed of writers in the West—"Stickers" he calls them—and how they are willingly submitting themselves to their places and conducting their literary explorations inward, to what sustains them spiritually and physically, which is not always an easy task.

TTW: But a blessed one. It's just so gorgeous here. I just got back from a wonderful teaching experience. The Utah Museum of Natural History is working with the Wasatch Community Gardens in an urban garden, specifically with young girls from age nine to fourteen. We're planting in the garden and keeping journals, and it has just been so moving seeing the interface of an urban life with a domestic life and a wild life that all comes together in a seamless way in that garden. To hear what these girls are writing and creating! The first day of class we planted basil, and today after four weeks we made pesto. To eat the garden! It was just so wonderful!

BW: Well you certainly know how to give these girls a transformative experience!

TTW: And the other side is that we passed out magnifying glasses last week, and one of the little girls promptly started a fire, to her great delight! I thought, okay, how are we going to work with this metaphor? We sort of stomped the fire out and poured water over it. And I said, talk to me about fire in your journal. And nine-year-old Savannah wrote a poem that went something like this: "I like to burn things up. / I love my life. / I hate the world."

BW: Whew!

TTW: This is the world we live in. Today, each one of the children wrote a letter to the garden, and without exception they were prayers of gratitude for the peace that is held there. So it's really so simple on the one hand.

BW: Care and affection and honesty. With all things great and small.

TTW: And charting the growth, the increments, day by day. It literally feeds us.

BW: The garden is such a fine way to do that. You've been spending some time in your own garden this summer, haven't you?

TTW: I have! And I'm stiff as I could be!

BW: That's because you went away on a vacation and found a crop of weeds when you got back!

TTW: It's so beautiful, Ben! You should see it. I just love the primrose that bloom every night. Brook and I just put up our chairs and watch it in awe.

BW: Evening primrose?

TTW: Yes. And Yarrow, Hare Bells, various kinds of Shades. It's so beautiful. The rest of our yard is completely wild. But it's a good patch and it recovers your soul.

BW: I can imagine.

TTW: It's quite an elegance of form. And the butterflies. That's what has been so amazing! Here we've been tending the plants, and in the morning we hear these little chirping sparrows in the understory, and we've got these beautiful little Sphinx Moths and Mourning Cloaks. It's just so thrilling! It's the first thing I do when I get up. I get up in the morning and run out and say, All right, who's blooming today?

BW: You never know who's going to surprise you next! We live on the edge of town, and I just went out in the field beside our house the other morning to pick Sarah a bouquet of Queen Anne's Lace, White Aster, Cattails, and tall prairie grasses. I love doing that.

TTW: It is about love isn't it?

BW: Yes it is. But we have such a hard time letting those wild places grow here in Iowa because we've lived so long with the norm of excessive cultivation. Now we're slowly coming to realize what treasures this region possesses, this Tall Grass Prairie and Oak Savanna ecosystem. Its remnants are a magnificent vision of possibility.

TTW: I think as our perception changes, hopefully our relationship with the places we live will change. And that's the power of these personal narratives that we're seeing now. I think about how we're told a story and then we tell our own, and it's sort of a chain reaction. That's the one thing I've seen in Congress this year as we've been working as a community to try to stop this wilderness bill. So many of the members of Congress have forgotten that intimate connection to place. They are themselves as uprooted as any person I know, living in the Washington Beltway, in a concrete, tunnelled existence, dealing only with issues of power and compromise. I think it will be up to the people to bring that intimacy back to Congress, whether it is about health issues or environmental issues. I almost feel like we have to reeducate our leaders as to what a connected life is, because it is so foreign to them. That bedrock democracy is ours, yet I fear we are losing that, either through our cynicism or our fatigue or the distractions of our lives. If we remember as communities, as citizens and individuals, that it is in our nature to respond and that our voices do matter—that collectively we can deliver a message from the heart—then we will in time recover that fugitive faith we were talking about.

BW: You wrote somewhere that "When the bond between heaven and earth has been broken, only stories can mend it." Each of us has a role in storytelling, don't we?

TTW: That's right. Of course, the other side of storytelling is listening. And so perhaps our greatest task right now is to listen. To the land. To each other. To what is really trying to be heard within our communities, from the children to our elders, so that these voices aren't silenced. But the joy of listening requires also patience and a concentration. We've been taking care of my grandfather who just turned ninety. He was just saying the other night as our family gathered, that as difficult as old age is, there are great advantages, and one of them is the capacity to listen. That was so moving to hear.

BW: Especially coming from the one to whom we should be listening.

TTW: Yes. There were all these various conversations going on and we were all engaged in familiar chatter, and all of a sudden when Jack said that, immediately what we wanted to do was listen to him. Tell us your stories. Tell us what you know. Tell us how to behave. There were four generations present. By saying that one of the gifts of age is the capacity to listen, he granted the younger generation permission to ask the questions so that in fact we could reciprocate.

BW: Thereby emphasizing that we always need to be listening.

TTW: There's a funny story a friend from Wyoming told me a couple of years ago. In the middle of the night they had gotten out of bed when they heard this peculiar sound. They recognized it as the beeping sound a backhoe makes when it's backing up. You know, the beep beep beep beep beep beep.

BW: I know the sound.

TTW: So they called the sheriff and said, "We're home. It's late. There's obviously a construction site nearby. We cannot sleep. Would you please come out and find whoever is engaged in this activity at such a crazy time of night." The sheriff asked for their address and came out, and sure enough they heard this beep beep beep beep beep beep. They went around with their flashlights but couldn't find any signs of any machinery. And then a neighbor who heard all the commotion came out and asked what on earth they were doing. They said they were looking for this crazy backhoe or truck that was backing up in the middle of the night and driving us all mad. The neighbor happened to be a naturalist working for Grand Teton National Park, and he said, "Have you never heard a screech owl before?"

BW: Oh Lord!

TTW: Have we become so mechanized that we no longer know the night sounds of owls?

BW: And so urbane that we can no longer appreciate the sight of Evening Primrose or Night Blooming Cactus?

TTW: Right.

BW: Can these hearts of stone become flesh again? Can these dry bones be made to live?

TTW: Those are the questions.

BW: I wonder if the fugitive faith comes nearest when things appear to be their darkest, when much of the world seems to be sleeping?

TTW: I feel like we're so lucky to be alive at this time to bear witness to these things, because it is a transition time. There is just enough wildness in our midst that we can still point to it and say, "This matters." And to ask each other, "Are we large enough as a species to allow others to survive and coexist as part of our community." Fifty years from now we may not have those options, and that's why I think it's so important that we ask these questions now. With both a poetics of place and a politics of place in mind. As we've been saying, Ben, it will require us to be both fierce and compassionate.

PART 4

THE RESURGENCE OF SPIRITUAL, ENVIRONMENTAL, AND COMMUNITY RENEWAL

Conserving and Renewing Community

KATHLEEN NORRIS

Kathleen Norris lives with her husband in Lemmon, South Dakota. She is the author of Dakota: A Spiritual Geography *and* The Cloister Walk; *she is also an award-winning poet with three volumes of published poetry, including* Little Girls in Church. *Kathleen has for twelve years been a Benedictine oblate of Assumption Abbey in North Dakota and has twice been in residence at the Institute for Ecumenical and Cultural Research at St. John's Abbey in Collegeville, Minnesota. With over 200 monks in residence, St. John's is the largest Benedictine Monastery in North America. It is situated on 2,500 acres of wetlands and lakes, prairie and oak savanna, and extensive forests which are sustainably managed as a natural habitat arboretum for place-based environmental education. We discussed the connections between writers and place, and what such settled monastic communities of contemplatives on the land might have to teach our culture today. "There does seem to be something in the human spirit that is attracted to a community that is a little bit aside of the mainstream of society . . . that respects silence and contemplation and certain kinds of communal living. . . . Some monasteries have been based in one place for more than a thousand years. That's fidelity. It means you're going to take care of the place and your relationships there. . . . We should bring our experience of monastic renewal to our own community, even though doing so may be the hardest of monastic disciplines."*

BW: Over twenty years ago, you left New York City and returned to South Dakota to live and write. In *Dakota: A Spiritual Geography*, you remind us that the word "geography" derives from the Greek words for earth and writing, and you say that writing about Dakota has been your "means of understanding that inheritance and reclaiming what is holy in it." What is there about restoring the connection between writing and place—about cultivating a literature of place—that is necessary and holy?

KN: When I lived in New York City, there were people from all over who really made it their home, who really did acclimate themselves, in an ecological sense, to the region. They really cared for the city in wonderful ways: promoting programs there, writing about it, etc. But I always sensed it wasn't really my place. And then the possibility of moving to South Dakota opened up. It was partly family duty. I was the one person who could possibly do what my mother wanted, which was to go out and live there for awhile until she decided what she wanted to do with her grandparents' estate. They owned a farm and they had a little house in town. That was twenty-two years ago, and she never will have to make up her mind about it. I'm there. But as a writer, somehow I also decided that it was my place. There are a lot of family roots there, family ghosts, things I knew I would want to contend with as a writer. I moved into the house my grandparents had lived in for sixty years, where my mother grew up. As a writer I knew that was fertile ground for me. So South Dakota was a place I had to write about. The landscape I had remembered as a child still loomed very powerfully in my imagination while living in New York City. Now, for the first time, I was going to be living in the reality of that place. If you're a writer I think you just have to write about your own world to describe what's at hand. I began to realize I hadn't seen a lot of descriptions of that particular part of the country, and certainly not through white eyes. Yet that was who I was and where I was, so I started writing about the place.

BW: What's holy about that occupation?

KN: In a place as remote as western South Dakota, there is something humbling about realizing that we really are creatures of the natural world. That we are very dependent on that world and have very little control over it. It offers a perspective that is holy in some sense. It's humbling, which is a good thing, because I know when I've been traveling around to cities like Washington, people imagine that they can fly planes up in the sky and get people to distant places on time and everything falls into place on a schedule. People are in a hurry, and it's easy to lose sight of how little we actually control. That's one of the reasons I like living where I do. There's a feeling of holiness there because nature is so extreme in the Dakotas, that you're always reminded of your place in the world. Human beings have a place, but in the natural scheme it's a fairly limited one. The sky is much bigger than we are. The ground is enormous and vast. There is so much going on that we really don't control. And when we try to control certain elements of nature it is usually disastrous. That's how I see my connection to the Dakotas because I am certainly aware in traveling so much that it's easy to lose sight of a lot of those larger realities in the urban environment.

BW: I suspect a lot of your readers appreciate *Dakota* as a personal narrative that traces your spiritual formation upon coming home to the Plains. Readers are interested in the role that landscape, rural culture, local Christian community and Benedictine monasticism have played in defining your religious sensibilities. What do people say they find most instructive about your story?

KN: Well, it's been nearly three years since publication, and I still get between five and ten letters a week. A number of people who have roots in the Dakotas are happy to find a book about the region. There just hasn't been much, and that's the reason I wrote it. I was a poet for years before I turned to prose. But during the farm crisis years in the mid-'80s, I began to think that if I didn't describe this place and this time and what was happening around me here, perhaps nobody would. I just felt that I was the one who should sit down and do this. A lot of people seem to appreciate the poetic nature of my language, the way I describe the landscape. Of course I am a poet and a frustrated painter, and I think it shows in *Dakota* because I'm basically painting a landscape with words. Some people have made the mistake of thinking I've got the spiritual nature of things all figured out. I get these letters saying, "You have spiritual peace now, so tell me about it." Those letters usually come on a day when I'm frustrated doing dishes and laundry and nothing's working right, and I don't feel I have much peace at all. But of course people are searching for religious significance, spiritual depth in their lives.

Many people like myself have been and still are very frustrated with institutional churches. What happened to me in this little town was that I figured out these institutions were really just people. While some people are difficult to get along with, the institution, at least at the local level, was where the action was. I realized I needed to start building a community, that having a religion or a spirituality of my own wasn't enough. So I actually joined a church, which I thought was probably a crazy thing for me to be doing, and a lot of my friends thought it was crazy, too. That story alone has triggered a lot of response from people who said, "I'm longing for something. The Bible makes me angry." Which is a good response to the Bible, because it means that at least we're engaged with it then. Or, "I look at these churches and I don't like what they're doing." You know, people looking at churches with political agendas. They want good ideas to come out of the mouths of their ministers and it may not happen all of the time, so there is this low-level frustration often expressed. So when I talked about the monastery and the small town church, it seemed to hit a nerve with people. That was something they had been looking for and it sounded good. One lady wrote, "I want to mark the year with something more besides seeing the seasons change. I joined some women's clubs involved in some civic and social action, but it wasn't enough." That told me she really had a religious sensibility that wasn't being addressed. So I hear from a variety of people.

BW: I want to come back to the monastic experience, especially since it is the predominant focus of your new book, *Cloister Walk*. But let me ask you something about the Plains landscape in *Dakota*, because it's not just a backdrop for a storyline but a pervasive presence in your narrative. In thinking about the physical and spiritual nature of the Dakotas, what striking quality would you attribute to its character that has especially shaped your character? And how has this landscape come to inhabit your language more and more over the years?

KN: Hard to say. We're almost in the realm of poetry here, where you make connections in a non-linear way. I think both the rhythm of the monastery and paying more attention to the rhythms of sunrise and sunset have grounded my work in a more natural rhythm. My first book of poems is extremely cerebral, with a lot of interior landscape that really doesn't make much sense to anybody but myself, which happens a lot with poets right out of college. Referring to the difference between my first and second book of poems which were published ten years apart ('71 and '81), one of my friends said that when I moved to South Dakota it was like I discovered gravity. I became more grounded. Which made a lot of sense to me. I think he was referring to the concrete particularities rather than the pretty abstract and cerebral sort of thing I was rewarded for in school. Out here I had to contend with the real world a little more. I think that about sums it up.

BW: Somewhere in your book you quote Jim Lein who describes Dakota as a place that gives one a "sense of planet," where you can really feel the curvature of the earth.

KN: I'd written a poem called "The Middle of the World," about two people out at night on the prairie. It's a marvelous time. If there's a full moon you can see the shape of the landscape. If not, you're totally focused on the sky. But I always have this sense of being in the middle of the world when I'm out on the prairie at night. That's what I've been talking about all along, because when you're in the Dakotas you've got the bigger picture. You really do feel like you can see the curvature of the earth. It is like looking at the ocean, a vast space out there that just is. Like God, the great I Am. Well the planet is like that also, and you feel it there.

BW: There's really no reason your section of the Plains region shouldn't share a little of the Big Sky title that Montana garnered through the writing of A. B. Guthrie.

KN: That's right. You can watch storms moving just like you can at sea. The ocean and plains metaphor can always be overdone, but the comparison is real to a surprising extent.

BW: This makes me wonder about nature's role in spiritual formation. In what ways has your interior life been nurtured by the landscape around you? How is your inner life a reflection of the outer life?

KN: I don't know how to answer that exactly. When I was first attracted to Benedictine liturgy, one of the older monks said, "The morning and the evening are the hinges of the day." Morning and evening prayer are especially important liturgies for a lot of Benedictines, even more than the Eucharist. That's interesting particularly when you consider that with Catholics the Eucharist is always the central feast and celebration of the day. Yet a lot of Benedictines still say, "Morning and evening prayer are the hinges of the day." Given my own inclination as a morning person, the hour right before dawn has become very important for me. I like to try to be awake then. If I can't go for my regular walk because I'm traveling, I still like to observe what's going on, even if it's outside a hotel window in a city. There's some kind of power with that time of day. That's when I might read the psalms or some scripture and get in gear for whatever the day has coming. There is something about that hour before dawn. The light seems much more beautiful to me. The French call it the blue hour, both dawn and dusk. Being aware and paying attention at that time, walking or praying, has an effect on me for the rest of the day. It affects my writing. That sense of waiting is a part of it. Waiting for this incredible light of daybreak. That hour nourishes and sustains me. Some kind of quiet time seems to be a universal need. We just don't survive very well without it.

BW: So in the landscape of the Dakotas, and in the natural rhythms and diurnal cycles of the day, monastic liturgy finds its rhythms. And you find yours within them. As we greet the dawn and raise our voices in morning prayer, we add our song to the songbirds of daybreak.

KN: Yes! And in some ways you see it in silence also. The Trappists are doing that more and more, of literally sitting from darkness into the dawn. Waiting. Marking that time in silence. Thomas Merton and a number of Trappists make eloquent comments about that, of sitting or standing in a cold church and just waiting.

BW: We're already talking about it, but the most unusual subject that crops up in the *Dakota* narrative, the one that became the focal point of your new book *Cloister Walk*, is your relationship with Benedictine monastic communities in the Plains region. Without diminishing the influence of land, ancestors, and local culture on your religious growth, you reserve enormous gratitude for the 1,500-year-old tradition of Benedictine monasticism that feeds and grounds you spiritually these days. You obviously find much that is worth emulating in these land-based religious communities of which you are an oblate, a lay associate. What do Benedictine communities have to teach those of us who care about an enduring culture?

KN: One of my friends, whom I quoted in the new book, said, "Monastic people just spring up like weeds." They seem to be fairly indestructible. No matter what's happening with churches or with politics outside or inside the monastery, monastic institutions somehow survive. Christian monasticism is about 1,700 years old, and of course Buddhist monasticism is much older, as is

Buddhism itself. But there does seem to be something in the human spirit that is attracted to a community that is a little bit aside of the mainstream of society, that's doing things a bit differently, that respects silence and contemplation and certain kinds of communal living. I think monasticism survives partly because it is a way of life. It isn't an ideology or even a theology, primarily. You've agreed to do certain things together. You haven't necessarily agreed to agree about everything, which is one of the things I find most distressing about American society, that we tend to divide or align ourselves around identities and labels: gay or straight, Republican or Democrat, conservative or liberal. So one of the fascinating things to me about monastic communities is that they harbor everybody but don't label each other, because if you label someone in a derogatory way, he or she is still going to be the person you're going to have to live with for years. Divisiveness is such an evil thing, so you live with difference, with contradiction. You don't have to talk everything out. In fact one of the hilarious things about the early desert stories concerns advising monks not to talk about scripture. Basically it's the same rule as you find in a bar; you don't have to discuss religion and politics if you want things to move along peaceably. To some people, I guess, that would seem like a foolish compromise if it meant everyone suppressed what they were feeling and were afraid to talk about these things. I don't sense that too much in monastic communities. It's more like, "We know we disagree and we're going to live together anyway." And that is a powerful witness right now in American society. I haven't really written about it, but maybe I will in my next book. I became interested in monastic community when I read Benedict's rule while my own little church congregation in South Dakota was going through a real divisive period. I thought the rule made sense for any group of people who want an institution that isn't self-destructive. Monasticism has something to teach us about longevity, the value of routines, and having certain communal activities like meals and prayers. While monks don't absent themselves lightly from these routines, monasteries do well on the level of practical tolerance. Monks and abbots may look uniform, and they do possess a kind of unity, but there's not much uniformity at all. That's been a real discovery for me that went against my stereotype of these people. You soon realize you can't get them to agree on anything. Talk to an abbot about how diverse Benedictines or Trappists are sometimes and you'll get an earful!

BW: By living in close quarters over a long period of time, longer than most nuclear families, it's not surprising that major differences and disagreements would arise.

KN: Major disagreements. Different personality types. All sorts of things. But Benedictines, and I suppose Cistercians also, have a vow of stability to the community of people. Normally that translates into one place, because monasteries tend to stay rooted in place for a very long time. But the vow of stability really means that you are committed to remain with these people no matter what. Now that is difficult, as anyone who has been married can tell you. To commit yourself for life to a particular group of people is a scary thing, but that's what they do.

BW: Let's explore this vow of stability a bit further. There are a lot of us who are waking up to the issue of material limits and increasingly questioning our cherished cultural beliefs in unlimited material progress. What might a contemplative practice accompanied by a vow of stability have to teach us in those regards?

KN: Well if you're really living a contemplative life, you're making time to think these things over. In the long run I think it helps people to make decisions that are not short-sighted. They can take the long view, so they're not going for short-term quick profits, which I think is one of the worst things about our culture. Businesses and their executives are rewarded for taking the short view, as are politicians. It's a real illness in our culture, not just American culture but human culture. You see other cultures like the Japanese doing this too, treating the ocean with short-sighted self-interest, as if it can't be hurt. But monastic life, contemplative life, pulls us back a bit, takes the long view, is willing to take a loss in the short-term to achieve long-term aims. In some ways that's a good definition of Christian life. That might be the most essential thing that monasteries have to offer, because they've always been counter-cultural, not so much concerned with a quick profit or living in an exploitive way in a place, because they want to stay there. There are many monasteries that have been based in one place for more than a thousand years. That means you're going to try to take care of the place and your relationships there. That's fidelity.

There is a lot of debate now in monasteries about ecological issues. St. John's has sent a monk to get a master's degree in forestry so they could have a sustainable land management plan for their 2,500 hundred acres, which are mostly lakes and forests. They've discovered some of the history of their own land which included wetlands, so they've taken to establishing wetlands again. They also have a prairie and oak savanna restoration project, and are planning to turn part of it into a natural habitat arboretum for place-based environmental education. They long ago prohibited motorized boating and any kind of biking, so they basically have a nature preserve already. But they decided they needed someone a little more knowledgeable who could educate the community on ecological issues. St. John's is almost like a monastic city with its university and theological center, with wonderful professors, a fabulous church and marvelous liturgy. But when a visiting African monk was asked what most impressed him about St. John's, he said "the garbage system." He was from Tanzania where they've often been careless about garbage, and the recycling system at St. John's is excellent, and this monk thought that was the most impressive feature. He'll probably get something like that going in his own monastery and university.

BW: In reading your new book, *Cloister Walk*, I have wondered if public interest in land-based monastic communities and religious orders is partly understandable in that they seem to offer an authentic answer to three cultural hungers that are converging in America. First is the hunger to reconnect ourselves to nature and place, to recover an affectionate and practical relationship with our environment. Second is a hunger for the spiritual life together with its contemplative dimensions, one that affirms the sacred in the ordinary. Third is the desire for settlement, for vows of stability to place, for a return to community in the deepest sense. As these yearnings converge, religious communities on the land suggest themselves in exemplary ways, because they integrate these practices.

KN: It's true, they can. When they are functioning well they certainly do.

BW: Is it all of these qualities together that draw people to monastic communities?

KN: I think there are a lot of reasons. I've been talking to people in different monastic communities on the East Coast whose guest facilities and retreat houses are booked up six months to a year in advance. People want to go to monasteries to get their batteries recharged. It's like "a spa with a difference." I've even heard people talk about it that way. A spa that really takes into account one's religious and spiritual health and sensibilities, a real community offering real hospitality without a profit motive. Monasteries are obviously different from businesses that want to offer what a spa can offer. But there is that sense of release that people get there, the silence that sinks in, all of which people need.

Like others, I've been tempted to let those weekend or week-long monastic retreats substitute for the need of real community when I get back home. Obviously, my marriage is where my vows are, my deepest commitments. I also live in a small town where I'm a member of a Presbyterian church. So I have commitments there. When I leave the monastery and come back home, it's those commitments that should be strengthened. The one thing I always fear in America, and I find it in myself, is a kind of individualism that wants to say, Okay, I'm getting something wonderful out of the monastery and that's all there is to it. I think that's worse than foolish because it denies what a monastery is really all about. The monastery is a community. For visitors like myself, even if I stay nine months, we need to remind ourselves that our real community lies elsewhere. It may be a community that we don't necessarily want—a college English Department, a church that frequently frustrates us, or difficult neighbors—but it's the one we have and the one that needs us. We should bring our experience of monastic renewal to our own community, even though doing so may be the hardest of monastic disciplines. The community where you are is what you have. Make your peace with that.

BW: But the monastery is the antithesis of American culture, which is more individualistic than communal, more active than reflective, more mobile than settled, more urban than rural. Are land-based religious orders and monastic communities putting us in touch with an ancient sensibility we are losing? Is that what draws people to monastic retreats? Is that why it all comes together for you here?

KN: Certainly, for me, monasticism is where it all comes together. But primarily it comes together in the liturgy. When you keep returning to the psalms, which have everything, you're grounded in human emotions, in human community, and in nature. It's all there in the psalms, and that's what keeps drawing me back. In a sense, everything that monastic communities do is centered in the liturgy, which is centered in the psalms. That is the work they do. It is what Benedict calls the work of God. The other work they do is connected to that, but really grows out of it. The worship and the liturgy are the center and always have been.

BW: Does that mean manual labor is of secondary value?

KN: Not secondary, but that it arises out of the liturgy. You could have a commune of people farming, but it wouldn't be a monastery unless those people were returning to the psalms several times a day, praying together every day, eating and working together every day. Benedict certainly emphasizes manual labor, as the Trappists and Cistercians still do, where running a farm and doing some kind of labor is still important, but he always starts with praying the psalms. So all the work they do comes out of who they are, and who they are is formed by the psalms and the liturgy and the worship, which I think is probably the hardest thing for people to understand. You say you go to church five times a day, and to most people that just sounds boring because that is how they experience church. But they're not reading stuff that is as lively as the psalms. It's an entirely different experience. They're usually getting preached at, which doesn't often happen in monasteries.

BW: Something still doesn't quite fit for me, and I want your help in understanding it. I'm trying to square the obvious public interest in monasticism as attested by your recent books, with the equally obvious disdain that many spiritual seekers and writers express for the local church, though both are ancient examples of Christian faith communities. Is it just a case of American infatuation with monasticism on the one hand, and American adolescent rebellion against the churches we've grown up with on the other? Or is it something more subtle and substantive than this?

KN: It's hard to say. There's always a tendency to romanticize monasticism, to romanticize Indians out in the Dakotas, and sometimes to romanticize farmers and ranchers. We may not like Christianity, but monks are okay. They're good people. But we don't want to relate to ordinary Christians who just trudge off to church on Sunday. That's a real dangerous dichotomy to get into, and I've seen it in my own attitudes before I became familiar with the little church in Lemmon. I didn't go to church for twenty years before that and had all the stereotypical dismissive attitudes about Christians and the Church. But again, it's an issue of community, of knowing what your community is. If you can't find other people you can do things with, there might be something really wrong. I know we find people who have this incredibly privatized spirituality, but Judaism and Christianity don't really allow for that. They're both very communal religions. If you have a wonderful intellectual and theological stance that doesn't allow you to get along with anybody else or live with other people, you're going to have a hard time. You may end up with a terrific superiority complex. Like one kid said to me one time, "Well how can you stand to go to church with all those hypocrites?" And I finally had to reply that the only hypocrite I really have to worry about is myself. To admit that you are just one of many seems to be extremely difficult for Americans. It's also one of the difficult things about monastic formation. We're in danger anytime we make another group exotic. The poet is exotic, a very creative person—as if other people aren't. The monk or the nun is exotic, a very spiritual person—as if other people aren't. So I look for ways to work on that, because I certainly get real frustrated with the local churches, and I get extremely frustrated with the national churches. If you are a human being, somehow you have to figure out how to contend with institutions. That is just part of life. As a Christian, institutions are part of religious life, because Christianity is communal. Just as the Pentecost experience that gave rise to it was a group experience. Just as the Jewish tradition that Christianity inherits is communal in character. So that's a real and necessary struggle for anybody.

BW: What might monasticism have to teach the Church writ large in our day, or the parish or congregation as a model of local religious community?

KN: Respect for the ordinary. It's an odd thing to say, but respect for the daily routines. Respect for community on a daily basis. Not community as some abstract ideal, but community as people that are actually living together and frustrating each other and making a life together. Also a respect for prayer. An openness to the scriptures. Monastic life is a total immersion in scripture. I think Benedictines and monastic people have a real respect for the power of words and sacraments. When you see how words are manipulated by the news media and advertising, how callously words are used by politicians, how the culture uses words, I think there must be some kind of corrective going on in monasteries. It is very refreshing to sit and recite poems four or five times a day with people, to let the words just sink in, rather than always having someone trying to interpret or manipulate them for some other end. There is very little preaching in the monastic day. You may have a five-minute homily during the Mass, but that will be it. The rest of the time you're listening to the words of scripture, letting them in, letting them change you. So the recognition that words have the power to change us, that we can have daily routines that are not boring rituals but are life-sustaining, that we can live in communities that are life-sustaining; all of that is there in the monastic model.

BW: If religion, as you say, is in our blood and in our dreams, is essential to our identity and survival, then it would appear we can't escape it even if we tried. Your life and work suggests there is much to be learned by reentering the living landscapes of our religious traditions in search of what Lettie Russell called a "useable past" on which to build. What must our attitude be as we approach this lifelong work?

KN: I guess I'll rely on the wonderful Benedictine concept of listening. If we're really paying attention, it means we're willing to listen to our ancestors, to our traditions. One of the things that sustains me are the psalms which are 3,000 years old, and the Christian monastic forms I love, which are 1,700 years old. Those people, those traditions, have something to say to me now. The Christian tradition offers something if I'm just willing to listen, as opposed to shutting myself off as I did for years, when I fell for the convenient media stereotypes and knee-jerk resistance to religion and the Christian tradition. For those who still think Christianity is ecologically unsound, or doesn't make sense, or some other thing they want to reject out of hand, I tell a story about a friend of mine who wanted to become a Buddhist monk. He went to Thailand to do that, and they told him that Buddhism wasn't his tradition. They said, "You should go become a Christian monk first and then come back and check with us, once you really know your own tradition."

Women and Regenerative Culture

MIRIAM THERESE MacGILLIS

Miriam Therese MacGillis is a member of the Dominican Sisters of Caldwell, New Jersey. She is the director and co-founder of Genesis Farm, one of a growing number of regional learning centers where lay and ordained people of good will are coming together in search of more authentic ways to live in harmony with the natural world and each other. Genesis Farm was an early pioneer in Permaculture and Community-Supported Agriculture. The Farm also conducts a fully accredited residential program in Earth literacy called "Exploring the Sacred Universe" which, both experientially and intellectually, draws on the New Cosmology of Thomas Berry. Sr. Miriam has lectured widely and served as a consultant to many land-based religious orders of women that are forging a strong practical link between their spiritual identity and efforts toward sustainable community and sustainable agriculture. This conversation took place while Sr. Miriam was in Eldridge, Iowa, consulting with sisters of the Carmelite order. At one point she said, "You see individuals within congregations who for a long time have been grappling with these issues. They've pushed just about every button in the old paradigm to see if they could make it work, and it's not working. Now they are on fire to begin refounding their order and practices in a new context."

BW: I understand that some of the seeds for regenerative agriculture and the ecological movement, for bioregionalism and the decentralist economics of E. F. Schumacher, were being planted over fifty years ago by Vincent McNabb. A Dominican priest, writer, and visionary social activist, McNabb once said that the future of civilization and religion depends on the return of contemplatives to the land. What was McNabb's point? And how has he influenced Dominicans and other religious orders in their practical search for environmental, spiritual, and community renewal?

MM: I've read that McNabb was a fiery eccentric who was on the leading social edge all the time. He used to set up a soap box in Hyde Park and hold forth. He would have been what we call a Luddite, a decentralist who was against the whole industrial program. He was deeply Catholic, so he was always talking about the Catholic social order, a common sense order that he saw disappearing around him in the disintegration and oppression of families and children and villages and farms and the land. He really believed that the basic reference point for people living a good life was the land, living close to nature; because if we all become disconnected from what sustains us, there isn't much hope for civilization. So that was his rallying cry to both the Church and to contemplative orders.

BW: Calling us, both literally and metaphorically, to return to our roots.

MM: Yes, because the abstract cultures we've built, that we perceive to be integral cultures, are really disconnected. They were just poison to his eyes, producing poverty and dislocation in England and Ireland and elsewhere. As we can see all around us, it's ongoing.

BW: What impact has he had on your own community at Genesis Farm and on other contemplatives who are joining you in this return to the land?

MM: He is one of many who have contributed to a growing awareness among women's communities across America—and certainly among Dominican congregations in the East—that the issues of land are really significant. Yet it is the work and writings and ideas of Thomas Berry that have really influenced that sensitivity more than anything else.

BW: As I understand it, Genesis Farm has been a leader in what appears to be a growing movement of land-based religious communities that are demonstrating how we might reconnect ourselves in practical ways to what sustains us physically and spiritually. Each in its own way is demonstrating how we might live within the limits and possibilities of our place, our bioregion. Because of your work at Genesis Farm, you've been called upon as an advisor and counselor to many of these communities.

MM: Yes, I have. When a religious community talks with me about their land and asks me to look at it with them, I am always happy to do that. What I often find in these congregations is a deep sensibility that this land shouldn't be sold, that this would be the worst thing they could do. And so I usually share something of our experience at Genesis Farm, beginning with the permaculture workshops we first conducted there in 1986. The permaculture approach opened up for us a way of seeing new design patterns that could be implemented to reinforce the way we relate to our land. One example that has been really vital for us was establishing a community supported garden in 1987, a very new idea at the time. We were fortunate to have a skilled biodynamic farmer who came to us and helped make this possible. As that began to have a life of its own, the implications became clearer and clearer—that our land was the basis for shaping regional community. So when we look seriously at options like these, then suddenly there's a real alternative to the sale of land.

BW: A fascinating study on land-based religious orders, commissioned by the National Catholic Rural Life Conference, confirms this rich tapestry of alternative practices rapidly emerging among orders of women religious. While there are some communities of men making the shift in thinking and practices you've described, they are the exception rather than the rule. So the contrast overall between communities of men and women is startling! Among religious orders of women in America, there appears to be a remarkable transformation underway in theology, spirituality, and sustainability practices. And there is a common pattern to the changes. First, women are making a place for the new cosmology in their religious metanarrative. This renewed spirituality is anything but ethereal or abstract; it has a practice and a practicality. You can see this demonstrated in the way they are reordering community life and their relationship to the land, in keeping with a sustainable economy. That's the second pattern, the actual demonstration of these new guiding principles. The third pattern is that many of them are attempting to reach out to other people and institutions in their region, whether through community supported agriculture or a host of other educational efforts. So they are involved in transformative education regionally.

MM: Yes. And what's remarkable is the thinking and the forces that are giving impetus to all these new practices in sustainable agriculture and sustainable community. The major force is the new cosmology, the new universe story of Thomas Berry. Certainly among those with whom I've worked, it's clear that the new universe story is prompting these changes. I was just talking with the Carmelite sisters here in Iowa about Al Fritsch, the Jesuit in Kentucky who is with Appalachian Science in the Public Interest. Al helps religious communities with natural resource and energy audits, and helps them design new plans around that. What's so fascinating is that most of the communities he's invited into are communities of women. And the single most common thread is the new universe story. It's also interesting because while Al doesn't buy into this new paradigm, its impact is self-evident and he acknowledges it.

It all begins with a "directional statement." Every six years or so, the general chapter of each religious community reevaluates its understanding of its founding charism—its spiritual identity—as well as its mission and purposes through what is called a directional statement. In this process of discernment, many communities have reflected on Berry's writings, and this has had a fairly big impact, helping resolve a series of questions about how best to relate to the earth, and clarifying new ministries. How they relate to their lands becomes self-evident in that process. A new directional statement typically expresses solidarity with the poor, addresses women's issues through health care and numerous other examples, and increasingly emphasizes interdependence with the earth, with creation. That's where the discernment of their lifestyle, their pur-

chasing habits, the way these are affecting their schools and colleges and universities and nursing schools and everything else starts to evolve. But ultimately
it always gets back to the land. Maybe it's just that forty acres sitting up there in
New York State that used to be a camp and now is being rented out to a farmer.
Then someone says, "We can start a new center there, and community supported agriculture," etc. I don't know where it's all going to lead, but that's the
pattern I keep seeing.

Take St. Mary of the Woods in Terre Haute, Indiana, for example, where the
whole congregation nationwide and in Canada has looked into the new story as
central to who they are defining themselves to be. The community that runs
that particular branch in Indiana has already made this commitment, and the
Sisters of Providence College based there has become an earth literacy center.
They've also developed their farmland in keeping with these principles, including a community supported garden, and Marriott food service is now under
contract to buy fresh produce from the garden in supplying the academic
institution's needs. It's really coming along. And it all begins with those few
individuals and the importance of community discernment. There are individuals within congregations who for a long time have been grappling with these
issues, and they've pushed just about every button in the old paradigm to see if
they could make it work, and it's not working. And now they are on fire to begin
refounding their order and practices in a new context. I think we are right on the
edge of that happening nationally.

BW: Why do you think this major shift in worldview and practice in religious orders on the land is being more readily embraced by communities of
women than men?

MM: I don't know for sure, but I have a couple of hunches. The men's
communities are mostly clerical orders, and their clerical status has so much to
do with their identity. If they own lands, there are usually massive institutions
on them. Since the Church as a whole is in crisis management, trying to enable
what has been created to continue, without the energy underneath to sustain it,
I think they're just exhausted by the work it takes, the psychic energy, the effort
to maintain what they're doing. I don't think women have had that same investment. It's true they've had institutions, but I think it comes out of a different
experience. Catholic women have never had the burden of a clerical status, and
so they're not in a hardened state now because of it. In addition, the whole
feminist way of thinking and being has affected them so profoundly over the
last twenty years that they're much freer. They can identify with what's going
on around them easier, and they are looking for new ways to live in response to
our times. Those would be some of my theories.

BW: Do you think there is some conscious awareness of the moral role
these land-based religious orders might play as a catalyst for change in their
regions?

MM: The idea of being of service, of providing an infrastructure that doesn't presently exist, is very normative for religious communities of women. That's basically what women's orders have always done; they create alternatives. It's just as natural as breathing for us. So there is a connection. You just get out and try to do it, yet with great sensitivity not to dislodge the past. I don't see anywhere this need to cut themselves off from their tradition. In fact, it's an extension, but on different terms. What has happened to women is that they have come to their own truth. They're not going to give the substance of their lives to what isn't the truth, and they're also not going to cut themselves off.

BW: A Franciscan sister with whom I'm acquainted said that if you look at the long record of women's religious orders over the centuries, you see that they are frequently on the leading edge of change as founders of new institutions, whether in health care or social services or what have you. This seems to be happening again, with new models for just and sustainable society emerging at the level of local community and local economy.

I want to talk a moment about the subject of charism, of spiritual identity. It appears to me that most religious orders have not only a Christian identity, but a founder's identity. They seem to be drawing on a central image in that identity which illuminates the environmental crisis for them and empowers their work of earth healing and restoration. For one order it may be the image of the spilled blood of Christ that further hallows the earth, for it is now the earth that is on the cross, the earth for whose passion we are responsible, the earth that needs our healing response. Or it may be the Benedictine sanctity associated with the vessels of the altar, an image that when stretched becomes an altar of unhewn stone, the altar of the earth itself. The vessels are creaturely, human vessels, along with the many tools by which we mediate our relationship to the sacred earth.

MM: Yes, that is what's happening. The meaning within the original vision has been opened up. It's as though the jar has been broken so that the essential can be expanded and enlarged. What the new universe story does is break us from a humanly oriented spatial consciousness and move us toward becoming whole, so that we have to redefine what neighbor means and who the poor are. What many of us now see is that the earth is the neighbor, the earth is the voiceless, the oppressed. It's not a displacement of those humans who are still voiceless and oppressed, but an enlargement of these realities. And a reconnection.

BW: It stretches our sense of the sacred and the desecrated. It spreads that sacred net to cover a wider embrace.

MM: And as that becomes more and more clear, you begin to see that the old cosmology, with its perception of reality and its hierarchical and ultimately patriarchal model, is the source of the problem. When you see this as an historic process of development, it helps us deal with some of the anger, which yields to compassion and understanding and tolerance toward a way of thinking that we have all internalized and believed. It's not a conspiracy against women and children or the earth. It's just what it is.

BW: I understand, at least among Catholic religious orders, that increasing numbers of lay people are seeking vows as lay associates or oblates in monastic communities, in essence committing themselves to live in some kind of extended community together. If this is correct, what do you think accounts for this phenomenon?

MM: I'm not sure about the vowed part. I think there are more covenants and commitments and rituals and ceremonies for people drawn into inclusion, not in the monastic way but in the extended way. Part of what happened is that religious communities saw the handwriting on the wall, that the forms they were living in were dying. If they wanted the charism and meaning of that service to continue, it had to leave the exclusive sense and roles in which sisters have carried it. The last thirty years of post-Vatican II thinking and renewal triggered that in the '60s, by saying to religious, You must get back to the essence of the charism of Christ, and then you've got to get back to the essence of the charism of your founder. Whatever that is, take the essentials of that and apply them to this moment in history. With that came a new clarity about what an imposition patriarchy had placed on women. Once we could identify that, we could also see that most of the founders never meant to be monastic. Founders were just widows and ordinary folk who wanted to get together and do something, but the only model for a religious institute that was available was the monastic. So the bishops immediately took control of them, put them in monasteries and habits, and imposed the whole rule on them. We never realized what was happening; it was incremental, and no one ever questioned it. But once people went back and questioned that in our day, they said, Wait a minute here. Even the outward signs of taking off the habit and such were done to take back the essence of what the vowed life was—living simply or in a celibate state, but in community, so that the wisdom of the whole could curb the excesses of the individual. Universally reaffirming that impulse for service to which all are called—I think that was the major shift. Because we were just never clerical, and were always laity ourselves, even though we took a vow, it was easy to make that connection. By opening up this common body of the church in the neighborhood and region, and doing the work that needs to be done there, most women religious would say, "That's what it is to be human." Again, we just unlocked it.

BW: So women religious have been recovering the essence of what human community is all about, and the essence of the charism has made it possible to address these issues more effectively.

MM: But it was a long, thoughtful discernment process, and not easy. Most of us would probably not want to go through it again. There was a worldview that we had internalized, and we had to take it apart inch by inch not knowing what we were doing.

BW: Kathleen Norris's recent books, *Dakota: A Spiritual Geography* and *The Cloister Walk*, tend to confirm my sense that more people today are seeking out monastic communities and religious communities on the land for spiritual growth. Do you think there is something uncommonly authentic about the life of these communities—in that they have not forgotten their relationship to the land as both a source of their spirituality and a practical outlet for their livelihood and economic necessities—that now draws the world to them?

MM: When Thomas Berry talks about the industrial age as a time of entrancement, he's saying that we've been totally entranced with technology as a way to escape the demands of living life. Now we've come to a time when more of us see that the satisfaction promised hasn't been delivered. The absolute disruption to everything is so obvious in the breaking apart of everything. How much longer can you sustain an illusion? I think people are wholesale coming into a recognition of that, even though there may not be a way they can articulate it or an alternative that could offer something different. But I think it's happening everywhere. The back-to-the-land movement in the '60s was an attempt to do what had been done in utopian communities earlier. There's always been a longing to live in that kind of community setting in the context of the natural world.

Religious communities on the land bring a long tested history of structures that facilitate that. The essence of this, part of it anyway, are the vows that make fidelity, stability, and long-term commitment possible. Otherwise it's too easy to move away when the going gets tough. After centuries of experience, religious communities also demonstrate a capacity to empower the individual to experience community as a dimension of self, which leads to the betterment of both. The sharing of goods and work is a part of this. But most important, there has to be a vision, deeper and more profound than any one of the members, to which you can give your life. Without each of these ingredients, the deepest kind of community is very difficult to sustain.

I know when I first began at Genesis Farm, I wasn't as clear about this as I am now. But I knew there was no way Genesis Farm could be an intentional community, because we had written into our first proposal that it was open to all people of goodwill. I knew what it was like to live for 25 years in community with a vow of stability, and obedience, all of that, and it was still difficult. I couldn't imagine how you could get people from different cultures to agree on anything that's sustainable. So it was our intention to absolutely and clearly say, "We are not an intentional community. We are a learning center." Our mission is to provide some way of dealing with this new vision. Along the way, the community has evolved on its own, but only through an internalization of the process. No agenda has been set or expectations put on anyone. Maybe in fifty years, when people have internalized the full implications of the new story, maybe there will be new forms of community that will be stable enough, but it will have to come from a deep place of inner freedom willing to move through a whole lot of shifts. If it happens it happens. In the meantime, some dimensions of that new way of being community are happening, and the commitment of people to it is just extraordinary. So we're living through the refinement and clarification of that, but it's not our agenda to know or control the outcome. It's just happening. The agenda is to be a center and grapple with this, to do our farming, and let what happens happen.

BW: Is this phenomenon confined to North America, or are we seeing this with communities in Europe and elsewhere?

MM: I don't know a whole lot about Europe. At our last two-week program we had three people from Ireland, one from Australia, and one from Colombia out of a total of fourteen. I know more about England and Ireland, where I have worked for a couple of years with Irish religious congregations. It's really in the heart and so instinctual in Ireland. Especially among the women. The women are right there! There is so much power in the women's communities! Whoa! They're getting it. The context of the earth is very, very strong. In fact, I'll soon be returning to Ireland to spend time with Irish Dominican women who have land at Wycklow in the most beautiful setting. They have an old school that was on a farm, with barns still standing, and these enclose fields and orchards, apiaries, and a greenhouse. The academic programs got too big and now they're falling apart. The sisters are older and they just can't keep up with it. But for some reason, they have been holding on to the vision that Wycklow can become a new foundation for their work in Ireland and their relationship with that land, especially with Irish agriculture which is now so threatened by the EEC. It's horrendous what is happening to the farmers in Ireland! So they get it! They get it! I'm so excited because they've been busy developing a board for rethinking the whole thing and getting some government funds to reestablish the barns and creating something like the learning center that we have at Genesis Farm.

BW: These developments at Wycklow put me in mind of Iona and Lindisfarne. These early Irish monastic communities once played a vital role in cultural renewal during a period of momentous social change. Are today's land-based religious communities consciously developing a role for themselves as regional centers for spiritual, ecological, and community renewal?

MM: I think so. But it's still tentative because it's so unusual, so new. There's some timidity, but the answer is still, yes.

BW: Yet among these Irish women and others you describe, there appears to be a fire, a determination, a powerful internal sense that this is their work and that now is the time.

MM: A keen sense that it has to happen. Yet what happens is they get nervous because they think they don't know how to form this by themselves, or they think they're too old for it. So what has to get clarified is that "You're not gonna do it. All you have to do is hold the space open with the vision and the clarity, and others will come into it and claim it with you."

Africa's Independent Churches and the Earthkeeping Movement

INUS DANEEL

Inus Daneel, who divides his time between Boston, Zimbabwe, and South Africa, has long studied and been a part of the African Independent Churches, as well as the African Earthkeeping Movement. The latter is an extraordinary partnership between the independent churches and traditional religion. As such, he is the founder of AAEC, the Association of African Earthkeeping Churches (representing 2 million people in 130 churches led by their bishops), and AZTREC, the Association of Zimbabwean Traditional Ecologists (representing 1 million people led by their chiefs and spirit mediums). He is also founder and director of the umbrella organization that coordinates these two movements, ZIRRCON, the Zimbabwe Institute of Religious Research and Ecological Conservation. ZIRRCON'S objectives are: (1) research on religion and environment; (2) training of ordinary people in a very basic form of environmental education from various religious perspectives; and (3) organizing, mobilizing and empowering communities to engage in environmental projects. In this and other ways there are fascinating parallels between Inus Daneel's life and work and that of the Thai Buddhist monk, Pra Kru Pitak Nanthakun, including their use of ritual to help people heal the Earth and themselves. Inus says that these people he loves are "incurably religious," so there is "nothing like religion to motivate people to change their lives, particularly in Africa. . . . We are changing attitudes and beliefs, and binding this into the heart of the Church; that when there is a sacrament, when Christ is focal, the cosmos is also focal."

BW: What can you tell me about the African Independent Churches in Zimbabwe and in South Africa?

ID: The African Independent Churches are real churches that are now more mainline than the so-called mainline or western forms of Methodism,

Anglicanism, and the Catholic Church. Those might be mainline in terms of historic traditions and so forth. But in terms of growth rates in Africa and in terms of contextualizing the message of Christianity in Africa, I would call the independent churches mainline churches. They're now mainstream. They are also growing faster than the other churches at present, and have much more vivid appeal for the African people.

BW: What is it that distinguishes the African Independent Church movement?

ID: It's a big story. I have spent all my life with them and have written many books about them. I could never complete interpreting them. It's such a rich phenomenon, and so very difficult to say exactly. But I would say that it's black leadership. They have liberated themselves from white missionary tutelage, from that part of Christianity, in favor of their own genuine type of Christianity. And since they were looked down upon by many of the mission churches as separatists or as non-churches or as non-Christian, I acted as a catalyst in helping them build a new ecumenical movement during the war years, which was difficult, because a lot of people were dying. This was during the Chimurenga liberation struggle, from 1972 to independence in 1980.

BW: So you've been very close to this movement throughout this time?

ID: Yes. As the founder of the movement I had to stay very close. I was raising the funds for it. We had 90 independent churches and 90 bishops toward the end of that phase. Then I went to the University of South Africa as a missiologist and was professor there. When I came back to Zimbabwe in 1984, I started doing research on Chimurenga, on the involvement of both Christianity and traditional religion in the liberation struggle. And in that process together we became very conscious of the fact that the lost lands that they were fighting for, which they won back politically, were being lost ecologically because of overpopulation, deforestation, and such. And so we were challenged to look at the liberation struggle of the environment, for if we don't extend the liberation struggle of the old war into the new phase of reviving nature, liberation is not complete.

BW: What were the environmental conditions then?

ID: In the rural areas where I was doing research, in Masvingo Province which is the most densely populated province in Zimbabwe, the Gutu and Chibi districts had vast tracts of land with little or no trees left. It's a problem inherited from colonial times when people were pushed together in certain areas, with too many small farmers forced to grow more and more. Increasing numbers of people were confined to limited communal lands, while most of the good land was held by white farmers. We had to think of the future, and how we could get more farmland from the existing lands. Yet that's no good if people who are used to communal lands and subsistence farming move into those areas and just turn it, as in Kenya, into another patch of fifteen acres which gets overworked and devastated. That's one side of the coin, and the other is how to restore the land that is already devastated, because the majority of the people still live on that land and will continue doing so. So we started with tree planting. But we also want to promote wildlife conservation and reintroduce game into the areas where there is nothing left. We also want to protect water resources. We are committed to those three aims.

BW: "We" being the leaders in the African Independent Churches?

ID: Yes, and the traditionalists, because the chiefs still have considerable authority in their areas, together with the spirit mediums who represent the founder ancestors of that particular group. The chief never functions without the spirit medium, because the old political system of rule was based very much on ancestor veneration, those senior ancestors of the territory who gave that tribe or group a certain identity, and history, and that story was often recounted by the spirit medium.

BW: So you're working with the independent churches as well as traditional chiefs and spirit mediums?

ID: Yes. Getting those two groups to talk and work together was something that a lot of people would criticize and say was impossible. But we formed AZTREC, the Association of Zimbabwean Traditional Ecologists, which is the traditional group. And we formed the AAEC, the Association of African Earthkeeping Churches, for the independent churches in the movement that are working with Christian earthkeeping principles. These two are working together. There is ecumenism of a Christian nature amongst the independent churches working toward a common aim of earthkeeping, yet both groups are also working toward earthkeeping, interacting with each other and feeling a sense of unity despite the diversity in religion. Sensing that it's one world. That we all breathe the same air. We all sit in the same shade of the trees. It's an equalizer, meaning that while you recognize religious identity, which is important, there comes a time when people want to do certain ceremonies together, because they respect each other.

BW: So it took a pressing environmental problem to bring these two communities together around a common task.

ID: Yes. But it's only through the lifelong commitment of many people that you gradually grow into this. It's not something you can do overnight. I've been able to capitalize on a vast network of contacts because I've worked with the independent churches for thirty years. And since I have studied traditional religion, having actually been the first white ever allowed to participate in an oracle at the cult caves in 1967, I have established contacts with traditionalists over the years. I've had entrée and identification with the whole scale of traditional religion, along with the independent churches. So it's a magnificent process of earthkeeping that is taking place. During treeplanting ceremonies the traditionalists will talk to the ancestors, and include a wide variety of dance and song. But it's also modern because they bring the school children in to perform and say their recitals and their own songs. It gives the old culture and religion a new context, a reinterpretation. They know I am not a traditionalist, but they know I am sympathetic.

BW: Let me make sure I understand who is part of this earthkeeping movement. There are the traditionalists, led by the spirit medium community and the chiefs, and the African independent churches led by bishops. Is the government also involved?

ID: Yes, but let me first say that the movement is diffuse. If you look at the chiefs, many of them are Christian and attend churches. But they also attend traditional religious ceremonies because they feel they should do so as leaders of their people. So there is a wide range of people inside AZTREC, some of them Christian. And then you've got 130 churches in AAEC, some of them coming from the African Independent Church movement formed in earlier days. So you've got two movements, but AAEC is focusing largely on earthkeeping and income generating projects. The government is involved insofar as they've got the national tree planting day, for example, run at the request of Mungabi once a year. But we have a lot of nurseries now with many more trees than Mungabi's forestry commission, so we provide 60,000-70,000 trees for this national tree planting day. So I've told you about two movements. The umbrella organization for them is ZIRRCON, Zimbabwe Institute of Religious Research and Ecological Conservation. That is our research unit. Having started with research, I have built a team of field research workers, including many women, who can work with AZTREC on the traditionalist side, as well as the churches of AAEC. Women span these two worlds very easily, more so than men. So you need something like ZIRRCON that is a little more neutral and more removed, with which to raise funds, handle administration, etc.

BW: Are some of the women who were working for independence during the war years as freedom fighters and spirit mediums involved in this new movement?

ID: Yes. Most of the people that I work with have been involved with the liberation struggle. There are outstanding, prominent women involved in the movement and with ecology generally. But ZIRRCON is institutionalized. We run ten nurseries. We have an annual budget of $3 million. At present there are 30-40 salaried people, so ZIRRCON is much bigger than any particular individual.

BW: So ZIRRCON is an organizing center for the earthkeeping movement in Zimbabwe, and its nursery work and coordination efforts are really being done through these different faith communities, if I may put it that way.

ID: That's right. There is nothing like religion to motivate people to change their values, particularly in Africa. I would say that African people are incurably religious. And I say that as one of them, not as a kind of judgment. And it was proved during the liberation struggle. Not until such time as the spirit mediums and the independent churches and the others really came into play, particularly traditional religion, did the people become united and motivated to work as a nation on behalf of freedom and liberation. That was when they started believing they could win this war. Knowing that, I realized that if you want to mobilize something really worthwhile in that part of the world, that is the way to do it, and that is what we did. And being religiously oriented myself as a missionary, I've worked out the new theology of the environment as they do it, and I'm quite convinced that earthkeeping is an integral part of the mission of the Church. It's fascinating. For example, the independent churches developed a new ritual for tree planting. They call it "mapolasanyika," that is "to heal the Earth." The traditionalists say, "mafrukasanyika," that is "to clothe the Earth." It's the same thing, but distinguishes them as differently structured religious rituals. When it starts raining, they sometimes conduct their rituals together, sometimes separate. The church service is a Eucharist where the tradition is to prepare yourself properly, by confessing your sins before the Holy Spirit, because the Holy Spirit is the active agent that sees what's in you. So then you confess your ecological sins, which you normally don't confess—of chopping trees without planting trees, or river bank cultivation which is not allowed because of siltation and drying up of the river banks. They now say that it is the Holy Spirit that convinces them of these sins. They've never done that before. So after they confess those sins, they pick up a seedling, move to the communion table, receive the bread and wine, and confess unity in the body of Christ. So it's not as if the old communion is superseded. It is a full communion ceremony, but you do that with the tree in hand. And Christ's body is not only the body of believers but also the Earth itself. You've dug the holes over there. That is the spoiled body of Christ. That is the cosmos. But you've got this tree. You consume the bread and wine and now you're empowered by Christ, the earthkeeper. He is the savior. He is still the traditional one who asks for conversion, but if you are converted, you cannot be fully converted unless you're also a steward of the Earth. That's part of conversion, part of reconciliation. Conversion is not just me, God, going to heaven, and that kind of thing.

BW: So it's more than just being reconciled with your human brother.

ID: You are being reconciled with your brother and your sister the Earth, the tree. The women call the trees their sisters. And the men call them their brothers. So as they proceed now in procession to plant the tree, before they put it in the Earth, they say, "You my brother, have strong roots. Grow tall, give us shade. Give us fresh air, oxygen. We will take care of you, we will water your roots." And in that way there is dialogue between the plant and the person, like Francis of Assisi, but it wasn't taken from there. There are just these parallels. So they plant the trees. And then they dance, and have their songs, many of them improvised because they are very versatile. And then, it's healing the Earth, "mapo-lasanyika," and it's also healing the people. Because Christ the healer has come for the totality of life. That is what we believe. At the end of the ceremony, the earthkeepers themselves have ailments and all sorts of problems, and so we start the laying on of hands while there's music and drums. I don't pretend to be a healer because I haven't got a special gift of healing, but when I sometimes open my eyes there's an endless queue of people coming. And so I lay on hands and I pray with the prophets. You've been dealing with the soil and so your hands and fingers still have soil on them and now they're laying on the heads of people as you pray. So the healing extends throughout the cosmos. It's very wholistic and very liberating.

BW: And very holy?

ID: And holy. I get totally rid of my inhibitions and become a healer by the grace of God. I don't know how it works. To me it's just being part of the liberating process which they experience and I experience. I have been writing a book that analyzes the sermons of black people in that situation, how they see the Church, and its mission. There is still conversion, but now it is related to the mission of keeping the Earth. It's just being enlarged. The Church is recovering the age-old thing which is always dormant there, but which we've neglected.

BW: What is that? What is that age-old thing the Church is reaching for?

ID: They always take it back to the Genesis story where God tells his people to look after his garden, and they extend that to Noah and the Ark, and therefore it is that age-old task of us under the rainbow. It's still the garden of Eden, but we've spoiled it here where all the trees were chopped, and here we are on this barren Earth. But we can do something about it as Earth stewards, and we're not proper Christians if we don't, though they don't say it like that. They say, "We are the wizards of the land," meaning we killed the land. Now that's a terrible admission, because if you say I'm a witch or a wizard, it's the worst thing you can say in Africa. But if you mean it in terms of ecology, it means that you are really confessing destruction in its vilest form. And it shows how these people are aware of the terrible nature of their own contribution toward destruction. They don't always see what the solution is because the few million trees we've planted so far are a symbolic thing. We haven't got the means and resources to restore everything immediately. Nevertheless we've begun. So the first sermons express feelings of nostalgia for the past, and fatalism that the whole place is going down the tubes. Now many of them say in their sermons, "No, we can do something about it." They have the feeling that they've grabbed their destiny, because they can see that we are already harvesting some of the trees we planted in 1988, when the movements were formed. We are also planting indigenous trees on a large scale, but they're much more finicky and require more care afterwards. But you can put these bluegums in on their head with the roots up, and they will still grow! And you can harvest the eucalyptus woodlots for the firewood in the correct way and they grow again, and they are seeing this. They're not only planting for their own use, but also for aesthetic purposes. They're also planting wild fruit trees for the first time, in recognition of the age-old thing that their ancestors had ecological hopes and roots, which they have now transgressed. So you see it's swaying between the poles of the old traditions and Christianity. Christians are also part of restoring the old holy groves, even though they possess particular traditional religious meaning, because they are sensitive to this treading upon the holy ground of their people even though they weren't Christian. And it's wonderful to see that sensitivity. They do it in remembrance and love for their own people, and for the soil.

BW: To hear you describe how this grief and contrition can be turned around to produce a redemptive effect in the human heart and on the land is so encouraging. And to see you doing that by enlarging the central symbols of liturgy is very powerful.

ID: We are changing attitudes and beliefs, and we are binding this into the heart of the Church; that when there is a sacrament, when Christ is focal, the cosmos is also focal. When we do liturgy, or anything that's highly motivating in the Church, it is never unrelated to the totality of this sort. As with the big healers of people who have now become healers of the Earth with their own nurseries. Their headquarters are hospitals of the environment. Because the tools to heal are not only holy water, which you can still throw over the area you're going to plant, but also the trees. So you germinate your own trees, which becomes a program of the Church. You still have your patient colony, but your patients are getting involved in cultivating trees. That's a big difference, and I'm very happy when I see that.

BW: Having appointed Solomon Zenaka as the new director of ZIRRCON, you're here at Boston University on sabbatical to complete some research and writing. What will you do when you return to Zimbabwe?

ID: I have for years been thinking about the need for an African Earthkeepers Union as a way to devise new indigenized structures, like ours in Zimbabwe, that enable religion to inform and stimulate earthkeeping action. I've drafted the constitution, and the committees are there, but I'm sitting here, and unless the funds are raised to get the people moving, it's not going to get off the ground. But the African Earthkeepers Union is fermenting because we need a movement of chiefs and grassroots people on the ground with a lot of authority, whom you don't find at conferences with their university and government "experts." You need a few experts to make you aware of what you can do. But they don't mobilize people. They don't mobilize the masses. We need to extend something of this thing which we have in Zimbabwe where the chiefs, the traditional authorities, the churches, and rural Africans themselves can have a platform and work together and go back with inspiration and start fresh new things for earthkeeping throughout Africa. I think that is very important to do. If you look at the wilderness situation, such as the magnificent Zambesi Valley, it's being devastated. I was on the Zambian side during the war when the Mozambique people just flooded into that area. They've now got banana plantations all the way into the Zambesi River itself, a devastation as far as siltation is concerned. There is no buffalo, no elephant, no rhino, no nothing on the Zambian side. And the hippo is all on that side of the river because they get killed on this side. While the African Earthkeepers Union could stimulate ZIRRCON type initiatives, it should also take on a few big projects like the wilderness work of the Zambesi Valley, trying to influence the government and get the people in power to help, to relocate some people from those areas so that nature can restore itself, because we're just destroying everything! Zimbabwe, by contrast, has had the policy of 10 percent of total land for wildlife.

BW: A tithe, so to speak?

ID: Like a tithe.

BW: So the African Earthkeepers Union would not only nurture more grassroots movements, as ZIRRCON has done, but engage the government to address large-scale wilderness restoration projects.

ID: It would empower a people's movement that can prevail on governments to help save Africa from this endless destruction and this harmful process where nobody is taking responsibility. Yet it can be stopped, just as you can start mobilizing people and planting trees on a large scale, such as the 2 million people represented by the 130 churches in Zimbabwe. And the 1 million people that the traditionalists have access to or influence over. That's a lot of people.

BW: What in your life has prepared you to understand the importance of this work and to accomplish it in this way?

ID: I think that my whole life has been a big adventure so far, yet it never crystallized in terms of what I anticipated. I never got ordained, though I studied as a missionary and I am a missionary. But this commitment toward ecumenism and building the independent churches was not an academic idea. Whereas I had now become a doctor and had thoughts that maybe I should go on as a missiologist, it never worked like that. I never took a parish. I never went to a university at that stage though they offered me a chair related to missiology. Instead, what I have studied in the field has dominated. My calling was for something totally different. In a sense it was like going and living with the outcast people. They were not recognized as churches. And it was painful to do that and see the reaction from the missionaries who thought you were going to play a meaningful role in the missionary movement from the perspective of the Dutch Reformed Church. But it was a better challenge for my kind of talent, and I came to terms with that through the struggle in the war which gave me a life experience I could never have had in any other way. That prepared me for the earthkeeping mission.

I don't know how to explain it, but I am not a true academic. I am much more adventurous. I do a bit of academia, but the basic thing is back among the people. They are my peers. The university never became my peer group, because my real commitment lay back in the rural areas of Zimbabwe. I must also say that my conditioning in missions had been pietistic and conversion oriented. So looking at nature, it's still as if that is sometimes of lesser importance than the human being's spirit, and yet over the past decade I have learned that you can never separate these things. I've lived too long with the dualistic approach of western philosophy, and I have learned by way of my exposure to Africa's way, of the wholism of Africa, that dualism is nonsense. Although part of me still hankers after that soul-saving ministry, which is still a priority, my task is now more earthy in a sense, and my spirituality is more earthly. Not so high, but in the soil. I still suspect myself sometimes of using that as a cheap way out. But on the other hand, earthkeeping is so enriching that I don't doubt it to be central and focal in the mission of the Church. It is worthy of pursuing. I had problems with that, coming from a pietistic background. But it is so enriching. And humbling.

BW: You talked earlier about the image of Christ taking on cosmic form. Did your image of Christ have to change in the process to see that this humble work was indispensable to the salvation of the community?

ID: I think that dawned on me the first time I planted trees and still had dust on my hands and then was laying hands on people, praying for people and seeing their faces. But it takes so much money to get the nurseries going and so much of my ministry to do all that, that the laying on of hands is now marginal. When I could somehow, through God's grace, combine the two, then I felt free. But the old demon of the model missionary that I grew up with still assails me at times, and then I have to be liberated. It's like conversion; it takes place all your life, not just once. So it's a rough process. But I've lived for a long time on the edges, doing the counterpoints to what people expected me to do. If you live beyond the expectations of a field like mine, you will find some people disappointed, those who can only think of God's kingdom being soul salvation. Those are people I love and care about, yet to become a nonperson in their eyes because I see something else is not easy. I pay a price. But I have never doubted that the price I pay is the price of God's mercy, not anything else. And God's mercy can sometimes make you a nonperson with certain communities. If you've lived with expectations regarding those communities, that too can be hurtful.

But liberation is its own reward and overcomes self-pity, which is the most dangerous thing in all this world for any person.

To get beyond self-pity and start celebrating is what the independent churches have taught me. They've taught me a lot more than I've taught them. Celebrate life itself! When I see the celebration around the tree planting and the joy and the presence of the Holy Spirit as they see it—and I believe the Spirit is there— then I come away from those experiences tired from planting, yet joyful. Again, it's the two worlds coming together. You see the soil on your hands, and the man whose head is between your soiled fingers is a man whose body is emaciated with AIDS. There are many such people, whose life is at an end, who interpret that in the medium of witchcraft. And when you're laying on hands, the ministry of Christ, the presence of Christ then acquires a new color, having seen the broken body of Christ in deforestation. I obtain strength from that same broken body, the "wounded healer," by standing at his table and getting liberation and salvation in the sacrament, and then taking responsibility in a sense for his body. Then, through grace, healing people. This is something of the totality of Christ's ministry to which we are called. I cannot fathom the totality of it, but in that very simple act of healing the Earth and then healing the human being, in that process I come to terms with the difference of what I am doing from what I expected to be doing earlier in life. And I'm saying I'm blessed and enriched and have no reason to indulge in self-pity because I have had a magnificent life so far.

BW: Coming back to the earthkeeping movement. Is there something about the character of the independent churches that makes them quite naturally embrace earthkeeping in a way that is perhaps more difficult for some of the western oriented denominational churches in your region?

ID: Zimbabwe's grassroots earthkeeping movement is in fact the independent churches and traditionalists. You can talk about specialists like environmentalists, who play a significant advisory role, but they are not the earthkeeping movement as far as we're concerned. The forces on the ground level, the people doing the job, are the independent churches and the traditionalists more than anybody else. This is the biggest earthkeeping mass movement in Zimbabwe, and probably in southern Africa. So the independent churches and traditionalists totally identify with it because that's where the initiative emerged. I'm not belittling other movements. But when we started in the '80s, there wasn't that much on the ground, and this quickly became the dominant earthkeeping movement in that part of the world. I would say there's a natural link, because the independent churches are spontaneously contextual. And in being contextual they divert to the wholistic worldview much easier than the denominational mission churches with their more western-oriented divide between spirituality and the world. The result is that in the wholistic approach, salvation and conversion apply all around. It is indeed an individual and a human thing. But it is also extended to stewardship for the Earth. In other words, you're not really Christian if you're not also involved in protecting and taking care of God's Earth. These are integral to one another. They require one another. And I think the independent churches have a theology of celebration, of living closer to the Earth as rural people dependent on a peasant existence and a subsistence economy. They are living much more directly related to nature than a lot of people in the cities. So tree planting out in the deforested areas is the predominant concern. It ties in with the worldview of the people there, and thus the independent churches have their stronghold in the rural areas of Zimbabwe.

BW: You mentioned earlier this wholistic view. Does it come through theologically in the sermons given by leaders in the independent church movement?

ID: Yes. For example, when the leaders talk about trees themselves, they identify with trees as their brothers. They talk about the things of nature, the life in nature, as on a par with humanity. They don't take literally this thing about humanity as the crown of creation, this triumphalism and dominion, where humans are responsible for ruling over nature. They explicitly indicate that we are on a par with nature. Yes, we have a responsibility, but it is one of service rather than dominion. They're more inclined to experience God's presence in nature, compared to us who have lost touch with nature. Our consumerism tends to make us stand away from nature, to have a much more utilitarian and remote kind of approach. But they live in nature and are much more directly dependent on nature. We're all dependent on nature, but we who live in the cities with western individualism tend to become more alienated than these people are. So I would say, by way of their own sermons and lifestyle, they have something in common with nature, a dimension which we seem to have lost.

BW: In exploring this practical link between religion and ecology, between the independent church movement and the earthkeeping movement, I want to ask you to expand your reference point beyond your region. As you look out across Africa, what do you see that is likened to or different from what is happening in Zimbabwe?

ID: I see other movements in Africa coming up. Wangari Mathai and the women of the Greenbelt Movement. The permaculture movement. The growth of NGOs. Concerned chiefs in Ghana. They're all concerned about the environment. And this ties in with my need to expand what we are doing by way of an African Earthkeepers Union. In South Africa, the Faith and Earthkeeping organization is modeled on what we are doing in Zimbabwe. A friend of mine, David Olivier, is leading that. And the three main objectives are (1) research on religion and environment; (2) training of ordinary people in a very basic form of environmental education from various religious perspectives (Christian, Baha'i, Islam, and so forth); and (3) organizing, mobilizing, and empowering communities to engage in projects like tree planting, cleaning up water resources in urban areas, and recycling of materials.

BW: So the objectives are research, training, and mobilizing—much like ZIRRCON?

ID: Yes. It's modeled on ZIRRCON, but is free to adapt and improvise to meet the needs of people in South Africa.

BW: Is the independent church movement extensive throughout southern Africa, and is David's organization working with them as well?

ID: Yes. But, of course, it doesn't have the kind of kick start that we had in Zimbabwe because of the networks I had developed over 30 years of involvement in the region. So it's a more laborious process there. But the independent churches are even more numerous in southern Africa than in Zimbabwe, comprising about 40 percent of the total black population. It's huge! You can imagine what a few good people could do if they were working at mobilizing the independent churches. Already it has triggered a whole process of generating new nurseries for trees and projects with immediate effect. So empowerment of the people on a massive scale throughout the continent is one of the keys to addressing the problem. Mobilization has become a strength in my own life, and we've developed a successful model in Zimbabwe, despite all the variations it might take if rooted elsewhere. And so I have the feeling that we should look at the continent as well and make a point of getting the good news out. It's a mission, you see. That being the case, as a missionary and a believer, one has no option but to look at it squarely and see how one is going to go about it. Perhaps if we can develop a strong link between South Africa and Zimbabwe, that might be the first stepping stone toward interaction through the Africa Earthkeepers Union. At least one building stone has been laid, and that may be all that is required as far as my personal involvement is concerned.

BW: So let it grow organically, as it has been growing already to a large extent.

ID: Yes. Let it grow organically. That phrase says much about the whole earthkeeping process.

BW: And pretty well describes how these institutions have emerged out of this process.

ID: It certainly does. They have grown up out of the soil. If you look at the people we are working with, even in the liberation struggle against colonialism, their closeness to the land and soil was the dominant theme.

BW: I've heard you say that repeatedly in the course of our conversation. It has grown out of the soil, and the peoples' connection to the soil, out of the liberation movement, out of the independent church movement, and out of the very religiousness of the people.

ID: And that soil at no point excludes religion. When we talk of the Earth as Westerners, we tend to see the barriers between things of the Earth and religiosity. This is why I am always fascinated by the African people. Being earthy and of the Earth is not being less religious. It's being *more* religious. And that to me is an inspiration, because I come from a Calvinistic background where the Spirit is sort of remote and elevated. Upness is God, and downness is demonic. But God's love for the cosmos has become for me an inspiration. He has loved it all. It's all his creation. It is we who have messed it up. But coming closer to nature is coming closer to God. That doesn't mean I replace the role of the Church or the Bible. But somehow that connection with the Earth is of the greatest significance. I think from our Christian background and perspective we've neglected that. And so it's also a sort of pilgrimage back into a lost dimension.

BW: Maybe the African Independent Churches can assist us with that. Maybe their missionary role now is to offer this grounded theology back to the denominational and mission structures that first helped spawn them.

ID: Yes. In our own missiology, we have totally neglected the fact that the independent churches and the African people themselves have been missionaries par excellence. Not only in Church growth in the traditional sense have they played a big role, but now with an environmental mission they are again in the forefront. And to a large extent this has flowed out of their being an authentic Church. Because it is not unnatural for them, they are developing that side of mission which we have long neglected. To me it's quite fascinating to see the use of the Eucharist and confession and things like that as missionary tools that take the people to that old thing, to the realization of what is inherently there anyway. And to see how that affects their spiritual lives, because to the extent that we are healing the Earth, we are spiritually healing ourselves. It's always been like that. As you turn the focus away from yourself you become whole yourself. To the extent that you only focus on yourself, you're closing in on yourself and dying. The same with the Church. But now the Church is moving into this vitally important field, and it's becoming the Church with more integrity in that process. And that, to me, is the liberation.

Reviving Ritual, Conservation, and Community in Thailand

PRA KRU PITAK NANTHAKUN

Pra Kru Pitak Nanthakun is a senior Buddhist monk from the northern part of Thailand and founder of the Haq Muang Nan Network, a non-profit society of those who "Love the Province of the Nan." Through the Network, he and others are mobilizing villagers to promote environmental awareness and responsibility through a systematic program based on education and the use of Buddhist traditions, including ceremonies that bless community forests and prolong the life of reservoirs and rivers. In a campaign that draws upon the community's shared values, they work their way down the Nan River Valley village by village, inspiring people to honor and protect the natural resources where they live and engaging local organizations to take up the work in those areas. They hope one day to extend their program from the northern mountains to the ocean. For these new pattern-setting social innovations, Pra Kru Pitak was named an Ashoka Fellow, linking him to an international network of public-service innovators in the developing world founded by MacArthur Fellow William Drayton. All this began when Pra Kru Pitak returned home to Khieu Muang to live in an ashram at age 17, and subsequently persuaded villagers to plant trees, conserve the forest, and establish a cooperative rice bank. His life, like that of Inus Daneel, demonstrates that regenerative powers can flow from revitalized rituals and liturgies in combination with strategies of community development and environmental conservation.

BW: When you were young and living in the village of Khieu Muang, you witnessed the destruction of the forest and its creatures as a result of inappropriate development. When did you begin to address these problems?

PKP: Please allow me to explain a little of my personal history. When I was young I moved to the subdistrict center, located about eight kilometers away from my home, in order to study. This was because the village I was from was very small. It was made up of only 22 households. The village lacked a school and the road in and out was difficult to travel because most of the area was forest. Animals and plants in the forest were abundant and this is what the villagers lived from. My family was large. I was the seventh of 12 children. Neither my parents nor my older brothers or sisters had gone to school. They had to go into the forest to farm and collect items from the forest to sell in order to support their families. I was sent to live at the temple in the subdistrict center where I was a pupil of the monk in charge. At the age of 7 I began to learn the Thai language. At the age of thirteen I became a novice. I then commenced to learn the dharma, the way of Buddhism. After 4 years of study, at the age of 16, I completed the highest level and accepted the call to teach those younger than me. I spent 4 years teaching those at the lower and middle levels. When the monk in charge saw that I possessed the qualities required to be a leader, I was sent back to my birthplace, Bahn Khieu Muang.

During the 10 years I had been away I had had few opportunities to visit my home. When I returned to Khieu Muang to live in the ashram on the mountain north of the village (which is today the temple in Khieu Muang), I could see that much of the forest had been destroyed. The villagers had begun to lack food due to the disappearance of the forest. Streams that flowed previously were almost dry. For the past two or three years the villagers had had to ask the district administration for assistance in bringing water to those in the dry areas. This was the point at which I began to develop my concept of forest conservation. The cause of the deforestation between 1969 and 1971 was the granting of concessions. Forest companies had cut down the large trees until they became hard to find, and then they pulled out. Smaller investors from nearby villages then came in to cut down the remaining trees for sale. In addition, sellers of firewood hired villagers from outside to cut down trees, both big and small, to use in tobacco curing houses and refugee camps, until the forest that had previously provided such refreshing shade and fresh air was almost gone.

I decided to do something to solve these problems beginning in 1978, at which time I was 17 years old. Once I returned to Khieu Muang, I began calling meetings to create an awareness among villagers of the importance of the forest and the damage that cutting it down brought about. This was the cause of a conflict with the village head and the schoolmaster, who together were selling illegally cut trees. In the end the schoolmaster moved away, as did the village head and his whole family. Neither were from Khieu Muang in the first place. The villagers then elected my older brother as the new village head, and he has served in that role for 20 years now. Together, my brother, the village committee members, and I surveyed the forest around the village in order to help set aside a village forest reserve. It was strictly forbidden for anyone to cut down or damage the forest. Should it be necessary to cut down trees, for example to construct public facilities for the community or to build a house, this was allowed. But it was necessary first to ask permission from the village committee.

Once permission was given it was allowed to cut only the amount of wood specified by the committee. For every tree cut down, five must be planted.

BW: Is there a history of community development and environmental conservation associated with the principles of Buddhism and its practice by novices and monks?

PKP: Buddhism originated in India through the experiences of the Lord Buddha. The coming of the Buddha may be compared to opening a container that had been closed, shining a light into an unlit container, shedding a light on the darkness, explaining the way to someone who is lost. Buddhism actually originated in order to solve the problems of society. Before the Lord Buddha became a monk he was a prince. He knew well the problems that villagers faced. As a consequence he wanted to help solve the problems of all the world's societies. But there were many obstructions. So he became a monk, since it was the only way to obtain the opportunity to think of solutions. He spent six years in deep thought until he came up with the dharma, the way of solving the problems of society, and attained enlightenment. He then spent the next 45 years, until he died at 80 years of age, spreading the Buddhist religion to forest communities and cities in 7 regions. Having been a rich person sitting on a large pile of gold and silver, the son of a great king, he attempted to bring himself down to the level of an ordinary person, unattached to anything, whose life is worth one baht. One baht with which to go begging. He then made his life worthwhile by working to develop society. He conducted his life very simply, living in a hut in the woods. His teachings were based on the principle of temperance: moderation in living and housing, moderation in eating, moderation in action.

Environmental conservation originated a long time ago; it is not something new. The Lord Buddha was an environmental conservationist before us, and the history of the religion has always concerned the forest. If we take the opportunity to study the history of the Lord Buddha—Prince Siddharta—we see that he was not born in a palace in the city, but in the Lumphiniwan National Forest. When the prince became a monk, he became a monk in the forest, where for six years he ate only fruit as he persisted in his quest to find tranquility. Having attained enlightenment, he began spreading the word of the dharma, traveling and living for the most part in the forest, close to the communities there, until returning to a forest close to his home. His converts gave land and made donations for the construction of temples in the forests, for example, Wat Pawelawan, Wat Papai, Wat Ampawan, Wat Pamamuang, Wat Bupparam, and Wat Padokmai. At the age of 80, the Lord Buddha passed away under a Po tree in the forest at Gusinara. His body was cremated on a mountain in the forest. As you can see, his whole life centered around the people and creatures and trees of the forest, for example the Po tree, the sacred tree that the Lord Buddha was born under, attained enlightenment under, and died under. At every Buddhist temple Po trees stand as a symbol.

The principles of Buddhist teaching and rules are many. The basis of his teaching is that monks should live simply, eat only what they require, spend only what they require, use natural resources only as required, etc. It emphasizes that monks should practice environmental conservation. For example, Buddhist principles forbid monks and novices to destroy the forest, build living quarters larger than required, build fires outside their living quarters that could result in burning down the forest or the temple, defecate or urinate near waterways or large deciduous trees.

All the activities that I have carried out have also been carried out by many other monks in Thailand, although their work may not be as widely recognized. But you must realize that monks in rural and urban Thailand today have many duties and serve in many roles: administration at every level; community and social development at every level; academics engaged in scholarly research and teaching; teachers of Buddhism and meditation; etc.

BW: You understand the power of religion in Thailand and its capacity to create an awareness of natural resource management. How do you coordinate environmental planning and bring groups of Buddhists together to promote conservation and preservation efforts in a way that makes use of the customs, culture, and religion of Buddhism?

PKP: I attempt to persuade many groups of people to come together. It is not necessary that they be Buddhist. Those of all faiths can join together to work for society and conservation of the environment. Everyone can participate. I myself am a monk who has learned the precepts of Buddhism, and most Thai people are Buddhist. Therefore we use local customs and Buddhist ceremonies as a mechanism to promote environmental conservation.

BW: So you have been using Buddhist rituals and liturgies to increase the commitment to forest conservation and sustainable use of natural resources. Could you describe these ceremonies, and what meaning these symbols and activities have for your people in their relationship or sensitivity to their environment?

PKP: Taking Buddhist ceremonies such as the ordination of monks ceremony, the "seub chatta" (life-prolonging) ceremony or the "tawai tan pha pa" (giving of robes) ceremony, and using them to conserve the environment is only a strategy or mechanism. Usually these ceremonies are used to initiate a person, but we apply it to the forest to help people understand the forest's importance, so that if someone cuts down a tree it will be seen as a sin, since the tree has already been ordained. Parts of the ceremony are very similar to the ordination of a person, but we add to it so that it becomes more potent or sacred on its own.

The "seub chatta" ceremony is normally used to prolong a person's life, to make one calm and happy, but we apply it to the rivers and waterways and village reservoirs to prolong their life. It helps people demonstrate their love for the river and convinces others to help conserve our waters by discouraging them from throwing wastes or releasing poisons into water supplies or cutting down the forest which would cause the rivers to dry up. It has even encouraged the villagers to set aside some sections of the rivers as non-fishing zones where no one is allowed to harm the aquatic life. One or two years after the ceremony we have seen that the water becomes clearer and cleaner and that the number of fish increases.

Before we perform the "seub chatta" ceremony on a river, we take pictures and survey the river and gather information, such as how long and wide it is, how many villages and subdistricts it runs past, whether there is garbage thrown into it or poison released into it. The information and pictures are displayed at the "seub chatta" ceremony in order to inform the participants and to help find ways of solving problems in the future.

On the day of the ceremony we invite as many visitors as we can through use of the mass media, for example radio, the public address network, invitation cards, and notices. Monks are invited to come and take part in the ceremony, and the most important monk in the vicinity is invited to be the chairperson. Important guests are invited, including the governor of the province, the head of the district, and other government officials, so that they are informed as well.

The "seub chatta" ceremony itself includes three tree forks and various items such as rice, savory sweet fish, and those things, like the rough hair of a dog, that can be found and gathered together from the village and the fields. The people ask the monks they respect or the village "doctor" to perform the duty of tying strings on the wrists of the participants and sprinkling holy water. Once the ceremony is completed there is sufficient rice and fish for all to eat. A committee is then selected to oversee conservation in the future. The final purpose of the ceremony is the collection of money for a community fund.

For this we use the "tawai tan pha pa" ceremony which is normally used as a way of raising money for the temple, but we apply it to the trees as a way of raising funds for taking care of the forest and purchasing seedlings to replace the trees that are cut down.

BW: How do the people feel who take part in these ceremonies?

PKP: In the opinion of most who take part, these ceremonies are good because they are successful, but how successful depends upon the village or community committee and the villagers in the area who manage the forest in the future. We also have to take time to explain and persuade the villagers through the use of such media as videos, slides, and pictures. But, over time, a common trend has become clear, that many people are coming together and the network continues to grow.

BW: Once the ceremonies have been carried out, who is responsible for taking care of the community forest, for example?

PKP: The villagers themselves in the vicinity. Once a forest has been or-dained, a conservation committee is formed that includes the village head, the subdistrict head or village leader as the chairperson and 5 to 10 committee members. This committee decides who has the right to cut down trees to build a house, for personal use or community use. They have the power to levy fines should someone cut trees where it is forbidden to do so, and the duty to lead the villagers in regularly surveying the forest and preventing forest fires.

BW: Can you tell me about the tree nursery at Wat Arranyawat and whether there are other temples that have applied this concept to their own reforestation work?

PKP: Originally we had no nursery as such. We would take the plastic bags that villagers used for donating food to the monks, wash them and dry them in the sun, punch holes in them, fill them with dirt and place seedlings in them. The seeds were first given to us by villagers who presented them to the novices. Once the novices had eaten, they would take the seeds and plant them under trees. When villagers returned to the temple we would give each of them one or many seedlings to take home to plant. Having done this for a long time it be-came well known, and people then began buying black plastic seedling bags for us to use. We depended upon the labor of the novices and children living at the temple, who used their free time from school to plant seedlings and distribute them. Seedlings left over were given to other temples in the countryside in "pha pa" ceremonies and later distributed to their villagers. As this activity spread, some people who observed our work felt pity for the trees because they were exposed to the sun in the hot season, since there was no nursery. So the Local Development Institute and the Village Foundation donated around 30,000 baht for the construction of a nursery in 1992. There are five or six other temples in the province of Nan who use the same concept in their work. There are also temples that do so in other provinces, but I do not know how many.

BW: How do you form groups and educate villagers about environmental conservation? Which local leaders and groups do you work with?

PKP: I depend on word of mouth, such as sermons and speeches I give in the course of my work and at various ceremonies I attend. Beyond this, there are people who come to the temple to make merit and seek advice, including children and young people. When I am invited to speak at functions, govern-ment or private, I try to add something about the conservation of the environment. At present the Haq Muang Nan Network and myself are trying to convince individuals from many organizations—Buddhist, government, private, and vil-lage-based—to come together to work and to exchange experiences and opin-ions. This includes youth groups that emphasize conserving the environment, and groups dedicated to occupational training and development, and preserva-tion of local culture.

BW: Can you summarize your vision and the strategy that guides your work?

PKP: My vision, my wish, is that people and nature can coexist together happily and without exploitation. I don't want people to take too much advantage of nature. I want every person to know simplicity, to know helping others, until all people, all races, love happiness and hate sorrow. I wish to see everyone experience the joy of sacrificing themselves in some way for others. I don't want to see people kill each other or live apart due to race or religion. Every group has the same rights. I would like to see all the people of the world turn around and become brothers and sisters and friends. I would like to see everyone get the opportunity to lift up someone less fortunate than themselves, to give them the opportunity they lack, without the thought of receiving something in return. I do the things that I am capable of doing and hope to die peacefully in my sleep.

As to our strategy and objectives, I and my friends are committed to our work. We try to find a common purpose and direction. Although our jobs and our responsibilities differ, and each person knows different things and has different abilities and experience, we are all intent on making the overall work successful and realize that we are all responsible together for ensuring that it is. We work to give, not to receive. This naturally results in increased cooperation.

BW: What is required to carry out this work of conserving Thailand's environment and developing its society into the future?

PKP: We need to have the cooperation of every sector. Those who are advantaged should help those who are not, perhaps through intellectual means, through advice or knowledge gained from experience, or perhaps by providing materials or funding as required. Money is an important factor with the work and the groups engaged in it. Although the Haq Muang Nan Network began with personal sacrifice and no monetary considerations, today we see that money is one thing that ensures the work will proceed smoothly into the future. Nevertheless, money is not the main factor. The main factor is those who are willing to sacrifice.

BW: Do you intend to expand your campaign of environmental conservation and preservation to villages and provinces and watersheds beyond the upper Nan River and its tributaries?

PKP: Yes. Before we carry out a "seub chatta" ceremony we try to go out and meet with the villagers who live close to the forest and river in order to bring about participation and create an understanding and agreement with our way of thinking. Once this is done we begin carrying out conservation and various ceremonies. After the ceremonies have been carried out it is necessary to form a committee to help supervise conservation in the future. Then we try to spread the news to other villages and communities. Since we carried out the first "seub chatta" ceremony on the Nan River in 1993 at least 40 non-fishing zones have been established along the Nan River and its tributaries. Groups from other provinces regularly come to observe these areas. In this way the network spreads naturally. We have seen that the various groups that come to observe the work of the Haq Muang Nan Network begin their own activities when they return home that imitate those of Haq Muang Nan, whether they be involved with conservation, ceremonies, or the formation of groups. Many times Haq Muang Nan is invited to participate as instructors or advisors.

BW: I understand that Haq Muang Nan Network, which you chair, is now made up of approximately 40 organizations in the Nan province, having originated in 1990 from exchanges between academics, monks, and villagers. What are the objectives and goals of the Network? What would have been the result if these groups had not come together to cooperate?

PKP: The objectives of Haq Muang Nan are for each person to love the earth they were born on, to be proud of their country and their culture, to help conserve and guard their natural resources and culturally valuable objects, and above all, to maintain their humanity. According to these objectives people from all groups, all races, all nationalities, and all religions who reside or have resided in the province of Nan are included. Every person should feel gratitude and realize the value of the earth on which they were born. I think that if everyone showed an interest and cooperated, there wouldn't exist the threats to our future destruction that are so urgent today, such as the destruction of natural resources, the swallowing up of local cultures, and the replacement of personal sacrifice with selfishness. People taking advantage of others in society and xenophobia have given rise to the disappearance of community spirit. In the future, the objective of Haq Muang Nan will be to try to become a community development institution, the Haq Muang Nan Foundation.

BW: What are the most important challenges that lie ahead in the future for Thai culture?

PKP: The barbarity that afflicts the whole world: selfishness, extravagance, and the breakdown of moral principles which have affected every segment of the populace and given rise to new values. Young people are turning to drugs, prostitution, harmful sexual behavior, etc.

BW: Where do you find your hope? What sustains you and your colleagues in your work?

PKP: My colleagues and I do not need to obtain our hope and encouragement from others. The best place to find encouragement is within oneself.

Afterword

It is good to take time to listen to one another's experience. It is good to speak from the heart.

In these interviews we are reminded that there is a moral ecology in life. We are responsible for its fabric, and it is torn. Yet if there are patterns to our problems, there are also patterns to their mending.

Those interviewed point to spoiled patterns connecting our crises of community, radical individualism, overconsumption, environmental destruction, and spiritual malaise. In our contemporary paradigm of technological control, we have effectively declared war on the world in this bloodiest of centuries and we are reaping the consequences of our acts. We are slowly, painfully learning about limits—the world's and our own. We are beginning to relinquish our preoccupation with self and our illusion of mastery over the world. We may be starting to grow up.

On the verge of a new millennium, these conversations raise our hopes that a powerful and irreversible sea change is underway in our spiritual life, in the environmental movement, and in our understanding of community. As William Reilly says, we are "looking for a system that values community more, one that involves an ethical extension of community that includes economy and nature as part of the same moral enterprise." We are engaged in restoration efforts, in the hope, as Thomas Berry says, "that all the children of the earth in the twenty-first century can walk serenely into the future as a single sacred community."

What does renewal require? If the old is in some ways the new, we are being called to walk humbly, do justice, and live in right relationship to that which sustains us physically and spiritually. On this path there is no scarcity, only abundance.

In reconnecting ourselves to what matters most, we have many resources to draw upon. Ultimately, as Parker Palmer wisely states, we must learn to "lead from within," which requires living from within ourselves. Or as Pra Kru Pitak Nanthakun says, we need to find our hope—and our satisfaction—within. "By going deeper," as Terry Tempest Williams says. By doing the things we are given to do, with the one precious life we have been given.

Where will we find reliable instruction? We need stories that are both large enough and particular enough to offer perspective on our dilemmas and give meaning to life. Some writers among us are looked to for their capacity to remember ancient human bonds and describe new realities in a way that helps us through times of great change. They help us clarify our vision and practice wisdom. A long lineage of sacred ancient texts does likewise.

And then there is the Earth, that indispensable teacher, upon which all language and writing—all "geo-graphy"—is based and all human systems depend. Beyond these sources of authority is the old One, the eternal One, the "depth dimension," the mystery and genius that stands behind it all, the "all-nourishing abyss" from which everything flared forth and because of which everything still holds together.

We need to remember that, despite the disintegration around us, "there lives the dearest freshness deep down things," as the poet Hopkins says about the regenerative capacities of nature. We need to recognize that religion endures, too, or at least our religiousness does. "It is generic to the human species," as Robert Bellah says. "It's not a question of the presence or absence of religion. Religion is going to be around. Tradition is going to be around. It's a question of what kind of religion. What kind of tradition." Since it is our nature to respond from the heart, the future of much depends upon how our generation will draw upon and shape this living tradition.

Bellah reminds us that we should not ignore our communities of faith and religious traditions as cultural resources, for they are at the center of the "lifeworld." Thus they may be our last best chance for conserving and renewing community and shaping a good society, one that does not presume it can better itself by destroying the earth or by widening the gap between rich and poor.

Yet it is also incumbent on religious institutions, which tend the archives of our deep memory, to open themselves to new life and to people with movement sensibilities, for we have much to give and receive from each other. This is a passionate conviction held by Paul Gorman and many others in this book—that religious traditions and the environmental movement need each other, not only for their own good, but that a culture of life might triumph over a culture of death.

From the first interview to the last, we hear men and women who are trying to "claim the fugitive faith we have allowed to run away from ourselves." We are trying to turn our attention back to first things so that we have a better idea of who we are and what conserving and renewing community is all about.

In opening ourselves to that fugitive faith, in reaching for that "age-old thing," we need to listen, as Kathleen Norris and Terry Tempest Williams suggest. We need to be obedient to the lifeworld and to have courage to resist death-dealing systems, as David Steindl-Rast and Robert Bellah suggest. And then we need to act, as Inus Daneel and Pra Kru Pitak demonstrate.

In reflecting on these conversations, I am convinced that we have the beginnings of a regenerative culture in our midst. Whether this extended community is best described as as "effective remnant" or a growing "movement that cannot be stopped" is up to each one of us and the Spirit in which we live and move and have our being.

Like prodigal sons and daughters, we are turning homeward, back into the circle of our being. From out on the margins, this movement flows today into the mainstream. Treasuring what we have learned as "edgewalkers," we now work for a better day by reshaping the moral purposes of the institutions through which we live. Having lived in a society whose systems are organized on the "logic of some derivative order," we are moving back to the primary order of the earth system, the earth household, the God household. As we do so, let us all take solace in Bill McKibben's words, "Grace still lives in the world and is always willing to meet us halfway."

May what we all long for come to us. May it embrace us and hold us forever. May we claim it as our dearest possession.

Benjamin Webb

Also in the Ecology and Justice Series